AQA
GCSE Physics

Editor: Graham Hill,

Graham Hill, Steve Witney

Hodder Murray

A MEMBER OF THE HODDER HEADLINE GROUP

Acknowledgements
Every effort has been made to trace all copyright holders, but if any have been inadvertently overlooked the Publishers will be pleased to make the necessary arrangements at the first opportunity.

Although every effort has been made to ensure that website addresses are correct at time of going to press, Hodder Murray cannot be held responsible for the content of any website mentioned in this book. It is sometimes possible to find a relocated web page by typing in the address of the home page for a website in the URL window of your browser.

Risk assessment
As a service to users, a risk assessment for this text has been carried out by CLEAPSS and is available on request to the Publishers. However, the Publishers accept no legal responsibility on any issue arising from this risk assessment: whilst every effort has been made to check the instructions for practical work in this book, it is still the duty and legal obligation of schools to carry out their own risk assessment.

Hodder Headline's policy is to use papers that are natural, renewable and recyclable products and made from wood grown in sustainable forests. The logging and manufacturing processes are expected to conform to the environmental regulations of the country of origin.

Orders: please contact Bookpoint Ltd, 130 Milton Park, Abingdon, Oxon OX14 4SB. Telephone: (44) 01235 827720. Fax: (44) 01235 400454. Lines are open 9am–5pm, Monday to Saturday, with a 24-hour message answering service. Visit our website at www.hoddereducation.co.uk

© Graham Hill, Steve Witney 2007
First published in 2007 by
Hodder Murray, an imprint of Hodder Education,
a member of the Hodder Headline Group
338 Euston Road
London NW1 3BH

Impression number   5 4 3 2 1
Year   2011 2010 2009 2008 2007

Contents

Introduction

Welcome to the AQA GCSE Physics Student's Book. This book covers all the Physics content as well as the key 'How science works' elements of the new specification.

Each chapter starts with a set of **learning objectives**. Don't forget to refer back to these when checking whether you have understood the material covered in a particular chapter. **Questions** appear throughout each chapter, which will help to test your knowledge and understanding of the subject as you go along. They will also help you to develop key skills and understand how science works.

Activities are found throughout the book. These will take you longer to complete than the questions, but will show you many of the real-life applications and implications of science. At the end of each chapter a **summary** evaluates the important points and key words. You will find the summaries useful in reviewing the work you have completed and in revising for your examinations. Don't forget to use the **index** to help you find the topic you are working on.

You will find **exam questions** at the end of each chapter, to help you prepare for your exams. These include similar questions to those in the unit tests.

You will sit three written papers for GCSE Physics: Physics 1, Physics 2 and Physics 3. These match the three sections of this book.

The book includes both **Higher-tier** and **Foundation-tier** material. Learning objectives and summary points that are needed for the Higher-tier exam are shown by a tick in a coloured circle (e.g. ✓). In the text, the sections of the book that you must include if you are taking the Higher-tier exam are shown with a thick coloured stripe on the right hand side of the page. Questions numbered inside a coloured circle (e.g. ②) would only be asked on the Higher-tier exam paper.

Finally, we would like to thank Gillian Lindsey, Becca Law and Anne Trevillion, all members of the Science Team at Hodder Murray, for their conscientious, perceptive and intelligent contributions to the production of this book.

Good luck with your studies!

Graham Hill and Steve Witney

Chapter 1
How is heat transferred and what is meant by energy efficiency?

At the end of this chapter you should:

✓ understand how heat (thermal energy) is transferred;
✓ know the factors that affect the rate at which heat is transferred;
✓ appreciate ways of reducing the transfer of heat into and out of bodies;

✓ understand how energy can be transformed (changed) from one form into another;
✓ appreciate that a device is more efficient if a greater percentage of the energy supplied is usefully transformed.

Figure 1.1 Using energy efficiently benefits the planet and saves us money.

How is energy transferred by radiation?

Energy is transferred from the Sun to the Earth by electromagnetic waves. (See Section 3.2.) These waves, which include visible light waves and invisible infra-red waves, can travel through a vacuum.

Although infra-red waves cannot be seen you can feel them. When infra-red waves are absorbed they cause a heating effect. This is why you feel warm in sunlight. Infra-red waves are often called thermal radiation, or just **radiation** for short.

All bodies transfer energy by thermal radiation. The hotter a body is, the more energy it transfers each second by thermal radiation. A warm object will radiate only infra-red, but at higher temperatures it may also emit visible light waves. At about 800 °C, an object may glow 'red hot'. In this state it is emitting infra-red waves as well as waves from the red end of the visible light spectrum.

All bodies emit and absorb thermal radiation. But which surfaces are better emitters and which are better absorbers?

Emitting radiation

Dark-coloured matt surfaces emit radiation at a faster rate than light-coloured shiny surfaces (Figure 1.3). (A matt surface is dull and non-shiny.)

The infra-red radiation emitted by a body can also be detected using an infra-red camera. The camera produces an image that shows different temperatures as different colours. (See also Section 3.3.)

> **Radiation** is the transfer of thermal energy (heat) from one place to another by means of electromagnetic waves.

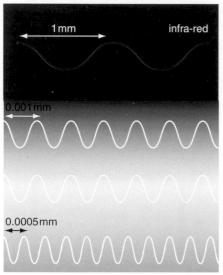

not drawn to scale

Figure 1.2 Very hot objects emit infra-red and visible light waves.

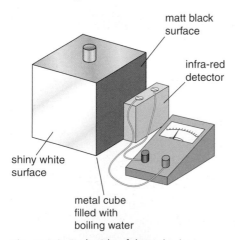

Figure 1.3 Each side of the cube has a different colour or texture but all the sides are at the same temperature. The infra-red detector shows the relative amount of infra-red radiation emitted by each surface. It shows the highest reading when opposite the matt black side of the cube, and the lowest reading when opposite the shiny white side of the cube.

Variables

A variable is something that is subject to variation, such as the different surfaces of the cube in Figure 1.3.

There are different kinds of variables:

Continuous variables can have any numerical value such as the length of a piece of string or the mass of a stone.

Discrete variables are restricted to whole numbers, for example, the number of layers of insulation or the number of atoms in a molecule.

Ordered variables have a clear order of size or mass or length, such as small, medium and large pairs of socks.

Categoric variables are different types of something such as the different surfaces of the cube in Figure 1.3 or the different sexes.

Later in this section we will meet two other types of variable – independent variables and dependent variables.

Figure 1.4 Electronic components are sometimes joined to a 'heat sink'. The heat sink has black metal fins which radiate energy away from the component, helping to keep it cool.

Figure 1.5 An infra-red photograph can show which parts of a building lose the most heat. The owner may be able to add insulation or take other measures to reduce heat loss.

Absorbing radiation

Objects heat up when they absorb thermal radiation more quickly than they emit it.

Figure 1.6 The outside metal of a dark-coloured car warms up more quickly in sunlight than the outside metal of a light-coloured car. A polished shiny car will not get as hot as an unpolished dull car.

The example given in Figure 1.6 shows that:
- dark-coloured surfaces absorb thermal radiation more quickly than light-coloured surfaces;
- shiny surfaces reflect more thermal radiation than dull, matt surfaces.

Good emitters of thermal radiation are also good absorbers of thermal radiation but poor reflectors of radiation.

❶ The window blinds in Ms Clymo's laboratory are matt black. The blinds are often closed. On a sunny day, Ms Clymo records the laboratory temperature every 15 minutes between 9.00a.m. and 11.15a.m. Her results are shown in Figure 1.7.
  a) At what time did Ms Clymo close the blinds in her laboratory? Explain fully the reason for your answer.
  b) At 11.00a.m. the laboratory is absorbing 10 kJ of energy every second from the Sun. At what rate must the laboratory be losing energy? Give a reason for your answer.
  c) Although Ms Clymo used a thermometer to measure the temperature, she could have used a temperature sensor and data logger. What are the advantages of using a temperature sensor and data logger rather than a thermometer?

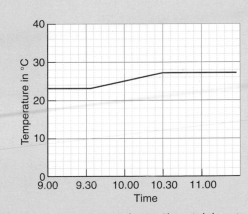

Figure 1.7 The temperature inside Ms Clymo's laboratory

  d) Estimate the probable temperature of the laboratory at 3.00p.m. Explain why your estimate is unlikely to be **reliable** (able to be repeated).

❷ What happens to the temperature of a body that emits more thermal radiation than it absorbs?

❸ Explain each of the following statements.
  a) Houses in hot countries are often painted white.
  b) Large storage tanks for gas and liquid fuels are usually painted white or silver.

  c) Hot food from a take-away restaurant is packed in shiny aluminium containers.
  d) Car radiators are usually painted black.
  e) The outside of casserole dishes used in ovens is often matt black.

Activity – Does the intensity of infra-red radiation increase as you move towards the source of radiation?

To answer this question, Ted designed a simple experiment. He used a thermometer to detect infra-red radiation. When the intensity of the radiation absorbed by the thermometer went up, the reading on the thermometer also went up.

The apparatus Ted used is shown in Figure 1.8.

Ted wrote this plan for his experiment.
- Place a thermometer with a blackened bulb 60 cm in front of the infra-red lamp and record the reading.
- Switch on the lamp.
- Wait two minutes, then take the thermometer reading again.
- Move the thermometer 10 cm at a time towards the lamp.
- Each time the thermometer is moved wait two minutes and then take the new reading.
- Repeat the experiment.

The temperature recorded before the lamp was switched on was 22 °C.

Distance from lamp	Thermometer reading		
	1st	2nd	Mean
60	37	38	37.5
50	41	40	40.5
40	44	44	44.0
30	51	50	50.5
20	73	73	73.0

Table 1.1 The data from Ted's experiment

The thermometer readings after the lamp was switched on are recorded in Table 1.1. These measurements are Ted's **data**.

❶ Why did Ted take the temperature before the lamp was switched on?
❷ Why did Ted use a thermometer with a blackened bulb, rather than a clear bulb?
❸ Why did Ted wait two minutes before taking each temperature?
❹ Give two reasons why the second set of temperatures was not exactly the same as the first set.
❺ Ted moved the thermometer 10 cm between

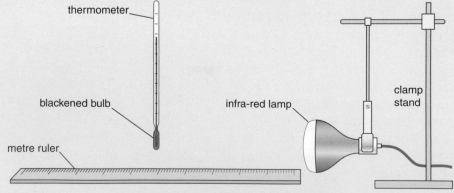

Figure 1.8 Apparatus used by Ted to investigate infra-red radiation

temperature readings. This is called the interval. What advantage would Ted gain by reducing the interval to 5 cm?

6 A results table should always include both the quantity measured and the unit in which the quantity is measured. What is missing from Ted's results table?

7 In an experiment, the **independent variable** is the quantity that you change. The **dependent variable** is the quantity you measure when you change the independent variable.
   a) Is the independent variable in this experiment distance or temperature?
   b) What is the dependent variable in this experiment?
   c) Is temperature in this experiment a categoric variable, a continuous variable or an ordered variable?

8 Ted repeated the experiment in order to improve the **reliability** of the results. Reliable results are results that you can trust because they can be reproduced. Are Ted's results reliable? Give a reason for your answer.

9 The **sensitivity** of a measuring instrument refers to the smallest change that the instrument can detect. A thermometer that can be read to the nearest 0.1 °C is more sensitive than one that can be read to the nearest 1 °C. Was the thermometer Ted used sensitive enough for this experiment? Give a reason for your answer.

10 Drawing a graph or putting results in a table often helps us to identify **anomalous results**. An anomalous result is one that does not fit the expected pattern. Are any of Ted's results anomalous?

11 The way in which we present results depends on the type of variable they represent. If the independent variable is an ordered variable or a categoric variable, the results are best presented as a bar chart. If the independent variable is a continuous variable, the results are best presented as a line graph. How would the results of the cube experiment in Figure 1.3 be best presented?

12 A set of results has a certain range. The **range of results** is from the smallest to the largest value.
   a) What is the range of Ted's results?
   b) How could Ted have increased the range of his results?

13 If the results or the evidence from an experiment are to be taken seriously, they must be **valid**. Valid results are reliable and they are only affected by one independent variable. Explain why the results and evidence from Ted's experiment are valid.

1.2 How is energy transferred by conduction and convection?

Radiation is the transfer of heat (thermal energy) by waves. Radiation does not involve particles of matter. Unlike radiation, the transfer of heat by conduction and convection does involve the movement of particles.

Conduction

Conduction is the transfer of heat (thermal energy) between materials in contact, or between different parts of the same substance, without the materials or the substance moving.

If you walk around barefoot, you will soon notice that ceramic floor tiles feel much colder to your feet than carpet. Your feet feel cold because they are losing energy to the tiles in the form of heat. This transfer of heat from your feet to the tiles is an example of **conduction**.

All metals are very good conductors, but materials like plastic, wood and glass are poor conductors. Gases are very poor conductors. These poor conductors are called insulators.

If one end of a metal bar is placed in a Bunsen flame, the heat from the flame is quickly transferred along the bar from the hot end to the cold end. This happens because metals contain both atoms and mobile electrons (electrons that are free to move).

At the heated end of the metal bar (Figure 1.9a), the energy from the flame:
- increases the kinetic energy of the atoms, making them vibrate faster and with a bigger amplitude. These atoms collide with their neighbours, passing on energy, so they also vibrate faster. This process transfers energy slowly through the bar;
- increases the kinetic energy of the mobile electrons. The rapid movement of the mobile electrons in the hotter parts of the metal is transferred via collisions to adjacent electrons. These, in turn, transfer energy to other electrons and energy is rapidly conducted through the metal.

Energy is transferred along a metal bar by a series of collisions between neighbouring atoms and by the movement of mobile electrons.

a) In a metal, energy is conducted quickly by fast-moving, mobile electrons.

b) In an insulator, there are no mobile electrons, so energy is conducted slowly by atoms colliding as they vibrate.

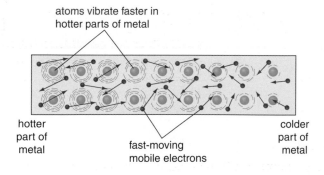

atoms vibrate faster in hotter parts of metal

hotter part of metal

fast-moving mobile electrons

colder part of metal

atoms vibrate faster in hotter parts of insulator

electrons are not mobile in the insulator

hotter part of insulator

colder part of insulator

Figure 1.9 Conduction in metals and insulators

In thermal insulators there are no mobile electrons. In these materials, the transfer of thermal energy relies on the collisions between neighbouring atoms (Figure 1.9b). This is usually a very slow process.

Convection

Convection is the transfer of heat (thermal energy) by the movement of a liquid or gas due to differences in density.

Convection is a second way in which thermal energy (heat) can be transferred from one place to another. Convection occurs in both liquids and gases (fluids). During convection, the warmer liquid or gas moves, transferring its extra energy with it.

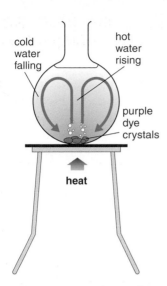

cold water falling

hot water rising

purple dye crystals

heat

Figure 1.10 Energy transfer in a heated liquid

❹ A metal jug and a plastic container are taken out of a refrigerator. They are both at the same temperature. Why does the metal jug feel colder?

❺ Explain, in terms of particles, how heat is transferred from a gas flame through the bottom of an aluminium saucepan to a liquid in the pan.

❻ Why are non-metals better insulators than metals?

Figure 1.10 shows what happens when water is heated.

As the water at the bottom of the flask is heated, the water molecules gain energy. This extra energy causes:
- the molecules to move around each other faster;
- the molecules to move apart and take up more space;
- the water in the warmer region to expand;
- the warm water, as it expands, to become less dense than the cooler water around it;
- the less dense warm water to rise.

As the warm water rises, cooler water flows in to replace it. In due course, this water also gets heated and rises. These movements of hot and cold water, due to changes in density, are called convection currents. Convection currents stop when all parts of the water are at the same temperature.

Figure 1.11 Which parts of the mountaineer are insulated best from the cold? Which parts of his body will lose the most heat?

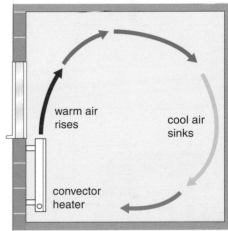

warm air rises

cool air sinks

convector heater

Figure 1.12 A convector heater creates an air flow in a room. Energy is transferred through a gas in the same way as a liquid.

Coping with the cold

Animals and humans try to cope with the cold in various ways.

A seal has a thick layer of fat all around its body. The fat is a good insulator, so it reduces the rate of energy transfer from the seal.

Animal fur traps pockets of air, which is a good insulator. On a cold day an animal will fluff up its fur to trap more air. In this way, it can stay warm even in very cold weather.

Humans wear clothes to keep warm. When it is very cold, it is wise to put on several layers of clothes. Air is then trapped between the layers as well as in the fabric of the clothes.

Figure 1.13 Trapped air in its fur keeps the rabbit warm.

7 Barbara, who runs Hot Snak, a takeaway food shop, is fed up with customers complaining that the coffee they buy goes cold too quickly. She decides to carry out a simple experiment to find a disposable cup which will keep coffee hot for at least 10 minutes. Barbara fills four cups, made from two different materials, with the same volume of boiling water. She puts lids on two of the cups, then waits for 10 minutes before taking the new water temperature.

Cup	Material	Lid	Temperature after 10 minutes in °C
A	Cardboard	Yes	60
B	Cardboard	No	52
C	Polystyrene	Yes	75
D	Polystyrene	No	66

Table 1.2

Table 1.2 shows the results of Barbara's experiment.

a) What did Barbara do to make this experiment a **fair test**? A fair test is one in which only the independent variable affects the dependent variable.

b) Barbara only recorded one set of results. Why would it have been better if she had repeated the experiment and obtained two more sets of results?

c) Which results should Barbara compare before deciding to use cardboard or polystyrene cups?

d) Which results should Barbara compare before deciding if it is worth providing a lid for the cups?

e) What type of variables are cardboard and polystyrene in Barbara's experiment?

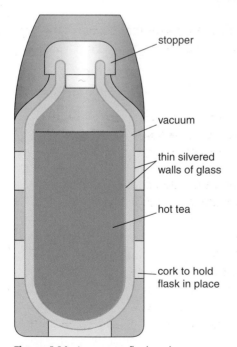

Figure 1.14 A vacuum flask reduces energy transfer

How does a vacuum flask keep hot drinks hot or cold drinks cold?

A vacuum flask keeps drinks hot (or cold) by reducing energy transfer by conduction, convection and radiation.

A vacuum flask reduces energy transfer by having:
- a vacuum between the double walls of the container to reduce energy transfer by conduction and convection;
- walls with shiny surfaces to reduce energy transfer by thermal radiation;
- a stopper made of a good insulator such as cork or plastic, to reduce energy transfer by conduction and convection.

Do all bodies (objects) transfer heat at the same rate?

The words 'body' and 'bodies' are general terms used to refer to any object or objects. Although a glass beaker, a metal spoon, and a wooden toy are different objects, each one can be referred to as a 'body'.

Heat (thermal energy) is transferred from a body to its surroundings when the body is at a higher temperature than the surroundings.

The rate at which a body transfers heat depends on various factors:
- the type of material the body is made from;
- the shape of the body;
- the dimensions (size) of the body;
- the difference in temperature between the body and its surroundings;
- what the body is in contact with.

a)

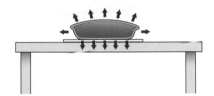

b)

Figure 1.15 a) Heat is transferred to the pie from the hot air inside the oven.
b) Heat is transferred from the hot pie to the surroundings.

Type of material
Bodies made from different materials will, under similar conditions, transfer heat at different rates. Two hot bodies made from different materials may start at the same temperature, but after a few minutes their temperatures will be different. The two bodies will transfer heat and cool down at different rates.

Shape
The rate of heat loss from a body depends on its surface area. Changing the surface area by changing the shape of the body will change the rate of heat transfer (Figure 1.16).

Dimensions (size)
The rate of heat loss from a body depends on the surface area of the body. But the rate at which the temperature of a hot body falls (or a cold body rises) depends on its surface area to volume ratio.

In general, for bodies of the same shape, the rate of temperature change increases as the size decreases. This means that smaller bodies cool down faster than larger ones.

Temperature of the surroundings
The bigger the temperature difference between a body and its surroundings, the faster the rate at which heat is transferred. The graph in Figure 1.17 shows how the heat lost from a hot water pipe increases as the temperature difference between the pipe and the surrounding air increases.

Figure 1.16 Cooling fins help to lower the temperature of the motorbike engine. They do this by greatly increasing the surface area of the engine, allowing more cooling air to come into contact with more hot metal.

What the body is in contact with
When a body is in contact with a conductor it will lose heat faster than when it is in contact with an insulator. In a building, heat loss is reduced by using insulating materials. (See Section 1.4.)

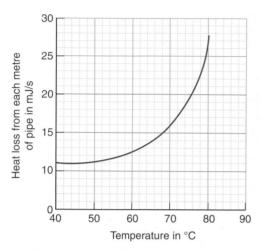

Figure 1.17 Heat loss from a hot water pipe

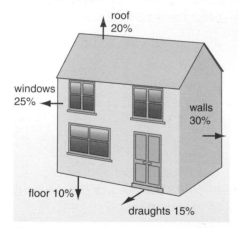

Figure 1.20 Heat loss from an average house

⑧ Figure 1.18 shows a section of a car radiator. Explain how the design of the radiator helps to cool the car engine.

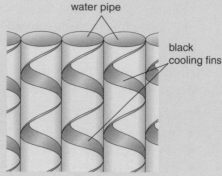

Figure 1.18

⑨ Figure 1.19 shows three ball bearings in a beaker of hot water. The ball bearings are left to reach the same temperature as the water. They are then taken out and placed on a table.
a) Which ball bearing cools down at the slowest rate? Explain the reason for your choice.
b) Explain how the rate of cooling of the ball bearings would change if instead of being placed on a table they had been put in a refrigerator.
c) Explain why the different sizes of the ball bearings can be regarded as an ordered variable.

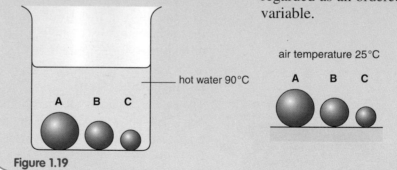

Figure 1.19

1.4

How can the rate of heat transfer be reduced?

Keeping your home warm

Keeping your home warm is not just about turning on the central heating or lighting a fire. It's also about reducing the amount of heat transferred from inside your home to the air outside.

Different amounts of heat are transferred through the roof, the walls, the windows, the floor and the doors of a house. These are shown in Figure 1.20.

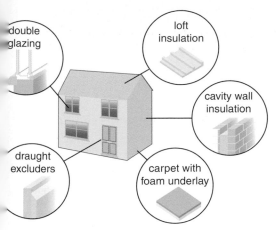

Figure 1.21 Reducing heat loss from our homes

Reducing heat transfer involves trying to stop conduction and convection. Figure 1.21 shows some of the methods used to reduce the heat loss from our homes.

Most methods of reducing heat transfer work by trapping air. If air is trapped in small pockets it cannot move far, so heat loss by convection is greatly reduced. This trapped air is also a good insulator, so heat loss by conduction is reduced (Figure 1.22).

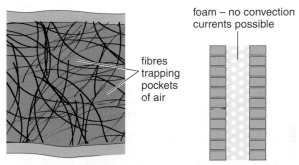

Figure 1.22 Air trapped by fibre wool and by foam

With double glazing both the air and the glass are good insulators so very little heat is lost by conduction. To keep heat loss by convection low, the layer of air between the glass sheets must be thin.

Draught excluders trap warm air inside the house and stop cold air coming in.

10 Give three ways of reducing heat transfer from a house.

11 Explain why fish and chips wrapped in layers of paper stay hot for a long time.

12 Figure 1.23 shows a pudding called 'baked Alaska'. The pudding is baked in a very hot oven for a few minutes. Why does the ice-cream not melt?

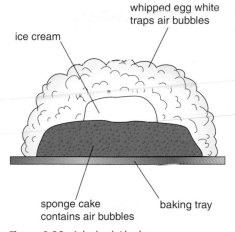

Figure 1.23 A baked Alaska

Saving energy, saving money

Installing any type of insulation costs money. However, once it is installed less energy will be needed to keep a home warm. This means that heating bills will be less, so you save money.

The time it takes to get back the cost of the installation from the money saved on the heating bills is sometimes called the 'pay-back time'. It may take 40 years for the money saved by having double-glazed windows to pay for their installation.

Example
Gurpal lives in a 1930s house which was built with very little insulation. Gurpal has just installed loft insulation. It cost £180. The insulation will

save Gurpal £45 each year on his heating bill. What is the 'pay-back time' for the insulation?

$$\text{pay-back time} = \frac{\text{cost of insulation}}{\text{money saved each year}} = \frac{180}{45} = 4 \text{ years}$$

So, Gurpal will get back the cost of installing the loft insulation in four years.

Generally, the shorter the pay-back time and the longer the insulation lasts, the more cost-effective it is. Over its lifetime, cost-effective insulation will save far more money on energy bills than the initial purchase and installation cost.

Consider Gurpal's loft insulation. After four years the insulation has been paid for from energy savings. But those savings continue until the insulation needs replacing. Assuming the insulation lasts 30 years and energy costs stay the same, the total amount saved on energy bills is £45 × 30 = £1350. All for an initial outlay of £180. This is cost-effective!

⑬ Table 1.3 gives information about different types of insulation.
a) Calculate the reduction in the rate of energy loss for each type of insulation.
b) Which type of insulation gives the largest energy saving for each pound (£) spent?

⑭ Table 1.4 gives the costs, savings and replacement times for two methods of reducing energy loss in the home.

Which method is the most cost-effective for reducing energy loss over 20 years?

Type of insulation	Installation cost in £s	Energy loss before installation in J/s	% Reduction in energy loss after installation
Cavity wall	450	1500	30
Loft	250	1000	40
Carpet	800	400	25

Table 1.3

Method of reducing energy loss	Cost to install in £s	Yearly saving in £s	Replacement time in years
Draughtproofing	75	25	5
Temperature controls on radiators	120	20	20

Table 1.4

More energy saving ideas

Close the curtains

Thick curtains stop cold air blowing into a room. They also trap air between the window and the curtain so that less heat is lost by conduction. Closing curtains costs nothing; what could be more cost-effective than this?

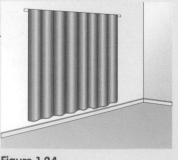

Figure 1.24

Insulate the hot water tank

Fit a thick jacket around the hot water tank. Fibres in the jacket trap small pockets of air so that less heat is lost by conduction and convection.

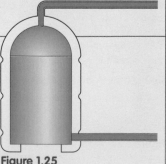

Figure 1.25

Career – building services engineer

A building services engineer is involved in the design and installation of water, heating, lighting, electricity and ventilation in a building. In fact a building engineer is involved in everything needed to make a home, school or workplace safe, healthy and comfortable. Building services engineers try to make buildings as energy efficient as possible by reducing waste energy to a minimum. In this way, they help to reduce both the use of our energy resources and any environmental pollution from the building. A building services engineer needs to understand the science of energy transfer so that they can advise builders and householders on the best ways to make a house energy efficient.

1.5 Energy efficiency

Energy from nothing!

We often hear that the Earth's non-renewable energy resources are running out. At the same time, we are encouraged to use more renewable energy resources and to develop these resources. But, wouldn't it be great if we could create energy from nothing? Unfortunately this is impossible!

Energy can be transferred (moved) from one place to another or transformed (changed) from one form into another, but it cannot be created or destroyed. This is a fundamental principle called the **law of conservation of energy**.

Energy is a bit like money. Money can make things happen when it is transferred from one person to another. In a similar way, energy can make things happen, but only when it is transferred.

Figure 1.26 Chemical energy in the muscles of the sprinter is transformed into kinetic energy, heat in her muscles and a small amount of sound energy.

Figure 1.27 A firework transforms chemical energy to light, heat, sound and gravitational potential energy.

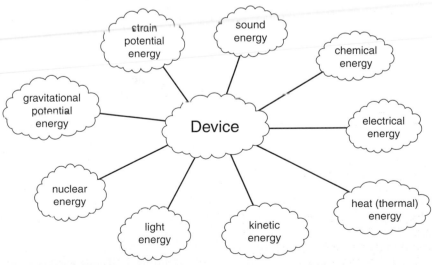

Figure 1.28 A device does not consume (use up) energy. It transforms energy from one form to another.

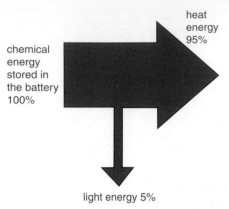

heat energy 95%

chemical energy stored in the battery 100%

light energy 5%

Figure 1.29 A Sankey diagram for a torch

A Sankey diagram can be used to show what happens to the energy transformed by a device or a machine. The wider the arrow in the diagram the greater the energy transformed.

Figure 1.29 shows that most of the chemical energy stored in the torch battery is transformed not into light but into heat. Only the light energy is wanted – the heat energy is wasted, but the total amount of energy stays the same. The energy has been conserved.

Any device that transfers or transforms energy also wastes some of the energy. The device transfers only part of the energy to where it is wanted and in the form that is wanted. This is the useful energy. The rest of the energy is transformed into forms that are not wanted. This is not useful and the energy is wasted.

A coal-burning power station is designed to transform chemical energy from coal into electrical energy. But it also transfers a lot of energy into heat, which is wasted.

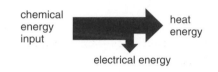

chemical energy input

heat energy

electrical energy

Figure 1.30 A Sankey diagram for a coal-burning power station

In every energy transfer or transformation some energy, however little, is transferred to the surroundings. This causes the surroundings to become warmer. As a result, molecules in the air gain kinetic energy and move a little faster. As the energy spreads out, any increase in temperature is usually too small to notice. The energy has been transferred to millions of molecules which all move a tiny bit faster.

As the energy spreads out, more molecules share the energy and it becomes more difficult to use it for further energy transformations. So the energy that started in a useful form is wasted, but it has not vanished.

In any energy transfer or transformation, some energy spreads out and becomes less useful to us.

⓯ A ball does not bounce back to the same height from which it is dropped. Explain how the law of conservation of energy applies to a bouncing ball.

⓰ Whenever Steve and Sue go out for the evening, Sue always switches the lights and TV off. Sue says that switching things off when you don't need them saves energy. But Steve is puzzled. Steve thinks that because energy cannot be destroyed it must always be there, so it cannot be saved. Explain carefully, using the idea of energy conservation, what Sue means by 'saving energy'.

How good is a machine at transferring useful energy?

The **efficiency** of a machine or device tells us how good it is at transferring energy into a useful form or forms. A device would be 100% efficient if the total energy going in were the same as the energy transferred in a useful form.

The **efficiency** of a device is the proportion of the energy input or energy supplied that is transferred into a useful form.

The efficiency of a device can be calculated using the following equation.

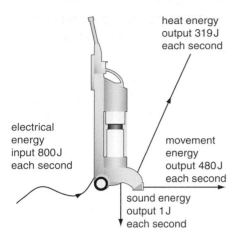

heat energy output 319J each second

electrical energy input 800J each second

movement energy output 480J each second

sound energy output 1J each second

Figure 1.31 The energy transfers produced by a vacuum cleaner

$$\text{efficiency} = \frac{\text{useful energy transferred by the device}}{\text{total energy supplied to the device}}$$

Example

A vacuum cleaner is designed to transfer electrical energy into kinetic energy. But it also transfers energy as heat and sound. What is the efficiency of the vacuum cleaner in Figure 1.31?

$$\text{efficiency} = \frac{\text{useful energy transferred by the device}}{\text{total energy supplied to the device}}$$

$$\text{efficiency} = \frac{480}{800} = 0.6$$

The efficiency is 0.6. Sometimes, efficiency is given as a percentage. So in this case it would be:

$$\frac{480}{800} \times 100 = 60\%$$

The greater the proportion, or percentage, of the energy that is usefully transferred by a device, the more efficient it is.

Low-energy light bulbs

A 100 W filament lamp is only about 5% efficient. Most of the electrical energy is transformed into heat. This energy is wasted.

Low-energy light bulbs are much more efficient at transforming electrical energy to light energy. Because of this a 20 W low-energy bulb can give out as much light as a 100 W filament lamp (Section 3.3).

17 An electric oven is described as being 70% efficient. What does this mean?

18 A diesel engine transforms 40% of the input energy to kinetic energy, 15% to sound and 45% to heat.
   a) Draw a Sankey diagram for the diesel engine.
   b) What is the efficiency of the engine?

a)

b)

Figure 1.33 a) A filament light bulb   b) A low-energy light bulb

Figure 1.32 This European Energy Label must be displayed on all new washing machines (as well as other types of electrical appliances). The information on the label allows you to compare the efficiency and running costs of different models.

Systematic errors affect all results in an experiment. The results are shifted away from the true value because the apparatus has an error in it.

A **zero error** is a type of systematic error where the instrument has a false zero reading.

Random errors cause readings to be different from the true value. These can be caused by faulty equipment, mistakes in reading scales or other human error. We can detect and compensate for random errors by taking many readings.

Activity – Investigating the efficiency of an electric motor

When an electric motor is used to lift a weight it transforms electrical energy into useful gravitational potential energy. Susan decided to investigate how the efficiency of this transfer depends on the weight being lifted. She used the apparatus shown in Figure 1.34.

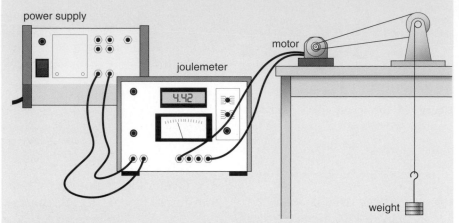

Figure 1.34 The apparatus used to investigate the efficiency of an electric motor

Susan used a joulemeter to measure the electrical energy supplied to the motor each time it lifted a weight 0.82 m. She then repeated the experiment, using a range of different weights. For each weight, she obtained two measurements and recorded the average. Her results are shown in Table 1.5.

Electrical energy input in joules	Weight lifted in newtons	Calculated efficiency as a percentage
15	2	10.7
17	3	14.2
21	4	15.3
26	5	15.5
33	6	14.6
46	7	12.2

Table 1.5 The results of Susan's experiment

❶ In Susan's investigation:
   a)   what range of weights was used?
   b)   what was the independent variable?
   c)   what was the dependent variable?
   d)   which variable was **controlled** during the investigation?

Remember, the independent variable is the quantity you change. The dependent variable is the quantity that changes because of this.

❷ Why did Susan take two measurements for each weight?
❸ Draw a graph of weight lifted (horizontally) against percentage efficiency (vertically).
❹ How does the efficiency of this motor depend on the weight being lifted?

A **control** variable is one that may, in addition to the independent variable, affect the outcome of an investigation. If a variable is controlled, then it is kept constant so that the investigation is a fair test.

How can 'waste' energy be useful?

In some devices and machines heat that would normally be transferred to the air, and wasted, can be usefully used. For example, some of the waste heat from a car engine can be used to warm the air inside the car.

The efficiency of a coal-burning power station is about 35%. Most of the energy from the fuel is wasted as heat. Although a combined heat and power (CHP) station is less efficient at electricity generation, it uses some of the 'waste' energy to heat water. Pipes carry the hot water to local buildings where it is used for heating. A CHP scheme is worthwhile where there is a steady demand for heating.

Laundries waste a lot of hot dirty water. Figure 1.35 shows how the heat from the dirty water can be used to warm clean water. This reduces the energy consumption and the cost of running the laundry.

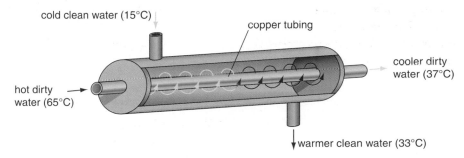

Figure 1.35 Using a heat exchanger reduces running costs.

Even the gas given off from sewage can be used. The gas is collected, burnt and the energy released is used to generate electricity.

⑲ The Sankey diagram in Figure 1.36 shows that a street lamp transforms electrical energy to light and heat. What is the efficiency of the street lamp?

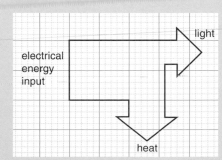

Figure 1.36

⑳ Erika has a very old but working freezer. Explain why it is probably more cost-effective to replace the freezer with a new 'A' energy rated freezer.

㉑ In a traditional power station 65% of the energy input is transferred and wasted as heat. Figure 1.37 shows the energy transfers in a combined heat and power (CHP) station.

Why is the CHP station more efficient than a traditional power station?

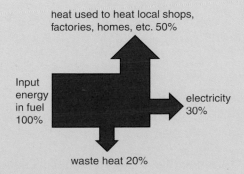

Figure 1.37

Summary

✓ Infra-red waves (thermal radiation) can travel through a vacuum.

✓ All bodies emit thermal radiation.

✓ Dark-coloured matt surfaces emit and absorb thermal radiation better than light-coloured shiny surfaces.

✓ Shiny surfaces reflect thermal radiation better than dull, matt surfaces.

✓ The transfer of heat by **radiation** does not involve the movement of particles, unlike the transfer of heat by **conduction** and **convection**.

✓ A material that contains free electrons is a good conductor of heat.

✓ Convection currents in a fluid occur because of changes to the density of the fluid.

✓ The rate at which a body transfers heat depends on:
  – the type of material the body is made from;

  – the shape of the body;
  – the dimensions of the body;
  – the difference in temperature between the body and its surroundings.

✓ The **law of conservation of energy** says: 'energy cannot be created or destroyed. It can only be transformed from one form to another form.'

✓ In any energy transfer or transformation, the energy spreads out and becomes less useful to us. Some energy is always wasted during the transfer or transformation.

✓ **Efficiency** is the proportion of the energy input or energy supplied that is transferred in a useful form by a machine or device.

✓ $\text{Efficiency} = \dfrac{\text{useful energy transferred by the device}}{\text{total energy supplied to the device}}$

EXAMQUESTIONS

❶ Figure 1.38 shows a cross-section through the outside wall of a house.

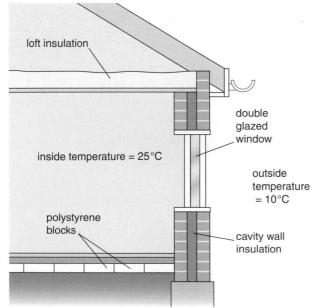

Figure 1.38

a) Explain how the polystyrene blocks under the floor reduce heat loss from the house.

(2 marks)

b) What happens to the rate of heat loss through the window when the outside temperature drops to 5 °C? Assume the temperature inside the house stays at 25 °C. Give a reason for your answer. *(2 marks)*

c) Table 1.6 gives information about four different ways to insulate a house.

Type of insulation	Heat loss before insulation in J/s	Heat loss after insulation in J/s
Floor	700	420
Loft	1600	940
Cavity wall	2200	900
Double glazing	1140	780

Table 1.6

Which type of insulation in Table 1.6 is most effective in reducing heat loss from the house? To gain full marks you must support your answer with calculations.

(2 marks)

❷ Marion and Jim have been asked to find out which of the three materials K, L or M would be the best for making a winter coat. They each produce a plan for their investigation.

Marion's plan
1   From each material, cut a rectangle 8 cm by 20 cm.
2   Wrap material K round an empty metal can; hold it in place with an elastic band.
3   Pour 200 cm³ of boiling water into the can; place a thermometer in the water.
4   Wait until the temperature reaches 85 °C then start a stop watch.
5   Take the temperature every minute for 10 minutes.
6   At the end of 10 minutes throw the water away.
7   Repeat the experiment with material L and then with material M.
8   Each time use 200 cm³ of water and wait until the temperature reaches 85 °C before starting the stop watch.

Jim's plan
1   Cut a piece of material from each of K, L and M.
2   Wrap the material from K around an empty metal can.
3   Pour in some hot water.
4   Start a stop watch and take the temperature every few minutes.
5   When the water has cooled down throw it away.
6   Start again with the other two materials.

a) Give four reasons why Marion's results will be more valid than Jim's results.   (*4 marks*)
b) Marion's results are presented in Figure 1.39. Which material should the winter coat be made from? Give a reason for your answer.
(*2 marks*)

❸ The Sankey diagram in Figure 1.40 shows what happens to the input energy for a television.
a) Calculate the efficiency of the TV. Show clearly how you work out your answer.
(*2 marks*)

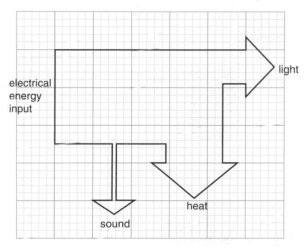

Figure 1.40

b) Joe is arguing with a friend about the conservation of energy. Joe says that since energy is conserved, it must always be there, so there is no point in switching things like a TV or computer off. Explain why Joe is wrong.   (*2 marks*)

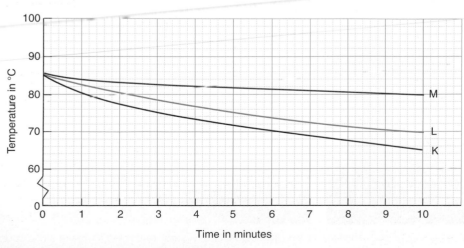

Figure 1.39 A graph showing Marion's results

EXAMQUESTIONS

Chapter 2
How do we generate and use electricity?

At the end of this chapter you should:

✓ know that electrical devices transform electrical energy to other forms of energy at the flick of a switch;

✓ know that the power of a device is the rate at which it transforms energy;

✓ understand how the National Grid transfers electricity from power stations to consumers;

✓ know how electricity is generated in power stations;

✓ know that electricity is generated using a variety of energy sources;

✓ appreciate that each type of energy source used to generate electricity has its advantages and disadvantages;

✓ be able to calculate the amount of electrical energy transferred from the mains supply and the cost of this energy.

Figure 2.1 Different energy sources are used to generate electricity. In the UK most electricity is still generated in power stations using the energy trapped in fossil fuels.

Why is electrical energy so useful?

In most homes there are various devices (appliances) which work by transforming electrical energy to other forms of energy.

In industry, electrical energy is a widely used source of energy.

Electrical energy is such a useful form of energy because it is easily transformed into other forms of energy, such as:
- heat (thermal energy);
- light;
- sound;
- kinetic energy;
- gravitational potential energy.

This is why we have so many devices that are designed to work from the electricity mains supply.

Figure 2.3 shows five everyday electrical devices and the energy transformations they are designed to bring about.

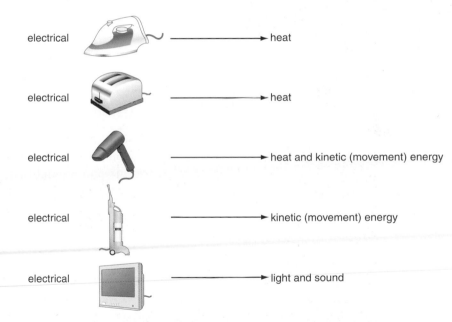

Figure 2.3 Some everyday electrical devices designed to transform energy

Figure 2.2 Many machines work by transforming electrical energy.

❶ Describe the energy transformations that each of the following electrical devices are designed to bring about.

- iPod
- mobile phone charger
- drill
- washing machine

❷ Name three devices designed to transform electrical energy into heat energy.

Electrical energy and power

The amount of electrical energy that a device transforms depends on two things:
- how long the device is used;
- the rate at which the device transforms energy (uses electricity).

The rate at which a device transforms energy is called its **power**.

Power is measured in watts (W) or joules per second (J/s).

Power is the rate at which a device transforms energy.

Figure 2.4 An electric jigsaw

Figure 2.5 The information plate shows the power of the jigsaw.

A device that transforms 1 joule of energy every second, from one form to another, has a power of 1 watt. So a 350 watt electric jigsaw (Figure 2.4) will transform 350 joules of electrical energy to other forms of energy every second it is switched on.

1 watt = 1 joule / second (1 W = 1 J/s)

Power can also be measured in kilowatts (kW).

1 kilowatt (kW) = 1000 watts (W)

Table 2.1 shows the power of some of the devices mentioned earlier in this section.

Appliance	Power rating in W
Lamp	60
Television	150
Toaster	250
Vacuum cleaner	770
Hairdryer	1200
Iron	1800

Table 2.1 The power rating of some everyday electrical devices

3 Each of the following appliances is used for 15 minutes.

1200 W hairdryer
100 W light bulb
1.8 kW iron
20 W radio

a) Which appliance transfers the most energy?

b) Which appliance transfers the least energy?

Give a reason for each of your choices.

Activity – Using electrical devices at home

1 Look around your own home. How many different devices can you name that work from the mains electricity supply? All you have to do is plug in and flick the switch.

2 Figure 2.6 shows two types of fan. Type A is a 230 V, 50 W mains operated fan. Type B is a 3 V, low-power battery operated fan.

Compare the advantages and disadvantages of using each type of fan.

Figure 2.6 Type A – mains operated fan. Type B – battery operated fan.

2.2 Paying for electricity

A **kilowatt-hour** is the amount of energy transferred to an appliance rated at 1 kW in one hour. This unit of energy is used by electricity supply companies.

4 Estimate the amount of energy you would save each year by replacing just one 100 W light bulb with a 20 W energy-efficient bulb.

5 Now estimate the amount of energy you would save each year if you replaced all the light bulbs in your home in this way. (Assume that all the light bulbs are 100 W.)

6 Finally, estimate how much energy we could save each year if everyone in the UK did this. (Assume there are 20 million homes in the UK, all with three bedrooms.)

7 Calculate the cost of using each of the following appliances. Assume 1 kWh of electrical energy costs 12p.
a) A 2 kW heater switched on for 4 hours.
b) A 9 kW shower used for 10 minutes.
c) A 2500 W kettle switched on for 2 minutes.
d) A 60 W light bulb switched on for 45 minutes.

Energy is transferred from the mains electricity supply every time an appliance is plugged in and switched on. This energy must be paid for.

Appliances with a high power rating (see Section 2.1) transfer a lot of energy from the mains electricity supply each second. For example, a 1.8 kW iron transfers 1800 joules of electrical energy every second. Any appliance with a high power rating costs a lot to use.

The cost also depends on how long the appliance is switched on for. The longer the appliance is on, the more it costs.

If the total amount of energy transferred to a home was measured in joules, the numbers would be enormous. Electricity companies measure the electrical energy transferred using a much larger unit. The unit they use is the **kilowatt-hour** (kWh).

The energy transferred by an appliance can be calculated using the equation:

$$\begin{array}{ccc} \text{energy transferred} & = & \text{power} & \times & \text{time} \\ \text{(in kilowatt-hours)} & & \text{(in kilowatts)} & & \text{(in hours)} \end{array}$$

Example
A 4 kilowatt electric cooker is switched on for 3 hours. How much electrical energy is transferred from the mains supply to the cooker?

$$\begin{aligned} \text{energy transferred} &= \text{power} \times \text{time (power in kilowatts and time in hours)} \\ &= 4 \times 3 \\ &= 12 \text{ kilowatt-hours (kWh)} \end{aligned}$$

Calculating the bill

The cost of using mains electricity can be calculated by simply multiplying the total number of kilowatt-hours of energy transferred by the cost of one kilowatt-hour.

$$\text{total cost} = \text{number of kilowatt-hours} \times \text{cost per kilowatt-hour}$$

Example
Between February and May a homeowner uses 247 kilowatt-hours of electrical energy. Assuming one kilowatt-hour costs 12p, what is the cost of using this energy?

$$\text{total cost} = \text{number of kilowatt-hours} \times \text{cost per kilowatt-hour}$$

$$= 247 \times 12p = 2964p = £29.64$$

Activity – Working out the cost of using electricity

Find the information plate on an electrical appliance that you have at home. The information plate will be on the outside of the appliance. There is no need to take anything to pieces!

1 What is the power of the appliance? Write the power in watts (joules per second) and in kilowatts.

2 Estimate how long the appliance is used in one week. Write the time used in seconds and in hours.

3 Calculate, in joules and in kilowatt-hours, how much electrical energy is transferred to the appliance in one week.

4 Calculate the weekly cost of using the appliance. (Assume 1 kWh costs 12p.)

5 Suggest a way to make your use of the appliance more energy efficient. For example, if the appliance is a dishwasher, you should only use it fully loaded.

 2.3 # The National Grid

A network of cables and transformers links our homes, offices, schools and factories to the power stations that generate electrical energy. This network is called the **National Grid**. The people who use the electrical energy are called consumers (Figure 2.7).

Electricity is transferred from power stations to consumers along the network of cables and transformers of the **National Grid**.

The National Grid links together all the major power stations as well as smaller electrical energy generators. This means that power stations can be closed for maintenance without disrupting the supply of electricity. Some power stations are used to supply energy to the grid only at times of peak demand. (Imagine the extra demand at half time in a televised world cup football match. Everyone wants a cup of tea or coffee.)

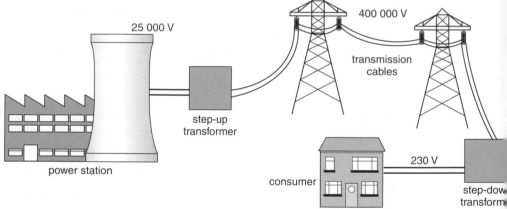

Figure 2.7 A simplified diagram of the National Grid network

Figure 2.8 Pylons carry the main cables of the National Grid to all parts of the country.

Every second, huge amounts of electrical energy are transmitted through the National Grid from power stations to consumers. The energy is transmitted using a high voltage. Using a transformer to increase the voltage across the cables reduces the current through the cables. Reducing the current reduces the amount of electrical energy transformed into heat in the cables. By reducing the energy lost as heat in the cables, the transmission of mains electricity is made more efficient. So, more of the energy from the power station gets to the consumer.

How should we generate the electricity we need?

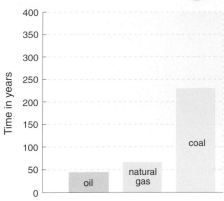

Figure 2.9 How long will the reserves of fossil fuels last?

The most common energy sources for generating electricity are coal, oil and natural gas. Coal, oil and natural gas are fossil fuels. Like all fuels, they store energy. But to release their energy, the fuels must be burned. It would take millions of years to replace the fossil fuels that have already been used. Because of this, fossil fuels are described as **non-renewable energy sources**. Once they are gone, they are gone forever.

Fossil fuel reserves are limited. Although some companies are always trying to find new reserves, fossil fuels will eventually run out. Figure 2.9 shows how long we can expect fossil fuels to last if we continue to use them at the present rate.

If we want the Earth's reserves of fossil fuels to last longer then we must start to use them more efficiently. This is crucial for oil and natural gas.

In comparison to fossil fuels, resources like the wind and the tides will never run out. These are energy sources that are replaced as fast as they are used. Because of this, the wind and the tides are described as **renewable energy sources**.

Although both non-renewable and renewable energy sources are used to generate electricity, most electricity in Britain is generated in power stations from non-renewable fossil fuels.

Coal or oil is burned to heat water and produce steam. The steam is made to drive turbines. The turbines turn generators and the generators produce electricity (Figure 2.10).

In a gas-burning power station there is no need to produce steam. Heat from the burning gas produces fast moving hot air which is used to drive the turbines directly.

Nuclear power stations generate electricity in a similar way to those that burn coal. But the fuel, mainly uranium or plutonium, is not burned.

> When **non-renewable energy sources** such as coal, oil and natural gas are used up, they are gone forever.
>
> **Renewable energy sources** will never run out. We can obtain renewable energy from the Sun (solar energy), from tides, waves and rivers (hydropower), from the wind (wind turbines) and from hot water and steam released from within the Earth in volcanic areas (geothermal).

8 Before the National Grid was set up in 1926, each area in Britain had its own power station. What are the advantages of the National Grid rather than smaller areas generating their own electricity?

9 Transformers are usually very efficient. Explain what this means.

10 Why does the National Grid transmit electrical energy at high voltage?

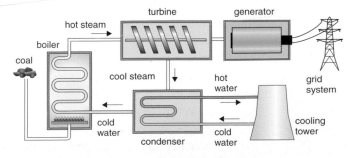

Figure 2.10 Using coal or oil to generate electricity

The breaking up or splitting of large atoms in elements like uranium and plutonium is called **nuclear fission**. When nuclear fission happens, energy is released.

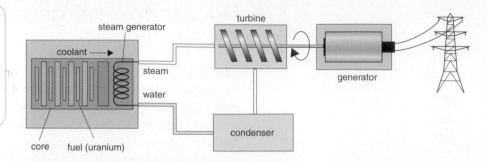

Figure 2.11 Using nuclear fuel to generate electricity

Instead the heat given out by the breaking up of uranium or plutonium atoms in **nuclear fission** is removed from the reactor by a coolant, and then used to turn water into steam (Figure 2.11). Nuclear fission is studied in more detail in Section 8.5.

2.5 Why are non-renewable fuels used to generate electricity?

Power stations that use non-renewable fuels can generate electricity at any time. It doesn't matter whether it is day or night, summer or winter. Provided the fuel keeps arriving, the power station keeps on generating. This makes non-renewable fuels reliable energy sources.

Oil- and coal-burning power stations are relatively cheap to build. Most of them have a very high power output of about 2000 megawatts (that's 2000 million watts). So a small number of power stations can provide power to millions of consumers.

After a power station has been closed down for maintenance, it needs to be started up again. The time it takes to get started up and generating electricity depends on the type of power station (Figure 2.12).

Coal-burning and most oil-burning power stations need to be kept running all the time. This is because the furnaces are likely to be damaged if they are allowed to cool down.

Nuclear fuel, which is relatively cheap, provides a concentrated energy source. One kilogram of nuclear fuel can release the same amount of energy as 20 000 kilograms of coal. The downside is the very high cost of building and safely decommissioning (dismantling) nuclear power stations.

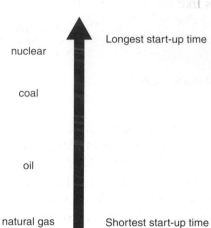

nuclear

coal

oil

natural gas

Longest start-up time

Shortest start-up time

Figure 2.12 Some types of power station start up faster than others.

⓫ How many 4 MW wind turbines are needed to replace a 2000 MW coal-burning power station?

⓬ Give one reason why gas-burning power stations start up quicker than coal-burning power stations.

How does the use of non-renewable fuel affect the environment?

Fossil fuels and global warming

Most of the heat (infra-red radiation) from the Sun that hits the Earth's surface is absorbed. Some of it is radiated back into space.

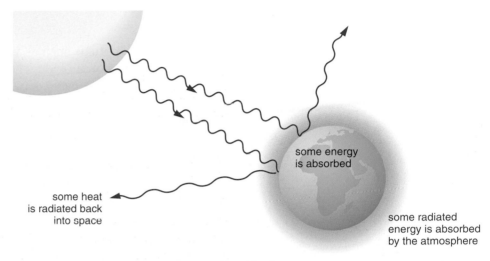

some energy is absorbed

some heat is radiated back into space

some radiated energy is absorbed by the atmosphere

Figure 2.13 Some of the Sun's heat is radiated back into space.

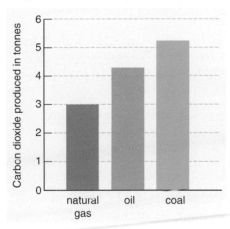

Figure 2.14 The amount of carbon dioxide produced for each kilowatt of power generated using a fossil fuel

(bar chart: vertical axis "Carbon dioxide produced in tonnes" 0–6; horizontal axis natural gas, oil, coal; natural gas ≈3, oil ≈4.3, coal ≈5.25)

The most penetrating heat rays from the Sun pass through the atmosphere and warm the Earth. These rays are absorbed by the Earth, which, in turn, radiates less penetrating heat rays. Under ideal conditions, the heat received from the Sun equals the heat radiated away from the Earth, and the average temperature of the Earth stays constant. But, during the last 150 years, the concentration of carbon dioxide in the Earth's atmosphere has increased. Heat rays cannot penetrate carbon dioxide as well as other gases in the air and, because of this, the less penetrating radiation from the Earth is blocked by carbon dioxide and prevented from travelling into space.

Fuel-burning power stations produce a lot of waste gas. The main constituent of this waste gas is carbon dioxide. So, as more and more fossil fuels are burned, more carbon dioxide enters the atmosphere. Many people believe that this has led to more heat being trapped and an increase in worldwide temperatures. This increase in worldwide temperatures is called global warming. There is clear evidence that the polar ice caps are melting due to this increase in temperature.

Fossil fuels and acid rain

When coal and oil are burned, sulfur dioxide is produced. This sulfur dioxide ultimately results in acid rain which damages buildings, kills plants and pollutes rivers and lakes.

Figure 2.15 Trees killed by acid rain

Figure 2.16 Oil doesn't have to be burned to affect the environment. An oil spill from a tanker can have a serious effect on wildlife and the environment.

Acid rain can be reduced.
- Sulfur can be removed from the fuels before they are burned.
- Sulfur dioxide can be removed from the waste gases before they enter the atmosphere.

Both methods of reducing acid rain are expensive and add to the cost of the electricity generated. Equipment to remove sulfur dioxide from the emissions at Drax, the UK's largest power station, cost £680 million!

Into the future

Like fossil fuels, biofuels such as woodchips, palm nuts, straw and olives also emit carbon dioxide when they burn. But unlike fossil fuels, they use up carbon dioxide as they grow. So, overall they add no extra carbon dioxide to the environment. Some power stations are now experimenting with blends of biofuel and coal. Elean Power Station in Cambridgeshire burns straw to generate 36 megawatts of power each year. In Queensland, Australia, a local electricity supplier burns 5000 tonnes of nut shells every year, producing enough electricity for 1200 homes.

Nuclear fuels and the environment

Nuclear fuels do not produce carbon dioxide or sulfur dioxide. Consequently, they do not add to global warming or produce acid rain.

Some people worry that nuclear power stations will leak radiation, but when nuclear power stations are working normally, little or no radiation or radioactive materials should enter the environment.

Fortunately, serious accidents at nuclear power stations are rare. But, when they do occur, radiation can be carried by the wind to a very large area.

Nuclear power stations do produce radioactive waste. This must be stored safely for long periods of time, sometimes for thousands of years.

❸ Explain why the use of biofuels to generate electricity would benefit farming communities and the environment.

Career – health physicist

Health physicists are responsible for monitoring radiation in power stations and the surrounding area. It's their job to make sure that people working at the power station are exposed to as little radiation as possible. They also monitor the local environment to ensure that the power station is not causing levels of radiation to rise above normal.

Activity – Nuclear waste? Not in our backyard!

Suppose you are the scientist on a committee asked to recommend the best way to deal with nuclear waste. The committee has put forward three possible options. All involve burying the waste.

Option 1: Bury and seal the waste permanently 500 m underground.

Option 2: Bury the waste 500 m underground but continue to monitor and, if necessary, retrieve the waste.

Option 3: Bury waste with a short half-life 100 m underground.

Some people don't want the area they live in to be chosen as a site for burying nuclear waste. They have started a campaign to prevent the waste being buried on their doorstep.

❶ What arguments might the campaigners use against burying nuclear waste in their area?

❷ What arguments and evidence would you use to persuade people that burying nuclear waste is a safe option?

❸ Explain why the committee has suggested that waste with a short half-life could be buried only 100 m below ground.

Look at Section 3.11 if you need help with this activity.

---

❶❹ How is the production of electricity in a coal-fired power station different to that in a nuclear power station?

❶❺ What economic factors need to be considered before building a nuclear power station?

❶❻ A 2400 MW power station uses nuclear fuel and 1 kg of the nuclear fuel produces 1 600 000 kWh of electrical energy.
   a) Calculate the power of the station in kilowatts (kW).

   b) How many kilowatt-hours (kWh) of electrical energy does the power station produce every hour?

   c) Calculate the amount of nuclear fuel the power station uses in one hour.

❶❼ Richard is considering buying some land to build a house on. The land is close to a nuclear power station. What evidence could a health physicist working at the power station present to Richard, to persuade him that it would be safe to live in a house built on the land?

Why use renewable energy sources to generate electricity?

Non-renewable fuels, like oil and gas, will not last forever. Reserves are running out. But the demand for electricity increases at an ever-increasing rate. Renewable energy sources need not burn fuels to generate electricity. The turbines that turn the generators use energy directly from the renewable source.

At the moment, Britain produces less than 3% of its electricity from renewable energy sources. The target, set by the government, is to increase this to 25% by the year 2025. But, how will this target be met?

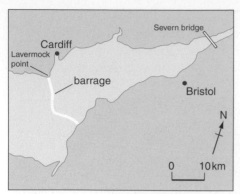

Figure 2.17 A tidal barrage across the River Severn could supply about 6% of Britain's electricity.

Using the tides

Every day tides rise and fall. Massive amounts of water move in and out of river estuaries. It is estimated that the energy of the tides could generate up to 20% of Britain's electricity.

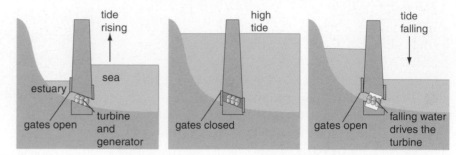

Figure 2.18 How a tidal barrage works

A barrage, which is like a dam, is built across a river estuary (Figure 2.18). The barrage has underwater gates which open as the tide comes in and then close to trap the water behind the barrage. When the tide goes out, a second set of gates are opened. Water rushes through these gates, driving turbines. The turbines turn generators which produce electricity. In some cases this system can be made even more efficient by also using the incoming tides to drive the turbines.

Of course, the amount of electricity produced by this method depends on the tides. The tides vary each day and change on a monthly cycle. However, tides are predictable, so the output from a tidal generator is reliable.

Tidal barrages have to be built across river estuaries. Because of this, they can disturb the flow of the river. This may destroy the habitats of wading birds and the mud-living organisms on which they feed.

Using waves

The UK is surrounded by the sea, and the potential for using wave energy to generate electricity is enormous. So, why are there so few wave power stations? The answer is simple. It is very difficult to harness wave energy and transform it into large amounts of electricity.

LIMPET (Figure 2.19), built on the coast of Islay, is an oscillating water column generator. The movement of the Atlantic waves forces air to drive a turbine, which then turns a generator (Figure 2.20).

Figure 2.19 LIMPET – the world's first commercial wave power station on the Scottish island of Islay has been generating electricity since November 2000.

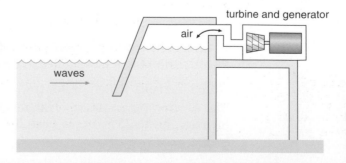

Figure 2.20 An oscillating water column generator

Activity – Generating electricity: the future

Because of the expense involved, scientists design and build smaller versions of their products for initial testing. These are called prototypes. After trials, they modify these prototypes before going ahead with the construction of a final product.

❶ Use the internet to find out how the two generator prototypes, Seaflow and Pelamis, work.
Start your search by looking at the following websites:
www.marineturbines.com   www.bwea.com
www.oceanpd.com

❷ Write a few sentences about each generator prototype.

❸ Which of the two prototypes do you think is the best choice for the future? Explain your choice.

Figure 2.21 The Seaflow generator, seen here, has been raised out of the water for maintenance.

Figure 2.22 Pelamis, moored off the Orkney Islands, moves with the motion of the waves.

Using hydroelectric power

The energy of a river can be used to generate electricity. To do this, a dam must be built across the river. Water is then trapped forming a lake behind the dam. When the trapped water is released it rushes downhill. The gravitational potential energy of the falling water is used to drive turbines, which then turn generators.

Hydroelectric power stations generate about 2% of Britain's electricity, but they produce about 10% of the world's electricity. Many of these schemes involve flooding large areas of land behind a dam. This may mean that:
- forests are cut down;
- farmland is lost;
- wildlife habitats are destroyed.

In China, the world's largest power project involved building a dam across the Yangtze River. The lake behind the dam flooded so much land that 1.5 million people had to move to new homes.

The demand for electricity changes during the day. When demand is high a hydroelectric pumped storage system can provide the extra electricity (Figure 2.26).

Figure 2.23 Hydroelectric power stations can be very large in size and generate vast amounts of power.

Figure 2.24 Between 1964 and 1968 the ancient temple of Abu Simbel in Egypt was moved, stone by stone, to higher ground. This prevented it being flooded by the lake created behind the Aswan High Dam.

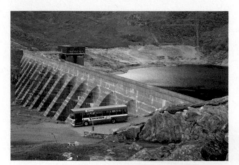

Figure 2.25 Ffestiniog Power Station is the first major pumped storage power station in the UK. It can produce enough electricity to keep North Wales going for several hours.

In just a few seconds, water which has been pumped into the top lake can be released. As the water falls to the bottom lake it drives a turbine, which then turns a generator.

At night, when more electricity is being generated than is needed, electricity is used to pump water back into the top lake. So, the energy has been stored and the power station is ready to generate again when demand is high.

⑱ What environmental problems are caused by building hydroelectric power stations?

⑲ Why do pumped storage power stations not increase energy resources?

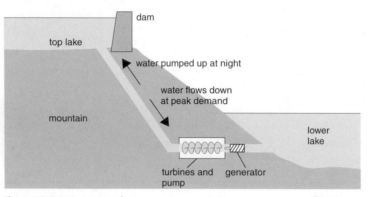

Figure 2.26 A pumped storage power station

Activity – Investigating a water-powered electricity generator

The model generator investigated by Anya is shown in Figure 2.27. The turbine rotates when a stream of water hits the cups. The rotating turbine turns the generator, which produces electricity.

Anya wanted to find out if the voltage output from the generator depended on the volume of water hitting the turbine each second.

Having made sure that the turbine was directly under the tap, Anya slowly increased the flow of water until the turbine just started to turn. Anya then placed a beaker in the water flow, timed one second, and then removed the beaker. Anya measured the volume of water and then tipped it away before repeating this step twice more. Her results are recorded in Table 2.2.

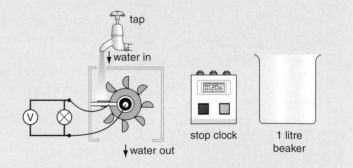

Figure 2.27 The apparatus used by Anya to investigate the generator

Attempt number	Volume of water collected in ml
1	42
2	52
3	68

Table 2.2 Anya's first set of results

① What is the mean (average) volume of water collected?

② Suggest a reason for the big difference between these values.

Juspal suggested that the experiment would be more **accurate** if Anya collected the water for 10 seconds rather than one second. She could then divide this by 10 to get the volume of water flowing in one second.

③ Why would the method suggested by Juspal improve the accuracy of the investigation? (An **accurate** result is one that is close to the **true value**, which is the value if the quantity is measured without any errors.)

Anya took the following steps to complete her investigation.
1 Turn the tap to give a steady flow of water.
2 Record the voltmeter reading.
3 Collect the water from the tap for 10 seconds.
4 Increase the flow of water and repeat steps 2 and 3.

The results of Anya's investigation are presented in Table 2.3 and Figure 2.28.

Voltage in V	Volume of water collected in 10 s in ml	Volume of water collected in 1 s in ml
0.25	680	68
0.30	720	72
0.50	780	78
0.60	880	88
0.70	940	94

Table 2.3 The results of Anya's investigation

④ Anya only took one set of results. Suggest why it would have been difficult to repeat the experiment to obtain a comparable set of results.

⑤ Do you think Anya planned a fair test? Give reasons for your answer.

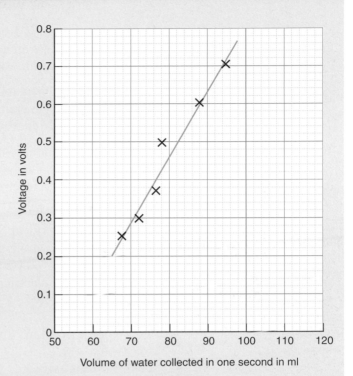

Figure 2.28 A graph of Anya's results

Not all of Anya's results lie on a straight line. What has been drawn is the line of best fit. Notice that some of the points are on one side of this line and some on the other. If all the points are to one side of the line it is not the line of best fit.

⑥ Suggest why the results do not give a graph with a perfect straight line.

The results of the investigation show a relationship or pattern between the volume of water hitting the turbine each second and the voltage generated. However the graph clearly shows that these two quantities are not **directly proportional**. For two quantities to be directly proportional the graph must give a straight line passing through the origin, the point (0,0).

⑦ Describe the pattern linking the volume of water hitting the turbine each second and the voltage generated.

⑧ Estimate the volume of water needed to generate 0.8 V. To do this you must assume the pattern continues as a straight line. This is called extrapolating the results.

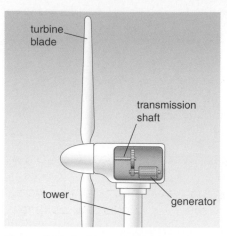

turbine blade

transmission shaft

tower

generator

Figure 2.29 Inside a wind-powered generator

Using the wind

Using energy from the wind is not a new idea. Over 1000 years ago, windmills were used to grind grain. In some countries, the power of the wind is still used to pump water from natural underground reservoirs.

In a wind generator, the turbine blades rotate when the wind blows. This turns the generator and produces electricity. So, a wind turbine transforms the kinetic energy of the wind to electrical energy (Figure 2.29).

One problem with wind generators is that the amount of electricity generated changes with the strength of the wind. If the wind is too light, little or no electricity is produced. This makes the wind an unreliable energy resource.

Wind energy applications vary from small units, which charge a battery, to large commercial wind farms with large numbers of wind generators providing power to the National Grid. Currently, only about 1% of Britain's electricity is generated using the wind, but this could increase to about 10%.

❷⓪ Why are the tides a more reliable way of generating electricity than the wind?

❷① Look at Figure 2.32. Why do you think the cost of generating electricity using wind turbines has fallen?

❷② The inhabitants of a small island need to replace their old power station. Half the residents want to build a coal-burning power station. The other half want a wind farm.
  a) State the reasons for and against a coal-burning power station.
  b) State the reasons for and against a wind farm.

Figure 2.30 Using a wind generator to charge the batteries of a boat

places where there is usually a strong wind

Figure 2.31 Generating electricity from the wind can be made more reliable by putting the wind turbines in places where there is usually a strong wind.

Figure 2.32 The cost of generating electricity using wind turbines

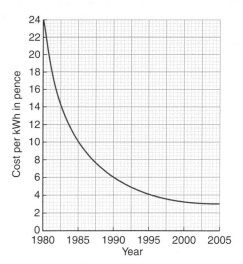

Figure 2.33 The conservationist Professor David Bellamy voices his opposition against placing the first giant wind turbine on the Mendip Hills in Somerset.

Figure 2.35 An offshore wind farm

Activity – Using wind power at home

You have decided to generate your own electricity using wind power. Before starting you need to know if this is a practical idea. Use the internet to research the information you need before deciding to go ahead. Use the British Wind Energy Association website (www.bwea.com) to help you.

Many people, including scientists, engineers and conservationists, argue that wind turbines are costly and inefficient. They also have a negative effect on the environment and wildlife.

Wind farms need to be where it is windy! This is usually on hills or along the coast in places of natural beauty. Some people think that the wind farms are ugly and spoil the view. So to some people, wind farms cause visual pollution.

Figure 2.34 Windy areas are often in places of natural beauty.

People living near wind generators also find them noisy. There is low-frequency noise from the rotating turbine blades and noise from the machinery inside the generator. So for some people wind farms cause noise pollution and, in certain cases, stress-related illness.

The costs involved in constructing a wind farm should not be ignored. Apart from the cost of making each turbine, materials are needed to build the base for each turbine and the access roads to and from them. Each base, for the largest type of turbine currently being manufactured, requires about 1000 tonnes of concrete. The production of cement for this amount of concrete will, in itself, pollute the environment.

Plans to site wind turbines offshore would greatly increase the amount of electricity generated by wind power in the UK. So far, three areas in the UK have been approved as sites for offshore wind farms. One of these, at Scroby Sands off the Norfolk coast, consisting of 39 giant turbines, will generate electricity for 50 000 homes.

Activity – For or against wind farms

The strength of local opposition to a planned wind farm of 26 giant turbines on a stretch of coastal marshland, near the Essex villages of Bradwell-on-sea and Tillingham, has led to the project being stopped.

People living in these villages and scattered farms were appalled by the plans. They said the plans would:

- destroy the unspoilt coastal marshes;

- threaten the thousands of migrating wildfowl and wading birds;
- create high levels of noise pollution from the turbines.

❶ Imagine you are a scientist working for a wind power company. What arguments would you use to persuade people to accept a wind farm in their area?

❷ Do scientists working for commercial organisations and environmental groups only look for evidence to support their own views? Give reasons for your answer.

2.7 Energy from the Sun and Earth

Energy direct from the Sun

The amount of electricity produced by a solar cell depends on the energy of the sunlight falling on it. If it's dark or cloudy, the energy of the light falling on the cell will be low and little or no electricity will be produced. Solar cells are therefore an unreliable way of producing electricity.

In some situations solar cells are the most convenient way to produce electricity. They are often used in remote areas, on satellites and in devices where only a small amount of electricity is needed.

Figure 2.36 A solar-powered MP3 player

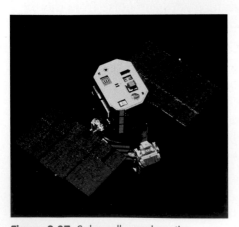

Figure 2.37 Solar cells produce the electricity to operate this satellite.

❷❸ Why are solar cells suitable for use with:
a) a mobile phone charger;
b) a satellite?

❷❹ Each square metre of land in the UK receives, on average, 200 joules of energy per second from the Sun.
a) What area of land would need to be covered by solar cells in order to generate 1 MW of power? Assume that solar cells transform only 15% of solar energy into electrical energy.
b) Would it be sensible to build a solar power station in the UK? Explain your answer.

❷❺ An African village uses solar cells to generate the electricity needed to operate the pump at a water well. Why are solar cells used to generate the electricity, rather than a petrol generator?

Energy from the Earth

Uranium and other radioactive elements are found inside the Earth. When atoms of these radioactive elements decay (Sections 3.8 and 3.9), they transfer heat to the surrounding rocks. This is called geothermal energy.

In areas of volcanoes, geysers and hot springs, water and steam heated by geothermal energy often reach the Earth's surface. The steam can be used to drive turbines connected to electricity generators.

Although the world's first geothermal power station, in Italy, started generating electricity in 1904, geothermal energy is under-used. At present the total worldwide geothermal generating capacity is only 8400 MW. But, this is gradually changing as more countries invest in geothermal energy. In the Philippines, one quarter of all electricity is now generated using geothermal energy.

Figure 2.38 Letting off steam the natural way!

26 The graph in Figure 2.39 shows how the demand for electricity in the UK varies over 24 hours.
   a) Why does demand increase after 6.00a.m.?
   b) The average demand during a 24-hour period is 6000 MW. How many hours was the actual demand lower than this?
   c) What type of power station could supply the additional power needed at peak times?

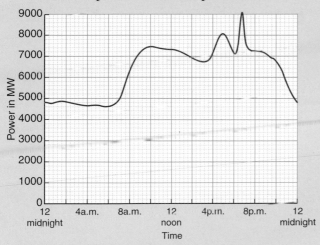

Figure 2.39 The demand for electricity is not constant.

27 Each year the global demand for electricity grows (Figure 2.40). How do you think the increased demand for electricity can be satisfied?

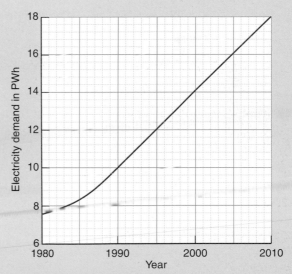

Figure 2.40 The actual demand for electricity and the forecasted demand for electricity between 1980 and 2010 (1 PWh is a million million (10^{12}) kWh)

Summary

✓ **Electrical energy** is easily transformed into other forms of energy.

✓ **Power** is the rate at which a device transforms energy.

✓ The power of a device is measured in watts (W) or kilowatts (kW).

✓ 1 watt (W) = 1 joule/second (J/s).

✓ The amount of electrical energy that a device transforms depends on the power of the device and how long it is switched on for.

✓ The amount of electricity transferred from the mains can be calculated using the equation:

energy transferred   =   power   ×   time
(in kilowatt-hours)   (in kilowatts)   (in hours)

✓ The **National Grid** is a network of cables and transformers linking power stations to consumers.

✓ **Non-renewable** and **renewable energy sources** can be used to generate electricity.

✓ The most common energy sources are fossil fuels – coal, oil and natural gas. Fossil fuels are non-renewable energy sources.

✓ Nuclear power stations generate electricity using the energy given out when uranium or plutonium fuels break up through **nuclear fission**.

✓ Renewable energy sources include the wind, tides, waves, falling water in hydroelectric schemes, solar energy from the Sun and geothermal energy from hot rocks.

✓ In most power stations an energy source is used to heat water. The steam produced drives a turbine, which turns an electrical generator.

✓ The energy from renewable sources can be used to drive turbines directly.

✓ Each type of energy source has its advantages and disadvantages.

EXAM QUESTIONS

❶ Table 2.4 shows data about a filament light bulb and a low-energy light bulb. Although the bulbs have different power ratings they both emit the same amount of light.

Type of bulb	Power in W	Lifetime in hours	Cost in £
Filament	100	1 000	0.60
Low energy	20	12 000	1.85

Table 2.4

a) Calculate, in kilowatt-hours (kWh), the amount of energy transferred to:
   i)   the filament bulb during its lifetime;
   ii) the low-energy bulb during its lifetime.
   (2 marks)
b) If each kilowatt-hour (kWh) of energy costs 12p, calculate the cost of using each bulb for its lifetime. *(2 marks)*
c) Which of the two bulbs is the most cost-effective? To gain full marks you must justify your answer with a calculation.
   (2 marks)

❷ An advertisement for solid fuel firelighters claims:

Be certain of a fast fire ...

... use H&S, the firelighters that give out more heat than any others

Figure 2.41

a) To test this claim, Paul plans an experiment to compare the heat given out by H&S firelighters with two other brands.
   This is Paul's plan for the experiment.
   • Take 1 g of H&S firelighter and place it on a tin lid.
   • Put 80 ml of water into a beaker.
   • Measure the temperature of the water.

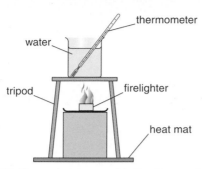

Figure 2.42 The apparatus used in Paul's experiment

- Use a match to set fire to the firelighter and then use the burning firelighter to heat the water.
- When all the firelighter has burned, measure the new water temperature.
- Repeat the experiment with the other two brands of firelighter.
  i) The type of firelighter is a variable. Is it a categoric or continuous variable? *(1 mark)*
  ii) Name two variables that Paul kept the same. *(2 marks)*
  iii) Give one reason why Paul wore safety goggles during the experiment. *(1 mark)*
  iv) Suggest how Paul could have improved the way in which he collected the data. *(2 marks)*
  v) Suggest one change Paul could have made to his choice of measuring instruments that would have improved the accuracy or precision of the experiment. *(1 mark)*

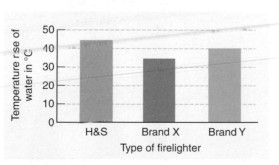

Figure 2.43 The data from Paul's experiment is displayed in this bar chart.

b) To compare his data, Paul drew the bar chart shown in Figure 2.43.
  i) Was the data collected by Paul sufficient to confirm the claim made by the maker of H&S firelighters? Give a reason for your answer. *(2 marks)*
  ii) Give two reasons why not all of the heat produced by the burning firelighter was transferred to the water. *(2 marks)*

❸ Mary wants to generate the electricity needed to run her own home. Having considered various options, including a petrol generator, she has decided to have solar panels installed on the roof of her house.
a) Use the following data to calculate the area of solar panels Mary needs to meet her electrical needs. Give your answer to the nearest whole number. *(3 marks)*

Electrical energy needed each year	3200 kWh
Average solar energy collected each day by 1 m² of solar panel	4 kWh
Efficiency of solar panel	20%

b) Explain why Mary should not rely only on solar panels to generate the electricity she needs in the winter. *(2 marks)*
c) Why should Mary keep her house connected to the National Grid? *(2 marks)*
d) Give one advantage of using a petrol generator rather than solar panels to generate electricity. *(1 mark)*

Chapter 3
What are the properties, uses and hazards of electromagnetic waves and radioactive substances?

At the end of this chapter you should:

✓ know that electromagnetic radiations travel as waves and move energy from one place to another;

✓ know that electromagnetic waves are grouped (classified) according to wavelength and frequency;

✓ understand that electromagnetic radiations and radioactive substances have many useful applications;

✓ appreciate that there are hazards associated with the uses of electromagnetic and nuclear radiations;

✓ understand how to reduce exposure to different types of electromagnetic and nuclear radiation;

✓ know that communication signals can be analogue or digital;

✓ know that all atoms have a small central nucleus, composed of protons and neutrons, surrounded by electrons;

✓ know that radioactive substances emit three main types of radiation (alpha particles, beta particles and gamma rays) from the nuclei of their atoms;

✓ understand the nature and important properties of alpha particles, beta particles and gamma rays;

✓ understand the term 'half-life'.

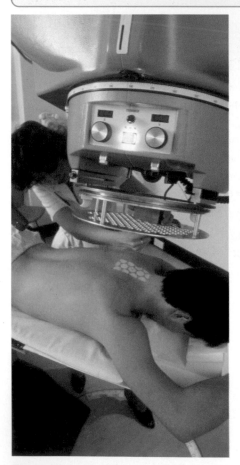

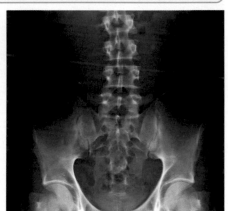

Figure 3.1 Some of the uses of electromagnetic waves and radioactive substances involve potential hazards as well as obvious benefits.

3.1 Looking at waves

A good way to visualise a wave is to use a stretched 'slinky' spring. In Figure 3.2 two people have stretched a slinky across the floor. While one end of the slinky is held still, the other end is moved from side to side. This sends a series of wave pulses along the slinky. The person holding the still end of the slinky can feel the pulses as they arrive. Each pulse carries energy but when the pulse has passed, the slinky remains exactly as it was before. None of the material of the slinky has moved permanently.

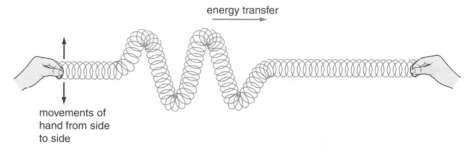

energy transfer

movements of hand from side to side

Figure 3.2 Wave pulses moving along a slinky

Figure 3.3 A Mexican wave passes around a stadium.

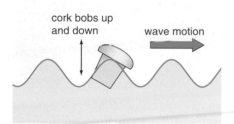

cork bobs up and down

wave motion

Figure 3.4 The cork bobs up and down as the water waves pass it by.

Waves move energy from one place to another without transferring any material (matter).

This is just like a Mexican wave at a sports event. As the Mexican wave rushes around the stadium you get the impression of something moving, but the spectators stay where they are.

When raindrops fall into a pond, water ripples spread out from the point where the rain hits the water. Again, you get the impression of something moving along but it is not the water. Energy is being transferred while the water vibrates up and down. You can see this clearly if you watch a cork bobbing up and down on the surface of a pond as waves pass it by (Figure 3.4).

All waves can be described in terms of three quantities – **wavelength, frequency** and **amplitude**. Being able to see a wave, like a water wave, makes it much easier to understand what these quantities are (Figure 3.5).

Wavelength is the distance from a point on one wave to the equivalent point on the next wave.

Frequency is the number of waves produced each second. It is also the number of waves that pass a point each second.

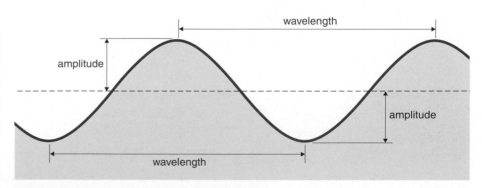

wavelength

amplitude

amplitude

wavelength

Figure 3.5 A wave moving across a water surface

Amplitude is the maximum displacement of a wave from its mean (middle) position.

Frequency is measured in units called hertz (Hz). A source producing one wave every second has a frequency of one hertz (1 Hz). If there are 50 waves in 10 seconds, the frequency is five waves per second, or 5 Hz.

The amplitude depends on the energy of the wave. The greater the amplitude, the greater the energy that the wave is transferring.

Wave speed and the wave equation

Suppose you are watching waves on the surface of a pond and three waves pass a particular point in one second (frequency, $f = 3$ Hz). Suppose also that the wavelength is 2 cm (Figure 3.7).

❶ Figure 3.6 shows wave pulses travelling at the same speed along two elastic cords. How are the wave pulses travelling along A different to those travelling along B?

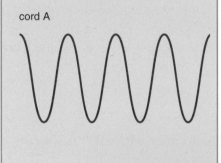

cord A

cord B

Figure 3.6

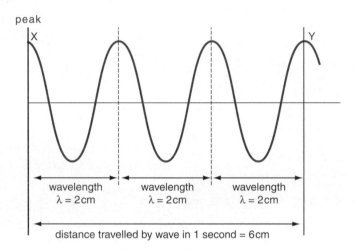

Figure 3.7

❷ The wave maker at a leisure pool makes one wave every 2 seconds. The wavelength of each wave is 4 metres.
a) What is the frequency of the waves?
b) Calculate the speed at which the waves travel across the surface of the water.

❸ When a stone is thrown into a pond, waves spread out across the pond. The speed of the waves is 0.3 m/s and their wavelength 5 cm.

Calculate the frequency of these waves.

Each wave peak moves forward by three complete waves every second. So, in one second the peak at X will have moved to Y. So the distance moved by a peak in one second is 6 cm.

Therefore, the speed of the wave = 6 cm/s.

In Figure 3.7 the speed of the waves can also be calculated by multiplying the number of waves per second (the frequency) by the length of each wave (the wavelength), i.e.

$$\text{wave speed} = \text{frequency} \times \text{wavelength}$$
(in metres/second)   (in hertz)   (in metres)

This is called the wave equation and it applies to all waves.

Example
Water waves with a wavelength of 0.6 metres make a moored boat bob up and down 2 times a second. At what speed do the waves travel across the surface of the water?

$$\text{wave speed} = \text{frequency} \times \text{wavelength}$$
$$\text{wave speed} = 2 \times 0.6 = 1.2 \text{ m/s}$$

The electromagnetic 'family'

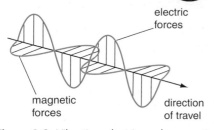

Figure 3.8 Vibrating electric and magnetic forces

Why electromagnetic?

Electromagnetic radiation travels as waves. But it is hard to visualise an electromagnetic wave. Just like water waves, they transfer energy. But unlike water waves, they do it without the need for a medium (a material to move through). The energy is carried through space by vibrating electric and magnetic forces moving along together. This is what we call an electromagnetic wave.

> The **electromagnetic spectrum** is the 'family' of waves caused by vibrating electric and magnetic forces, ranging from long wavelength radio waves to short wavelength gamma rays.

The electromagnetic spectrum

You already know a lot about one part of the **electromagnetic spectrum** – the part we call visible light. However, visible light is only a small part of the much larger electromagnetic 'family' (Figure 3.9). The electromagnetic family is a whole group of waves that together make up the electromagnetic spectrum.

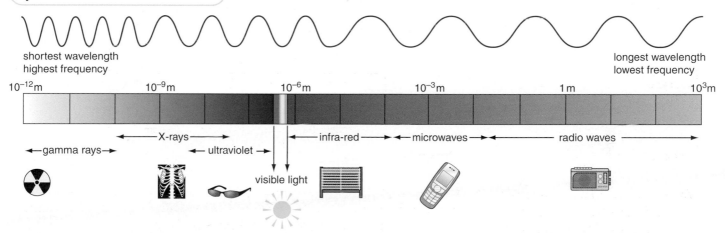

Figure 3.9 The electromagnetic spectrum – a 'family' of waves

There are no gaps in wavelength in the electromagnetic spectrum. Wavelengths run smoothly from one value to another, forming a continuous spectrum.

Despite having a huge range of wavelengths and frequencies, all electromagnetic waves have some important properties in common.
- They obey the wave equation (wave speed = wavelength × frequency).
- They can travel through a vacuum.
- They all travel through a vacuum and air at the same speed of 300 000 000 m/s. (This means that waves with the lowest frequency have the longest wavelength and waves with the highest frequency have the shortest wavelength.)
- They can all be reflected, absorbed or transmitted. But different wavelengths of electromagnetic radiation are reflected, absorbed or transmitted to different extents by different materials or types of surface.

4 Which parts of the electromagnetic spectrum have a higher frequency than ultraviolet?

5 A navigation system transmits radio waves at a frequency of 1.5 MHz.
  a) What is the speed of the radio waves?
  b) Calculate the wavelength of the radio waves.
    (1 MHz = 1 000 000 Hz.)

6 The waves which carry Radio 4 on the long-wave band have a wavelength of 1500 metres. Calculate the frequency of these carrier waves.

Electromagnetic radiation carries energy. When electromagnetic radiation is absorbed, the energy it carries will make the absorbing material hotter. It may even produce an alternating current (a.c.) with the same frequency as the radiation in the absorbing material.

Figure 3.10 The energy carried by infra-red radiation soon warms us up.

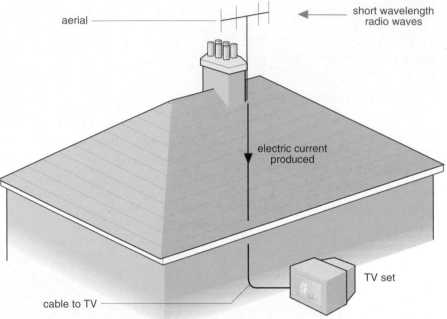

Figure 3.11 Electromagnetic radiation can produce an alternating current.

3.3 Using microwaves, infra-red and ultraviolet waves in the home

Microwave cooking

How does a microwave oven cook food? The answer might be obvious. You put the food in, push a few buttons and the food becomes hot. But of course it's not as simple as that. In fact scientists have more than one way of explaining how microwaves cook food. The neatest explanation is that microwaves, which can pass easily through materials such as plastic, paper and ceramic, are strongly absorbed by water molecules. The energy carried by the microwaves heats up the water. As most foods contain a lot of water, this gets heated by the microwaves and in turn cooks the food.

7 Explain why microwaves defrost frozen food rapidly.

8 Microwaves of frequency 2450 MHz are used to heat food. Calculate the wavelength of these microwaves.

9 Why is it important that microwaves don't leak from a microwave oven?

Food cooked in a conventional gas or electric oven is heated by conduction. This is a relatively slow process. Microwaves heat the food more quickly by penetrating several centimetres below the surface before being absorbed. So, using a microwave oven can reduce cooking times by about a quarter.

Activity – Sharon investigates microwaves

Sharon noticed that all the food containers she uses in her microwave are made from plastic. She thinks this is because microwaves lose less energy when they pass through a plastic container than they do through a ceramic container.

To test her idea, Sharon measured 250 cm³ of water into a plastic beaker. She placed the beaker in a microwave oven and heated it on full power for 2 minutes. Every 20 seconds Sharon stopped the microwave and took out the beaker. She stirred the water and took its temperature. Sharon then repeated the experiment heating the same volume of water, but this time in a ceramic coffee mug.

Table 3.1 shows the results which Sharon obtained when she used the plastic beaker.

Time in seconds	0	20	40	60	80	100	120
Temperature in °C	22	30	40	47	52	66	74

Table 3.1 Sharon's results with the plastic beaker

1. Draw a graph of temperature (vertically) against time (horizontally) for Sharon's results.
2. Sharon has one anomalous result. Which result is this? (Remember, an anomalous result is one that does not fit the general pattern.)
3. Why did Sharon stir the water before taking the temperature?
4. What was the temperature of the water after 50 seconds?
5. Estimate how long it would have taken for the water to boil.
6. Why is your answer to question 4 more reliable than your answer to question 5?
7. In Sharon's investigation, which quantity was the dependent variable?
8. Name one control variable which Sharon kept constant during the investigation.
9. The smallest scale division on the thermometer Sharon used was 1 °C. If Sharon had used a thermometer on which the smallest scale division was 0.1 °C would her measurements have been more accurate, more **precise** or more reliable?
10. Why did Sharon take a set of readings rather than just one at the start and one after 2 minutes?
11. Sharon thinks that microwaves lose less energy when they pass through a plastic container than they do through a ceramic container. If she is right, would her results using the coffee mug show a larger or smaller increase in water temperature? Explain your answer.

The **precision** of a measurement depends on the size of the smallest scale division on the measuring instrument. A smaller division gives a more **precise** measurement.

Figure 3.12 The infra-red radiation emitted by the heating element has been absorbed by the bread.

Infra-red radiation for cooking and detection

All objects emit and absorb infra-red radiation. The higher the temperature of an object, the more infra-red radiation it emits. Objects that absorb infra-red radiation become hotter.

We cannot see infra-red radiation. But an infra-red camera can be used to 'see' warm objects, even when we can't see them in the dark. The camera detects the different wavelengths of infra-red radiation emitted by a person, an animal or an object, and changes this into visible light that we can see. This type of camera is used by the army and police to spot people in the dark, and by fire crews to find people trapped in smoke-filled buildings.

Ultraviolet (UV) radiation

Ultravviolet radiation is emitted by any object at a sufficiently high temperature. In fact, objects emitting UV radiation must be white hot. The Sun emits UV radiation along with infra-red and visible light. UV radiation passes through some substances, but is partially or completely absorbed by others. Most types of glass are very good absorbers of UV radiation.

Some surfaces are good reflectors of UV radiation. If you go skiing it is important to remember that snow reflects up to 90% of the UV that hits it. As UV can damage the retina of your eyes, it's vital to wear glasses or goggles that give the right protection. Without these, you will end up developing snow blindness.

Figure 3.13 Sunbathing can be very pleasant, but you must take care to limit your exposure to the Sun.

Sunbathing

UV radiation given out by the Sun is partly absorbed by ozone in the Earth's upper atmosphere. The UV that passes through the atmosphere is what gives you a sun tan. When you get a tan, one type of skin cell is reacting to the UV, producing a brown pigment called melanin. Your skin changes colour and you have a sun tan. Your body produces melanin as its natural defence against UV. By absorbing UV, the melanin protects other cells from damage. But beware – melanin is not produced instantly, it takes time.

Figure 3.14 The fluorescent dial of this watch glows in the dark.

It is dangerous to overexpose yourself to UV radiation by being in the Sun for too long. It may cause your skin to age prematurely and increase your risk of getting skin cancer. Listening to weather reports, which include information about the UV level (the 'sun-index'), will help you to limit your exposure. But what else can you do? Here are a few suggestions:
- wear a hat with a wide brim;
- wear Sun-protective clothing. These garments will have a label giving the UPF (Ultraviolet Protection Factor);
- stay out of the Sun between 10a.m. and 3p.m.;
- slap on lots of high SPF (Sun Protection Factor) cream.

It's not all bad news though. UV enables your body to produce vitamin D, which is essential for healthy growth.

Energy-efficient lamps

Some substances can absorb the energy from ultraviolet radiation and then emit the energy as visible light. This is called fluorescence. Fluorescent paints and dyes, which seem to glow, work like this.

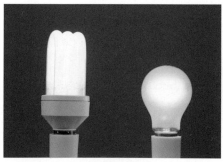

Figure 3.15 Fluorescent lamps are more efficient than ordinary lamps because they do not rely on a metal coil being heated.

Fluorescent lamps work by producing ultraviolet radiation. When electricity passes through the gas inside a fluorescent lamp, reactions occur and ultraviolet radiation is emitted. The ultraviolet radiation is absorbed by a chemical which covers the inside of the glass. The chemical fluoresces and visible light is emitted (Figure 3.16).

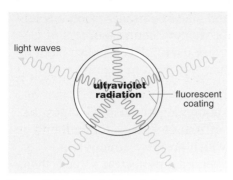

Figure 3.16 Ultraviolet radiation is absorbed and visible light emitted by the fluorescent coating inside the energy-efficient lamps.

⑩ Explain why it is difficult to get a sun tan inside a glass conservatory.

⑪ Why are fluorescent lamps often described as 'energy-efficient'?

Figure 3.17

Activity – Sensible sunbathing

A recent report has criticised travel agents for not doing enough to warn their customers of the dangers of sunbathing. Despite a sharp rise in the number of deaths from skin cancer, travel brochures still show lots of photos of scantily dressed, sun-tanned people lying around in the Sun.

Write a short article for the front page of a travel brochure. The article must warn people about the risk of skin cancer and, most importantly, give advice on how to reduce this risk. Of course, the article must not deter potential customers from taking a holiday in the sunshine.

Using X-rays and gamma rays in medicine

X-rays and gamma rays are at the short wavelength end of the electromagnetic spectrum. There is no sharp dividing line between the two. The range of wavelengths of X-rays overlaps that of gamma rays. Both types of radiation can penetrate and pass through some solid materials with very little energy being absorbed. Just like visible light, they also affect photographic film.

Both X-rays and gamma rays are ionising radiations. This means they can change the atoms of the materials they pass through. This is why they are harmful to us. When X-rays and gamma rays are absorbed by body tissues, their energy can remove electrons from some atoms, forming positive ions. This process is called ionisation. It can change the molecules that control the way in which a cell operates. This may result in damage to the central nervous system, mutation of genes or even cancer. So exposure to ionising radiations like X-rays and gamma rays must always be kept to a minimum.

X-ray photography

X-rays are absorbed by all body tissues to some extent. Bones, teeth and diseased tissues absorb more energy than healthy tissues, which X-rays pass through very easily.

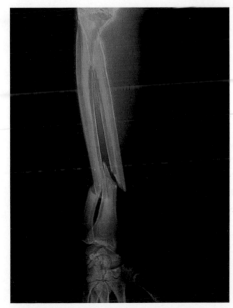

Figure 3.18 An X-ray photograph of a broken arm

In an X-ray photograph, bones, teeth and diseased tissues stand out because they absorb the X-rays and stop them affecting the photographic film. This makes X-rays very useful. Doctors use them to show where a bone is broken and dentists use them to identify tooth decay.

Radiographers, who operate the X-ray equipment in hospitals, must be protected from the dangerous ionising effects of X-rays. Often they work behind lead or concrete screens which are very effective in absorbing X-rays. If they cannot work behind a protective screen, then they wear a lead-lined apron. Lead is also used to protect the parts of a patient's body that are not being X-rayed.

Gamma rays

Gamma rays are widely used in diagnosing and treating diseases such as cancer. This is covered fully in Section 3.12.

⓬ Why is X-ray film kept in light-proof containers?

⓭ What precautions should a dentist take before X-raying a patient's tooth?

⓮ Why are X-rays and gamma rays described as ionising radiations?

Career – Radiographer

What does a radiographer do? Radiographers are involved in both the diagnosis and treatment of illness. A diagnostic radiographer uses a variety of techniques to produce images of our bodies. Using X-ray machines is just one part of the job. A therapy radiographer is an important part of the team that treats a patient. The radiographer will be involved in planning and delivering the treatment using high-energy X-rays and gamma rays. Working as part of a team, radiographers also need good communication skills. If you want to find out more about a career as a radiographer go to www.radiographycareers.co.uk or www.sor.org.

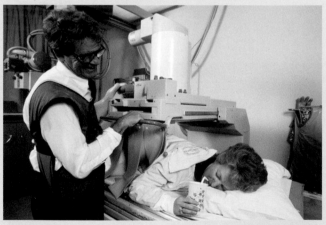

Figure 3.19 This radiographer, wearing a protective lead-lined apron, is preparing a patient for an X-ray.

3.5 Using waves in communications

Visible light, infra-red, microwaves and radio waves are essential for our communications.

Visible light and infra-red

Thin rods of glass, called optical fibres, are used to carry both infra-red and visible light rays. The fibres, no thicker than a human hair, consist of two parts – an inner core through which the light or infra-red travels and an outer layer that protects the inner core from being scratched. Once an infra-red or visible light ray is inside the fibre, it is reflected every time it hits the boundary between the inner core and outer layer. In this way, the ray travels from one end of the fibre to the other. It even follows the bends and twists in the fibre.

For communications, digital signals are produced by converting speech and electronic messages to light or infra-red impulses (see Section 3.6). These signals can then be transmitted along the optical fibres. Many telephone links now use optical fibres rather than copper cables. A single fibre is capable of carrying thousands of telephone conversations at the same time.

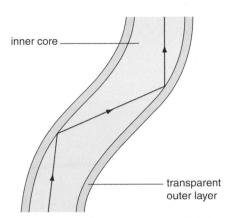

inner core

transparent outer layer

Figure 3.20 Reflection allows visible light and infra-red to pass along the optical fibre.

Microwaves and radio waves

The microwave and radio wave sections of the electromagnetic spectrum are divided into a number of wavelength bands. Together these bands cover a huge range of wavelengths, from 1 mm to over 100 km. The properties of the waves within each band determine the way in which the waves are used for communications.

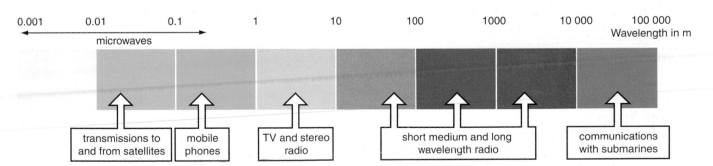

| 0.001 | 0.01 | 0.1 | 1 | 10 | 100 | 1000 | 10 000 | 100 000 |

Wavelength in m

microwaves

| transmissions to and from satellites | mobile phones | TV and stereo radio | short medium and long wavelength radio | communications with submarines |

Figure 3.21 Each band of the microwave and radio wave spectrum has a specific communications use.

Radio waves in the short, medium and long wavelength bands are transmitted around the Earth by reflections from the ionosphere (layers of ionised gas in the Earth's upper atmosphere). Radio stations, which use radio waves with wavelengths of 10 m or more, can therefore broadcast over very long distances with the shortest wavelengths travelling worldwide.

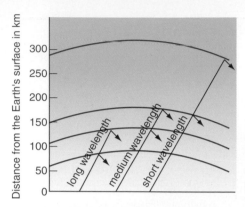

Figure 3.22 Different wavelength radio waves are reflected by different layers of the ionosphere.

More information can, however, be transmitted by shorter wavelength, higher frequency waves. So, stereo radio is broadcast using very high frequency (VHF) waves and television uses ultra high frequency (UHF) waves. Unfortunately, these waves are not reflected by the ionosphere, so their range is limited by the Earth's curvature. National broadcasts, using narrow beams of these waves, are made from communication towers such as the British Telecom Tower in London. These narrow beams are passed through a network of repeater stations throughout the country. At each station, the signal is transmitted in all directions to our homes.

Microwaves, with wavelengths of only a few centimetres, pass easily through the Earth's atmosphere. This means information can be carried by microwaves to and from satellites. Many people now receive their television programmes from signals carried by microwaves. These have travelled from a transmitter on Earth to a satellite and then back to a dish which acts as an aerial on the side of their house.

Nowadays, the commonest use of microwaves is in mobile phone networks. These microwaves are transmitted from place to place via tall aerial masts or from one continent to another via satellites.

Figure 3.23 Stereo radio and TV programmes are transmitted from telecommunications towers, such as the BT Tower in London.

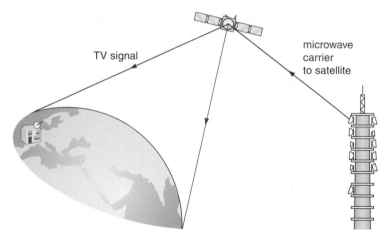

Figure 3.24 A satellite can transmit a microwave signal that covers a large part of the Earth's surface.

⓯ Explain how an optical fibre is able to carry a telephone conversation.

⓰ A TV programme in the UK uses a live satellite link to question a reporter in the USA. Why is there a delay between the question being asked and the reporter hearing it?

⓱ Why do most radio stations broadcast using waves with wavelengths between 100 m and 10 000 m?

⓲ What property of microwaves allows them to transmit information to satellites?

⓳ Which radio band can be used to communicate with a nuclear submarine on patrol in the North Sea?

Activity – Are mobile phones a health risk?

At present the simple answer to this question is that nobody really knows. But there are over 40 million mobile phones in the UK alone, so many people would like an answer.

In order to understand why mobile phones may present a health risk, we need to know how they work. Mobile phones are designed to transmit microwaves from an aerial in all directions. They must do this because the mast that receives and sends on the signal could be in any direction from where the phone is used. This means that some of the microwaves will travel towards us and penetrate our bodies, particularly our heads. As we learned in Section 3.3, microwaves are strongly absorbed by water and our bodies contain a lot of water. The energy absorbed by the water will raise the temperature of body tissues and may damage the cells (Figure 3.25).

Several scientific studies have suggested that there could be a link between mobile phone use and health problems such as tiredness, headaches, memory loss and brain tumours. Although the **evidence** from these studies is not clear-cut and conclusive, it indicates a need for more research.

> **Evidence** is data that has been checked and found to be valid.

In a report produced in 2005, Professor Sir William Stewart of the National Radiological Protection Board said,

'I don't think we can put our hands on our hearts and say mobile phones are safe. If there are risks – and we think there may be risks – the people who are going to be most affected are children, and the younger the child, the greater the danger.'

Following the Stewart report, a mobile phone specifically designed for children under the age of eight was withdrawn from sale in the UK. Some

Figure 3.25 Some energy from the microwaves is absorbed by the head and body.

people did not agree with this decision. Many parents want their children to have a mobile phone for emergencies. They argue that they worry less if their children can contact them at any time.

1. What does a scientist mean by conclusive evidence?
2. What reasons could a manufacturer give for producing a mobile phone for young children?
3. Why do you think a young child is more likely to be affected by the radiation from a mobile phone than an adult?
4. A study of 750 people in Sweden led to the suggestion that using a mobile phone for at least 10 years increases the risk of a tumour on the nerve between the ear and the brain by four times. The study has not been repeated.
   a) Do you think the number of people studied was sufficient to give firm evidence of a link between mobile phone use and developing a tumour? Give reasons for your answer.
   b) Why would it be a good idea to repeat the study?
   c) Why was the study restricted to people who had used a mobile phone for at least 10 years?
   d) If there was clear scientific evidence that using a mobile phone increased the risk of developing a tumour by four times, would you still use one? Give reasons for your answer.

Why are digital signals taking the place of analogue signals?

Digital signals are either 'ON' or 'OFF' and usually given the values 1 or 0.

Analogue signals vary continuously and can have any value.

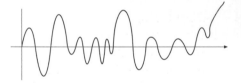

1 0 1 1 0 1 0 1 1 0 1

Figure 3.26 A digital signal is either 'ON' or 'OFF'.

Figure 3.27 An analogue signal produced by a microphone

20 Say briefly why digital signals are taking over from analogue signals.

21 Why is a radio often called a 'wireless'?

22 Describe what is meant by a digital signal.

23 Explain why the quality of a digital signal transmitted over a long distance does not change.

People have always wanted to communicate and nowadays it's easier than ever. Just pick up the phone, use your mobile or send an e-mail. We can communicate with people almost anywhere in the world and it is virtually instantaneous. But it hasn't always been this easy.

The telegraph was the first modern invention that allowed information to be sent using electricity as a message carrier. The signal was sent using a series of current pulses. These pulses were the first form of **digital signals**. In the USA telegraphy quickly became the fastest way of communicating over thousands of kilometres. But in modern terms, telegraphy was slow. At one end, an operator needed to code the message and then send the signal. At the other end, another operator wrote down the signal and then decoded it.

In modern digital communication systems, complex electronic circuits have replaced the operators. These circuits produce signals rapidly using only two electrical values, a high voltage pulse (ON) and a low voltage pulse (OFF). The number 1 is used to represent the 'ON' state and the number 0 the 'OFF' state. This allows any digital signal to be written as a series of ones and zeros.

The telephone, invented in 1876, was a major breakthrough in electrical communication. For the first time people were able to talk directly to each other. When you speak into a telephone, you produce sound waves. A microphone inside the telephone changes these sound waves into electrical signals. The amplitude and frequency of the electrical signals change as the amplitude and frequency of the sound waves change. These signals are called **analogue signals**. Analogue signals are waves with amplitudes and frequencies that vary continuously from zero upwards. In contrast, digital signals are integral values using the numbers 1 and 0.

In older telephone systems, copper cables carry the analogue signals to a receiver. The earphone in the receiver acts like a small loudspeaker. It changes the electrical signals back into sound. In modern telephone systems optical fibres, microwave links and radio links are replacing the copper cables linking 'sender' to 'receiver'. (See also Section 3.5.)

So communication signals may be either digital or analogue. But digital signals have certain advantages over analogue signals.

- Two things happen when any signal travels from a transmitter to a receiver. Firstly, the signal will get weaker. Secondly, it will pick up unwanted signals called 'noise' that interfere with and distort the original signal. With an analogue signal, different frequencies weaken by different amounts. So, during any amplification process to make the weak signal stronger, the original signal gets more and more distorted. With a digital signal, any unwanted 'noise' usually has a low amplitude. The receiver still recognises the original 'on' and 'off' states. This means that the digital signals received are not distorted and have a quality that matches the original signal.

- Computers work and communicate using digital signals. This makes it easy for a computer to process data in the form of a digital signal.

3.7 What are atoms really like?

Just over a century ago, scientists thought that atoms were hard, solid particles like tiny invisible marbles. Then, in 1897, J.J. Thomson discovered that the outer parts of atoms contained tiny negative particles, which he called **electrons**. As atoms were neutral overall, Thomson's discovery of negative electrons led scientists to think that the central part of an atom (the **nucleus**) must be positive. In 1909, Ernest Rutherford found evidence for positive particles in the nucleus and called them **protons**. Further experiments suggested that the nuclei of atoms must also contain neutral particles as well as protons. In 1932, James Chadwick, working with Rutherford, discovered these neutral particles and called them **neutrons**.

We now know that:
- all atoms are made up from three basic particles – protons, neutrons and electrons;
- the nuclei of atoms contain protons and neutrons;
- protons and neutrons have the same relative mass of one;
- protons have a positive charge, but neutrons are neutral;
- more than 99% of an atom is empty space occupied by negative electrons;
- the mass of an electron is about 2000 times less than that of a proton;
- the negative charge on one electron just cancels the positive charge on one proton;
- electrons whiz around the nucleus very rapidly. They occupy layers, or shells, at different distances from the nucleus.

The key points about atomic structure are summarised in Table 3.2.

Figure 3.28 J.J. Thomson (1856–1940) discovered electrons in 1897 when he was Professor of Physics at Cambridge University. In 1906, Thomson was awarded the Nobel Prize for Physics. Thomson was a brilliant teacher – seven of his students won Nobel Prizes for Physics or Chemistry.

Figure 3.29 Ernest Rutherford (1871–1937) found evidence for protons in 1909. In 1895, Rutherford left New Zealand to work with J.J. Thomson at Cambridge University. Later, he moved to Manchester University where he won the Nobel Prize for Chemistry in 1908. In 1919, Rutherford succeeded J.J. Thomson as Professor of Physics at Cambridge. Rutherford was a brilliant experimental scientist. His experiments always seemed to work.

㉔ Copy out Table 3.2 and fill in the blank spaces.

Particle	Position in the atom	Relative mass in atomic mass units	Relative charge
Proton	....	1	....
Neutron	Nucleus	....	0
....	Shells	$\frac{1}{2000}$	−1

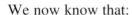

Table 3.2 The positions, relative masses and relative charges of protons, neutrons and electrons

The **nucleus** is at the centre of an atom. It contains positively charged **protons** and neutral **neutrons**. Negatively charged **electrons** orbit round the nucleus.

Protons, neutrons and electrons are the building blocks for all atoms. Hydrogen atoms are the simplest, with just one proton and one electron (Figure 3.30a). The next simplest atoms are those of helium with two protons, two electrons and two neutrons. Next comes lithium with three protons, three electrons and four neutrons (Figure 3.30b).

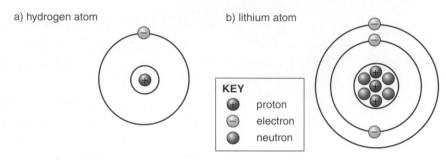

Figure 3.30 Protons, neutrons and electrons in a hydrogen atom and a lithium atom

Some of the heaviest atoms have large numbers of protons, neutrons and electrons. For example, gold atoms have 79 protons, 79 electrons and 118 neutrons.

Notice, in all these examples, that an atom always has the same number of protons and electrons. In this way, the positive charges on the protons just cancel the negative charges on the electrons and the atoms have no overall charge.

Atomic number and mass number

The only atoms with one proton are those of hydrogen. The only atoms with two protons are those of helium and the only atoms with 79 protons are those of gold.

So, the number of protons in an atom tells you which element it is. The number of protons in an atom is called its **atomic number**.

Hydrogen atoms have one proton. So, hydrogen has an atomic number of one, helium has an atomic number of two and gold has an atomic number of 79.

The mass of the electrons in an atom can be ignored compared with the mass of protons and neutrons. This means that the mass of an atom depends on the number of its protons plus neutrons. And the total number of protons plus neutrons in an atom is called its **mass number**.

Figure 3.31 If the nucleus of an atom is enlarged to the size of a pea and put on the top of Nelson's Column, the outermost electrons will be as far away as the pavement below.

The **atomic number** is the number of protons in an atom. All the atoms of an element have the same atomic number.

The **mass number** is the number of protons plus the number of neutrons in an atom.

> atomic number = **number of protons**
> mass number = **number of protons + number of neutrons**

㉕ Lithium atoms have three protons and four neutrons.
a) What is the atomic number of lithium?
b) What is the mass number of lithium?
c) How many electrons are there in a lithium atom?

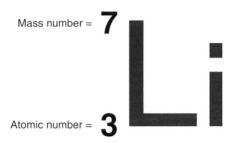

Mass number = **7**

Atomic number = **3**

Figure 3.32 The mass number and atomic number shown with the symbol for lithium (Li).

Sometimes, the symbol Z is used for atomic number and the symbol A for mass number. So, for lithium, Z = 3 and A = 7. Figure 3.32 shows how the mass number and atomic number are often shown with the symbol of an element.

All the atoms of one element have the same number of protons, the same number of electrons and therefore the same atomic number. But the atoms of one element can have different numbers of neutrons and therefore different mass numbers. These atoms of the same element with different mass numbers are called **isotopes**.

> Atoms of an element that have different numbers of neutrons, and so different mass numbers, are called **isotopes**.

For example, naturally occurring chlorine has two isotopes, $^{35}_{17}Cl$ called chlorine-35 and $^{37}_{17}Cl$ called chlorine-37. Each of these isotopes has 17 protons, 17 electrons and the same atomic number. They also have the same chemical properties because these are determined by the number of electrons. However, one isotope ($^{35}_{17}Cl$) has 18 neutrons and the other ($^{37}_{17}Cl$) has 20 neutrons. Therefore, they have different mass numbers and different physical properties because these depend on the masses of the atoms.

The similarities and differences between isotopes of the same element are summarised in Table 3.3.

Isotopes have the same	Isotopes have different
• Number of protons	• Numbers of neutrons
• Number of electrons	
• Atomic number	• Mass numbers
• Chemical properties	• Physical properties

Table 3.3 The similarities and differences between isotopes

㉖ Copy and complete the table below for the isotopes of carbon.

	Carbon-12, $^{12}_{6}C$	Carbon-14, $^{14}_{6}C$
Number of protons	6	
Number of electrons		
Number of neutrons		
Mass number		

(3.8) # Radioactive materials

Most **radioactive** materials that we use today have been synthesised by chemists, but some occur naturally. Large amounts of radioactive uranium and plutonium are used to generate electricity in nuclear power stations. Tiny amounts of these and other radioactive substances can be used to generate electricity in heart pacemakers. Radioactive materials can be beneficial, but they can also be harmful. They can cause cancer and also cure it.

> A **radioactive** atom is one that emits radiation from its nucleus.

Figure 3.33 Marie Curie began her studies of radioactivity with uranium compounds. From 1898 until 1902, she spent four years extracting radium chloride from the ore pitchblende. The radium in this was 2 million times more radioactive than uranium. In 1903, Marie Curie shared the Nobel Prize for Physics with her husband, Pierre, in the photo above. Then in 1911, she was awarded the Nobel Prize for Chemistry. She was the first person to win two Nobel Prizes. Marie continued working until 1934 when she died of leukaemia. This had been caused by the radioactive materials used in her research.

> An **alpha particle** is a helium nucleus, a **beta particle** is an electron released from a nucleus, and **gamma rays** are electromagnetic radiation.

A Frenchman, Henri Becquerel, and his Polish assistant, Marie Curie, carried out the first investigations into radioactivity in 1896. They discovered that all uranium compounds emitted radiation. This radiation could pass through paper and affect photographic film like light. Becquerel called the uranium compounds radioactive substances and he described the process by which they emit radiation as radioactivity or radioactive decay.

3.9

What is the radiation from radioactive substances?

The best way to detect the radiation from radioactive materials is to use a Geiger–Müller tube (Figure 3.34). When radiation enters the tube, atoms inside are ionised (changed into ions). These ions are attracted to electrodes in the tube and a small current flows. This current is then amplified and a counter is used to count the amount of radiation entering the tube. The amount of radiation is usually measured in counts per second or counts per minute.

Experiments show that radioactive atoms give out radiation all the time, whatever is done to them. The rate at which they decay is not affected by changes in temperature or by different atoms combined with the radioactive atoms. The radiation emitted consists of tiny particles and rays of electromagnetic waves which come from the nuclei of the radioactive atoms.

The nuclei of radioactive atoms emit three kinds of radiation – **alpha particles** (α particles), **beta particles** (β particles) and **gamma rays** (γ rays).

When radioactive atoms emit alpha particles or beta particles they become different atoms with different numbers of protons and neutrons in the nucleus. So, the emission of alpha and beta radiation leads to changes in the nuclei at the centre of radioactive atoms. This is different from chemical reactions, which involve changes in the electrons in the outer parts of atoms. When radioactive atoms emit gamma rays there is no change in the number of protons or neutrons in the nucleus but the atoms do lose energy. The energy is lost as penetrating electromagnetic radiation, similar to light.

The characteristics and properties of the three kinds of radiation are summarised in Table 3.4.

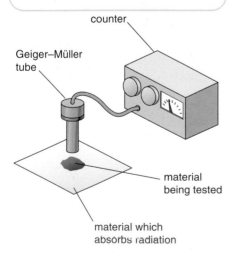

Figure 3.34 A Geiger–Müller tube and counter detecting radiation from a radioactive substance

Radiation	Nature of radiation	Penetrating power	Effect of electric and magnetic fields	Ionising power
Alpha particles	Helium nuclei containing two protons and two neutrons, $^4_2He^{2+}$	Travel a few centimetres through air, absorbed by thin paper	Very small deflection	Strong
Beta particles	Electrons, e^-	Travel a few metres through air, pass through paper, but absorbed by 3 mm of aluminium foil	Large deflection	Moderate
Gamma rays	Electromagnetic waves	Travel a few kilometres through air, pass through paper and aluminium foil, but absorbed by very thick lead	None	Weak

Table 3.4 The characteristics and properties of alpha, beta and gamma radiations

27 A scientist divided 3.0 g of pure uranium into three 1.0 g samples. He then converted these samples, without any loss of uranium, into separate samples of uranium oxide, uranium chloride and uranium bromide. He then measured the radioactivity of the three samples at the same time and temperature.
a) Are the three uranium compounds a categoric variable, a discrete variable or a continuous variable?
b) What is the dependent variable in this investigation?
c) Will the results for the three samples be:
i) exactly the same;
ii) more or less the same;
iii) very different?
d) Explain your answer to part c).

Notice the different penetrating power of the three radiations in Table 3.4. These differences in penetrating power are emphasised in Figure 3.35. Gamma rays are much more penetrating than beta particles and beta particles are much more penetrating than alpha particles:
- alpha particles cannot even pass through a sheet of paper;
- beta particles can pass through a sheet of paper but are absorbed by 3 mm aluminium foil;
- gamma rays can pass through a sheet of paper and 3 mm aluminium foil but are absorbed by thick lead. Because of this, radioactive substances are usually stored in thick lead containers.

Although alpha particles are the least penetrating, they have the strongest ionising power. On the other hand, gamma rays are the most penetrating but they have the weakest ionising power.

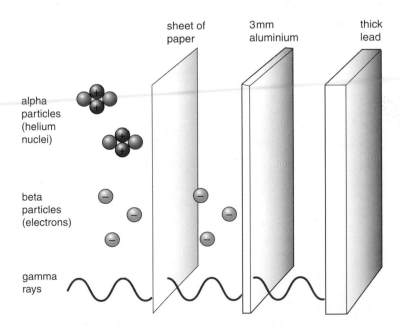

Figure 3.35 The relative penetrating power of alpha particles, beta particles and gamma rays

28 Figure 3.36 shows a thin beam of alpha particles being deflected by an electric field.
  a) Why are the alpha particles deflected towards the negative plate?
  b) Copy the diagram and assume that the source of radiation also emits beta particles. Draw the path of beta particles on your diagram. Remember that beta particles are negatively charged electrons and these are much lighter than alpha particles.
  c) Now assume that the source of radiation also emits gamma rays. Draw the path of gamma rays on your diagram.

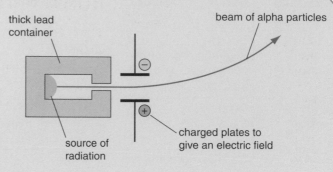

thick lead container

beam of alpha particles

source of radiation

charged plates to give an electric field

Figure 3.36 The effect of an electric field on alpha radiation

3.10 How much radiation are we exposed to?

The natural radiation that we are exposed to all the time from the Sun, rocks, our food and other sources is called **background radiation**.

Every day we are exposed to radiation from the Sun, from rocks and even from our food. This natural radiation to which we are exposed is called **background radiation**. As background radiation comes from various sources, it is higher in some areas than others. We are exposed to it all our lives. But normally it is very low and no risk to our health.

Although background radiation is very low, it must be accounted for in accurate measurements of radioactivity. This involves subtracting the average count rate for background radiation from the measured count rate of the sample being tested.

Figure 3.37 This environmental scientist is using a Geiger–Müller tube to check the levels of radioactivity in coastal soils.

29 An environmental scientist was asked to check the radiation from various plants along a path. First, she measured the background radiation by pointing her Geiger–Müller tube in different directions at six points along the path. She then measured the radiation level near six different plants along the path by holding her Geiger–Müller tube 20 cm in front of each plant. Her results are shown below.

Background radiation at six points along the path in counts per minute	58, 59, 58, 62, 60, 63
Radiation level in front of six plants in counts per minute	70, 64, 63, 60, 67, 66

  a) Why did she measure the background count at six points along the path?
  b) What value should she take for the background radiation in counts per minute?
  c) What is the average radiation level in front of the six plants?
  d) What is the average level of radiation emitted by the plants after correction for background radiation?

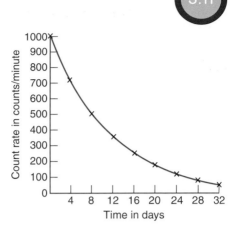

Figure 3.38 A radioactive decay curve for iodine-131

3.11 Radioactive decay

The breakdown of unstable radioactive nuclei is a random process. You cannot tell when an unstable nucleus will break down. If there are large numbers of unstable atoms, an average rate of decay will occur. So, if a sample contains 10 million radioactive atoms, it should decay at twice the rate of a sample containing 5 million atoms. As the unstable nuclei decay, the rate of decay will fall.

Figure 3.38 shows the decay curve for a sample of iodine-131. Doctors use this isotope to study the uptake of iodine by the thyroid glands. The shape of the decay curve is similar to those for other radioactive materials, but the scales on the axes can vary a great deal.

Notice from Figure 3.38 that:
- the count rate falls from 1000 to 500 counts/minute in 8 days;
- the count rate falls from 500 to 250 counts/minute in 8 days;
- the count rate falls from 720 to 360 counts/minute in 8 days.

> The **half-life** of a radioactive isotope is the time taken for the number of radioactive atoms to halve, or for the count rate to fall to half its initial level.

These results show that the time taken for the count rate of iodine-131 to fall to half its initial value is constant at eight days. We can also conclude from this that the time taken for the number of iodine-131 atoms to halve is also eight days. A similar constant pattern, in halving the count rate and the number of radioactive atoms, occurs with all radioactive substances. The time it takes for the count rate or for the number of atoms of a radioactive isotope to fall to half its initial value is called its **half-life**.

Half-lives can be determined by plotting graphs of count rates against time, like that in Figure 3.38, and then finding an average time for the count rate to fall by half.

Half-lives can vary from a few milliseconds to millions of years. The shorter the half-life, the faster the isotope decays and the more unstable it is. The longer the half-life, the slower the decay process and the more stable the isotope. Polonium-234 with a half-life of only 0.15 milliseconds is very, very unstable. Uranium-238 with a half-life of 4500 million years is 'almost stable'.

> **30** A hospital gamma ray unit contains 10 grams of cobalt-60. This has a half-life of five years. This means that half the cobalt-60 will have decayed after five years leaving only five grams of cobalt-60.
> a) How much cobalt-60 will be left after another five years (i.e. 10 years from the start)?
> b) How much cobalt-60 will be left after 15 years from the start?

What are the hazards of using nuclear radiation?

The particles and electromagnetic waves in nuclear radiation can cause the atoms in different materials to ionise. When an atom is ionised, one or more electrons are removed from it or added to it. If ionisation occurs in our bodies, the reactions in our cells may change or stop and cause disease. Because of this, exposure to ionising radiations can be harmful.

People who work with radioactive materials must be aware of the dangers from radiation.
- Low doses of radiation cause nausea and sickness.
- Moderate doses of radiation cause damage to the skin and loss of hair.
- High doses of radiation cause sterility, cancers and even death.

CHAPTER 3 What are the properties, uses and hazards of electromagnetic waves and radioactive substances?

Scientists and technicians who work with low-level radioactive materials must wear special badges containing photographic film sensitive to radiation. The film is developed at regular intervals to show the level of exposure.

The effects of radiation depend on its penetration, its ionising power and its half-life, as well as the length of exposure.

In general, gamma rays with their greater penetrating power are more harmful than alpha and beta particles. So, people who work with dangerous isotopes emitting gamma rays must take extra safety precautions. These include:
- shields of lead, concrete or thick glass to absorb the radiation;
- lead aprons, worn by radiographers who work continually with X-rays and gamma rays;
- remote-control handling of dangerous isotopes from a safe distance;
- reducing exposure to radiation to the shortest possible time.

Figure 3.39 This technician is wearing a special radiation-sensitive badge. This contains photographic film to show the level of radiation to which he has been exposed.

Activity – What are the long-term effects of radiation?

The data in Table 3.5 show the effects of radiation on uranium miners in Russia and on the people of Hiroshima after the atomic bomb in 1945.

❶ There were 100 extra deaths due to cancer in the 15 000 people living in Hiroshima after the atomic bomb had been dropped. This works out at one extra death per 150 people.
  a) How many people relate to one extra death among the uranium miners?
  b) Did the people living in Hiroshima or the uranium miners in Russia suffer the most?
  c) Does the data in Table 3.5 suggest that alpha radiation is more dangerous or less dangerous than gamma radiation?

❷ a) What was the source of radiation which affected the uranium miners?
  b) What form or forms of cancer do you think the miners suffered from? Explain your answer.

❸ It would be wrong to jump to conclusions about the data in Table 3.5 because it was not obtained by a fair test. The comparison of Russian miners with the people in Hiroshima was not carried out in a fair way.
  a) Explain what is meant by a fair test.
  b) State six reasons why it is wrong to compare the data for Russian miners with that for the people of Hiroshima.

Source of radiation	Type of radiation	Number of people studied	Extra deaths due to cancer caused by the radiation
Radon gas from decay of uranium	Alpha particles	3400 uranium miners in Russia	60
Radioactive materials from the Hiroshima bomb	Gamma rays	15 000 inhabitants of Hiroshima	100

Table 3.5 The effects of radiation on uranium miners and the people of Hiroshima

What are the uses of radioactive materials?

Radioactive isotopes are widely used in medicine and in industry. Their uses depend mainly on their penetrating power and half-life.

Medical uses

Although radiation can damage our cells, it can also be used to treat cancers. Cancer cells are damaged and killed more easily by radiation than healthy cells. This is because cancer cells grow and divide more rapidly than healthy cells.

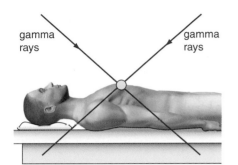

gamma rays   gamma rays

Figure 3.40 Treating lung cancer using gamma rays

Look at Figure 3.40. This shows how radiotherapy is used to treat a cancerous growth. The process requires penetrating gamma rays, which can pass through flesh and kill cancerous cells inside the body. It also requires an isotope with a fairly long half-life so that the gamma radiation can be adjusted to the same level over a few weeks of treatment. Cobalt-60 ($^{60}_{27}$Co), which emits gamma rays with a half-life of 5.3 years, is widely used.

Figure 3.40 shows beams of gamma rays from cobalt-60 being used to treat lung cancer. Gamma rays hit the cancer from several directions. This means the cancer gets a much higher dose than the surrounding lung tissue.

Skin cancer can be treated with less penetrating beta rays. This is done by strapping a plastic sheet containing phosphorus-32 ($^{32}_{15}$P) with a half-life of 14 days on the affected area.

Radioactive substances are easy to detect. They can be used in medicine to trace what happens to chemicals injected into our bodies. The isotopes used for this are often called tracers, which help doctors in the diagnosis of an illness. They must emit gamma rays, which can penetrate flesh and bone to be detected outside the body. Ideally, they should also have a short half-life so that the level of radiation in the body soon falls to a safe level.

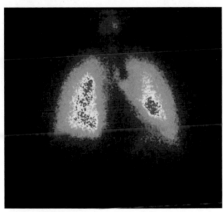

Figure 3.41 After injecting radioactive technetium-99 into a patient's blood, a doctor can study the blood flow through the heart and lungs.

Technetium-99 ($^{99}_{43}$Te) with a half-life of six hours and iodine-131 ($^{131}_{53}$I) with a half-life of eight days (see Section 3.11) are both used as tracers (Figure 3.41).

Most medical equipment, such as dressings and syringes, must be sterilised before being used. This is done by sealing the equipment in plastic bags and exposing them to intense gamma radiation from cobalt-60.

CHAPTER 3 What are the properties, uses and hazards of electromagnetic waves and radioactive substances?

Activity – Choosing radioactive isotopes for different industrial uses

Radioactive isotopes have a large number of industrial uses. These include their use in detecting leaks (Figure 3.42) and in thickness gauges (Figure 3.43). The choice of isotope is based on the type of radiation needed and a suitable half-life. This is also the case with medical uses discussed in Section 3.12.

❶ Look carefully at Figure 3.42.
   a) What type of radiation (alpha, beta or gamma) does this use require?
   b) Should the radiation used have a long or a short half-life? (Do you want the radiation to remain in the pipe for a long or a short time?)
   c) Why is the radioactive source described as a tracer when it is used in this way?

❷ Look carefully at Figure 3.43.
   a) What type of radiation (alpha, beta or gamma) does this use require?
   b) Should the radiation used have a long or a short half-life? (Do you want the level of radiation to remain at a constant level for a long time or to disappear fairly quickly?)
   c) What happens to the reading on the Geiger–Müller counter if the sheet of material gets thicker?

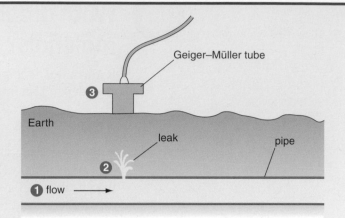

❶ Small amount of radioactive isotope is fed into pipe.

❷ Radioactive isotope leaks into soil.

❸ Geiger–Müller tube detects radiation and position of leak.

Figure 3.42 Using a radioactive source to detect a leak in an underground pipe

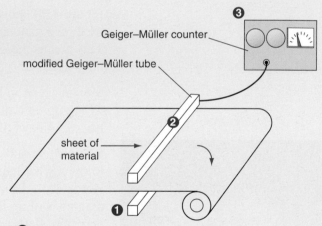

❶ Long radioactive source emits radiation.

❷ Long modified Geiger–Müller tube detects radiation penetrating the thin sheet of paper or plastic.

❸ Geiger–Müller counter measures radiation level. Information is fed back to adjust the thickness of the material if necessary.

Figure 3.43 Using a radioactive source in a thickness gauge for paper or plastic sheets

Summary

✓ All waves move energy from one place to another without transferring any material (matter).

✓ The **frequency**, **wavelength** and speed of a wave are linked by the wave equation:

wave speed (m/s) = frequency (Hz) × wavelength (m)

✓ The **amplitude** of a wave is its maximum displacement from its mean (undisturbed) position. The bigger the amplitude of a wave, the more energy it transfers.

✓ The waves which make up the **electromagnetic spectrum** have several important properties in common.
  – They obey the wave equation
  – They all travel through a vacuum at the same speed of 300 000 000 m/s.
  – They can all be reflected, absorbed or transmitted.

✓ When a material absorbs electromagnetic radiation it may get hotter.

✓ When electromagnetic radiation is absorbed, it may produce an alternating current in the absorbing material.

✓ Different parts of the electromagnetic spectrum have different uses.
  – Microwaves and infra-red can be used to cook food.
  – Ultraviolet (UV) radiation causes skin to tan, but it can also cause skin cancer.
  – X-rays and gamma rays have medical and industrial applications.
  – Visible light, infra-red, microwaves and radio waves are used in communications.

✓ **Analogue signals** are continuous waves that vary in amplitude and frequency.

✓ **Digital signals** have only two states, 'ON' and 'OFF'.

✓ Digital signals have two important advantages over analogue signals.
  – Digital signals are less prone to interference than analogue signals.
  – Digital signals can be processed by a computer.

✓ All atoms have a small central **nucleus** containing **protons** and **neutrons** surrounded by layers (shells) of **electrons**.

✓ All the atoms of one element have the same number of protons.

✓ The number of protons in an atom is called its **atomic number**.

✓ The total number of protons plus neutrons in an atom is called its **mass number**.

✓ Atoms of the same element with different numbers of neutrons and consequently different mass numbers are called **isotopes**.

✓ Some substances give out radiation from the nuclei of their atoms. These substances are said to be **radioactive** and the process is called radioactivity or radioactive decay.

✓ There are three main types of nuclear radiation emitted by radioactive sources:
  – **alpha particles**, which are helium nuclei, containing two protons and two neutrons with a relative charge of 2+;
  – **beta particles**, which are electrons with a relative charge of 1−;
  – **gamma rays**, which are very penetrating electromagnetic waves.

✓ The natural radiation to which we are exposed all the time is called **background radiation**. Normally, it is very low and there is no risk to our health.

✓ The time it takes for the count rate or for the number of atoms of a radioactive isotope to fall to half its initial value is called its **half-life**.

✓ The effects of nuclear radiation depend on its penetration, its ionising power and its half-life as well as the length of exposure.

✓ Radioactive isotopes have important uses in medicine and in industry. The choice of radiation for a particular use is dictated mainly by its penetration and half-life.

EXAMQUESTION

❶ Table 3.6 gives typical wavelengths for different parts of the electromagnetic spectrum.

Match each wavelength, **A**, **B**, **C** and **D** with the correct part of the electromagnetic spectrum numbered **1–4** in Table 3.7. *(4 marks)*

	Wavelength
A	0.00001 mm
B	0.0006 mm
C	18 cm
D	1.5 km

Table 3.6

Electromagnetic spectrum	
1	Microwaves
2	Ultraviolet
3	Radio
4	Visible light

Table 3.7

EXAM QUESTIONS

❷ a) Explain, with the aid of a diagram, the difference between a digital signal and an analogue signal. (*4 marks*)
b) Why do modern communication systems often transmit digital signals rather than analogue signals? (*2 marks*)
c) Draw a diagram to show how an infra-red signal is carried by an optical fibre.
(*2 marks*)

❸ Read the following extract taken from a newspaper article.
Plans for a mobile phone mast in the grounds of a local school have sparked anger amongst parents. Protestors opposed to the mast are worried about the potential health risks and believe that mobile phone masts will eventually be proved harmful. The parents feel that there is an urgent need for unbiased, *reproducible research* to be carried out and until this is done there should be no masts on school grounds. A spokesperson for the telecoms company said 'The mast will be unobtrusive and the health risks are unproven.'

a) Explain why mobile phone masts present a potential health risk. (*3 marks*)
b) What is meant by *reproducible research*?
(*2 marks*)
c) Give one reason why the evidence from a research project may be biased. (*1 mark*)
d) There are more than 30 000 mobile phone masts in the UK. Why does this make it difficult for scientists to prove a link between phone masts and health? (*1 mark*)

❹ Several people who work in hospitals and in industry are exposed to different types of radiation. Three ways to check or reduce their exposure to radiation are:
A wear a badge containing photographic film;
B wear a lead apron;
C work behind a thick glass screen with remote-handling equipment.

Which method (A, B or C) should be used by the following people?
a) A hospital radiographer. (*1 mark*)
b) A scientist experimenting with isotopes emitting gamma rays. (*1 mark*)
c) A secretary to a chief radiographer. (*1 mark*)

❺ A Geiger–Müller tube was used to measure a radioactive source with a half-life of 25 years. In five 10-second periods the following number of counts were recorded: 255, 262, 235, 258, 265.
a) Why were the five counts different? (*1 mark*)
b) In order to take fair measurement of the counts, some key variables had to be controlled. Name two variables that should be controlled. (*2 marks*)
c) Why were five counts taken? (*1 mark*)
d) Which one of the five counts is anomalous?
(*1 mark*)
e) Calculate the most reliable value for the number of counts per second. (*1 mark*)
f) Suppose five more 10-second counts had been taken. Would this make the result in part e) more precise, more reliable or more valid? (*1 mark*)

❻ Zak's teacher carried out an experiment to measure the half-life of protactinium-234. His results are shown in Table 3.8.
a) In the experiment, what was:
i) the independent variable; (*1 mark*)
ii) the dependent variable? (*1 mark*)
b) What instrument was used to measure the count rate? (*1 mark*)
c) What is the background count during the experiment? (*1 mark*)
d) Re-write the table, showing a corrected count rate at the times shown. (*1 mark*)
e) Plot a graph of count rate (vertically) against time (horizontally). (*3 marks*)
f) How long does it take for the count rate to fall from: i) 60 to 30; ii) 40 to 20; iii) 30 to 15? (*3 marks*)
g) Calculate an average value for the half-life of protactinium-234. (*1 mark*)

Time in s	Count rate in counts/s
0	66
40	44
80	30
120	20
160	13
200	9
240	6
280	4
320	4
360	4

Table 3.8

Chapter 4
What are the origins of the Universe and how is it changing?

At the end of this chapter you should:

✓ know that careful observations can stimulate further investigations and lead to important technological developments;

✓ understand that the results and information from scientific investigations can be made more reliable by repeated observations and the use of more sensitive equipment;

✓ appreciate the advantages and disadvantages of different types of telescopes;

✓ understand how the wavelength and frequency of light and other wave motions change when the wave source is moving;

✓ know that there is a red-shift in light from distant galaxies;

✓ understand how the observed red-shift provides evidence that the Universe is expanding and supports the 'big bang' theory.

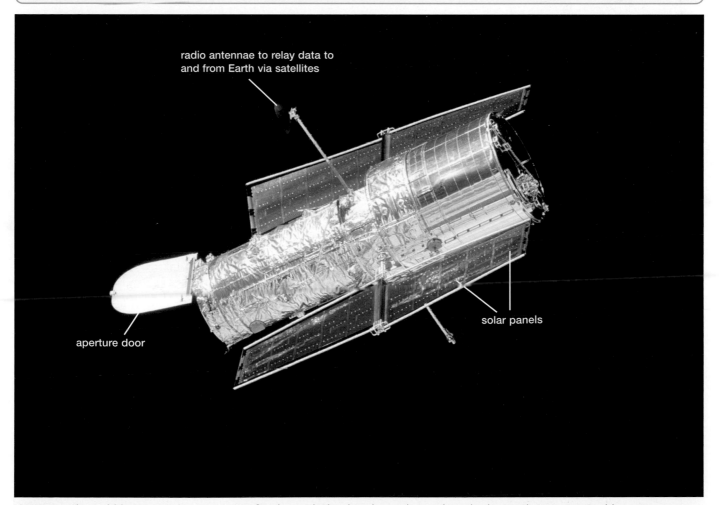

radio antennae to relay data to and from Earth via satellites

solar panels

aperture door

Figure 4.1 The Hubble Space Telescope or HST for short, which orbits the Earth, was launched in April 1990. HST enables astronomers to obtain clearer pictures than ever of the Milky Way and distant galaxies. HST is about the size of a bus. It was designed for launch and repair by astronauts from the Space Shuttle. They can replace worn out parts on the telescope, fit more advanced instruments and re-adjust its orbit.

CHAPTER 4 What are the origins of the Universe and how is it changing?

 ## Stars and galaxies

Betelgeuse, an old red supergiant star.

Rigel, a young bluish supergiant star.

Figure 4.2 Stars that make up the constellation Orion. The black outline shows the picture that the constellation is supposed to represent.

People have been looking at the stars for thousands of years. Stars are formed when clouds of gas (mainly hydrogen) get compressed. As the hydrogen is compressed, the temperature rises. Eventually, the temperature is so high that the nuclei of hydrogen atoms fuse together, forming helium. This nuclear fusion process emits immense amounts of heat and light. Of course, the Sun is the nearest star to Earth. But there are billions of other stars in the sky. Most of these stars are too far away to see, but if you look at the sky on a clear night, you will see hundreds of them.

People who watch and study the stars are called astronomers. Astronomers have grouped bright stars together in patterns and called them **constellations**. These constellations help astronomers and other star watchers to identify and find stars in the sky. Figure 4.2 shows the stars in the constellation Orion. In Greek mythology, Orion was a great hunter.

A **constellation** is a group of stars that forms a recognisable pattern in the sky.

❶ What is the difference between a star and a planet?

❷ Put the following in order of size from smallest to largest.

asteroid   galaxy   meteorite   planet   star   Universe

❸ Why can't you see millions of stars during the day?

❹ Why is the idea of constellations helpful?

Activity – Stargazing

The best time to observe the stars is on a dark, cloudless night, about two hours after sunset. It is often difficult to stargaze in cities because of the glare from city lights. It's much better to stargaze in country areas. It will take 15 or 20 minutes for your eyes to adjust to the dark, so don't give up if you can't see much at first.

Wear warm clothes for this activity because you will get cold sitting or standing still. Take a notepad, a pencil and a torch plus binoculars or a telescope. And **remember**, it's always important to go stargazing with an adult that you know.

❶ Use your binoculars or telescope to find the two well-known constellations, Ursa Major and Casseopeia, close to the Pole Star. These constellations can be seen all year round. First of all, look for Ursa Major, which is often called the 'Plough' or the 'Great Bear' (Figure 4.3). The two stars on the right of Ursa Major are known as pointers. These point towards the Pole Star.

❷ Sketch Ursa Major in your notepad as you see it.

❸ Look carefully at Ursa Major. Which one of the eight stars is, in fact, a double star?

❹ Now, find Casseopeia (Figure 4.4) and draw it.

❺ Make a sketch to show the position of the Pole Star, Ursa Major and Casseopeia.

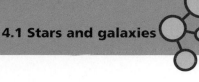

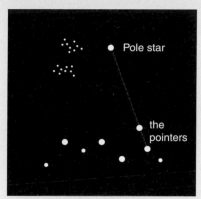

Figure 4.3 The constellation Ursa Major and the Pole Star

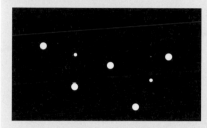

Figure 4.4 The constellation Casseopeia

6   If you watch the sky at night over a period of time, the positions of all stars and constellations change, except for the Pole Star. Why is this? (Remember that the Earth spins on an axis through the North and South Poles.)

7   Binoculars and telescopes help you to see much more detail in the night sky. Binoculars and telescopes have their own advantages. Which is better for being:
a) more powerful;   b) easier to use;   c) less expensive;
d) quicker to focus;   e) able to give a steadier image?

8   Now, try to find Orion and other constellations in the night sky. The best way to find constellations is from a sky map (star map). Go to the BBC Sky at Night website (log onto www.bbc.co.uk and search for 'sky at night' then search on 'sky maps'). This will allow you to view a star map for the period when you are looking at the sky. Alternatively, you can go to the same website and click on 'My space' followed by 'constellation guide' to view a particular constellation.

Careful observation of the stars and constellations using simple telescopes stimulated the early astronomers to make more investigations and this led to new discoveries.

Astronomers found that stars and constellations are not randomly scattered throughout the Universe. They are concentrated in large groups known as **galaxies**. Our Sun is just one of the 100 000 million stars in the Milky Way galaxy (Figure 4.5). If you could view the Milky Way from the side, it would look like two fried eggs stuck back to back – long and thin with a bulge in the middle. But, if you could view the Milky Way from above, it would look like a giant whirlpool with spiral arms. The Milky Way is spinning round slowly and our Sun will take about 220 million years to go round the centre of the galaxy. In millions of years' time, astronomers will see different stars at night.

The distances between stars and between galaxies are so large that it is pointless to measure them in kilometres. The distances are measured in **light years**. One light year is the distance that light travels in one year. The speed of light is 300 000 km/s, so one light year is roughly ten million million (10^{13}) km. The Milky Way is about 100 000 light years across. This means that it takes 100 000 years for light to cross its spirals.

> Stars are concentrated in groups containing billions of stars called **galaxies**.
>
> A **light year** is the distance light travels in 1 year. One light year is about ten million million (10^{13}) km.

CHAPTER 4 What are the origins of the Universe and how is it changing?

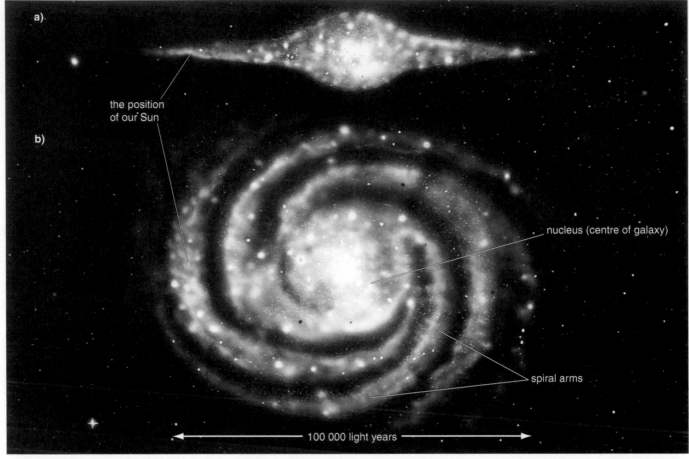

a)

the position of our Sun

b)

nucleus (centre of galaxy)

spiral arms

100 000 light years

Figure 4.5 a) A side view of the Milky Way and b) a top view of the Milky Way. On a clear, dark night, it is sometimes possible to see a broad, milky band of stars stretching across the sky. This is part of the Milky Way galaxy.

Activity – The Milky Way and other galaxies

Discover more about the Milky Way and other galaxies by going to the Discovery School Website at www.discoveryschool.com.

Then search on 'Galaxy Tour' or 'Milky Way'. As you view the website, plan and write a short report, of about 250 words, on the Milky Way and / or other galaxies.

(You will learn more about galaxies in Section 13.1.)

 ## Space watch

4.2

For thousands of years, people have gazed at the sky and wondered about the mysteries of the Universe. Since the Middle Ages, astronomers have used telescopes and binoculars to view the stars and constellations more clearly and more scientifically.

Today, extremely powerful telescopes allow astronomers to observe and study the Solar System, stars and galaxies throughout the Universe in great detail. The observations are made with telescopes that detect visible light or other electromagnetic radiations, such as radio waves and

X-rays. There are only two different types of powerful telescope – optical telescopes and radio telescopes – but some of these telescopes are based on Earth while others are mounted on artificial satellites orbiting in space.

Optical telescopes

Figure 4.6 The Keck telescopes in Hawaii are two of the largest optical telescopes in the world. Each one is eight storeys tall.

Optical telescopes produce images of stars and galaxies using light. These images are magnified using lenses and mirrors. Very large, powerful optical telescopes are housed in buildings called observatories. The Keck optical telescopes in Hawaii and the Hale optical telescope at Mount Palomar, in the United States, are so powerful that they are never pointed at anything as close as the Moon. These telescopes use huge concave mirrors with diameters of five metres or more. They are so sensitive that they can detect a candle flame 20 000 kilometres away and stars that we cannot even see. Some of these stars are so far away that their light takes millions of years to reach the Earth. When astronomers look at these stars, they are seeing them as they were millions of years ago.

It is very difficult to construct the large, accurate mirror in an optical telescope. Optical telescopes also need huge structures to support the mirror and allow it to move into different positions to pick up light from different parts of the sky.

The main problem with optical telescopes is getting the final image in a position where it can be seen without interference from incoming light rays. This is solved by placing a small flat mirror at an angle just in front of the focus of the concave mirror. The image can then be viewed through an eyepiece (eye lens) away from the incoming light rays (Figure 4.7).

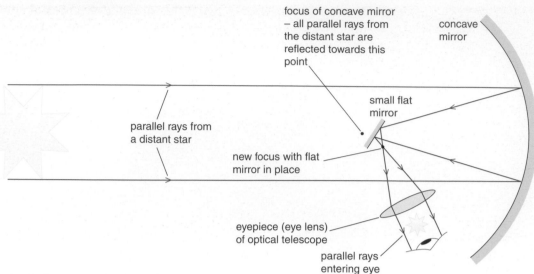

focus of concave mirror
– all parallel rays from
the distant star are
reflected towards this
point

concave
mirror

small flat
mirror

parallel rays from
a distant star

new focus with flat
mirror in place

eyepiece (eye lens)
of optical telescope

parallel rays
entering eye

Figure 4.7 The path of light rays in an optical telescope

Radio telescopes

In 1932, an American electrical engineer, called Karl Jansky, detected radio waves coming from space. This simple observation led to the development of radio telescopes. A new area of technology opened up leading to the discovery of pulsars and new galaxies. Pulsars are small stars which rotate quickly, giving off pulses of radiation.

Radio telescopes enable astronomers to study stars and galaxies even further away in space. These distant stars and galaxies give off radio waves, but they cannot be seen using optical telescopes. Radio waves are electromagnetic waves (tiny electrical and magnetic vibrations) which belong to the same family as light but they have much longer wavelengths and lower frequencies (see Section 3.2).

Radio telescopes have a huge concave dish to collect the radio waves given off by certain stars and galaxies (see Figure 4.8). The main dish directs the radio waves towards a secondary reflector, supported above the main dish. This, in turn, reflects them onto a receiver just above the centre of the main dish.

Like many other scientific measurements, there is always some variation in the strength and frequency of radio waves from stars and galaxies.

In order to make their data more reliable, scientists use rows (arrays) of several radio dishes and make repeated observations over days, months and even years.

Signals picked up by several radio telescopes over long periods are often fed into computers. The signals can then be converted into images ('pictures') of the stars and galaxies that are giving off the radio waves.

Figure 4.8 This group of 27 radio telescopes in New Mexico, USA is used to study stars and galaxies beyond the Milky Way. It is known as the Very Large Array.

Space telescopes

Since 1990, scientists have discovered how to put telescopes into space so that they orbit the Earth. These so-called space telescopes can be either optical telescopes or radio telescopes.

Space telescopes can be used to see much further and more clearly than telescopes based on Earth. This is because the Earth's atmosphere does not distort or block their reception of signals from space. By using space telescopes with larger, more carefully constructed mirrors, astronomers can measure smaller and more distant objects in space. Space telescopes are also more sensitive to weaker signals of light, radio waves and other electromagnetic radiations with lower amplitude and lower energy.

The first major space telescope was launched in April 1990. It is called the Hubble Space Telescope, or HST for short (Figure 4.1). It was named in recognition of Edwin Hubble (Section 4.4). HST is an optical telescope which orbits the Earth about 600 km above the ground. Astronomers on Earth can send instructions to cameras on board HST via radio antennae attached to its structure. The same radio antennae relay data and pictures of distant galaxies and planets back to Earth.

At present, scientists in Europe and America are working on the construction of space telescopes that have even more sophisticated functions than the Hubble Space Telescope. The USA's replacement for HST, named The Next Generation Space Telescope, is due for launch in 2009.

In order to understand space exploration further, we must now study what happens to sound and light waves when the source of the waves is moving.

5 What do you understand by the terms
a) optical telescope;
b) radio telescope?

6 What are radio waves?

7 Make a list of the relative advantages and disadvantages of optical telescopes and radio telescopes.

8 a) What is the big advantage of space telescopes over telescopes based on Earth?
b) Suggest three disadvantages of space telescopes.

4.3 What happens to sound waves and light waves when the wave source is moving?

Have you noticed as a police car or a fire engine rushes past you, that the noise of the siren changes? Figure 4.9 will help you to understand why this happens.

In Figure 4.9a, the source of sound, S, is stationary. Waves spread out from S and someone standing at A hears exactly the same sound as someone at B because they both receive the same number of waves every second.

In Figure 4.9b, the source is moving to the right. This distorts the waves which become closer together on the right and more spread out on the left. So, someone standing at C hears fewer waves per second than someone at D. The waves at C have a lower frequency and a longer wavelength than those at D.

A similar effect happens with other wave motions, such as light and radio waves, if the wave source is moving very quickly. If a source of light is moving away from you, the wavelength of the light increases. And if the source of light moves even faster, then the wavelength increases even more.

9 How is a source of light moving if its wavelength is longer than expected?

10 What can you conclude about distant galaxies if the wavelength of light from them is longer than expected?

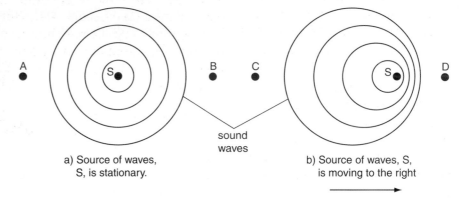

a) Source of waves, S, is stationary.

sound waves

b) Source of waves, S, is moving to the right

Figure 4.9 The sound waves from a) a stationary source; b) a moving source

4.4 Moving stars and galaxies

Stargazers have been aware that stars moved across the sky for thousands of years. Early in the twentieth century, astronomers realised that our Solar System was just a very small part of an enormous galaxy of stars. They also realised that the Universe contained millions upon millions of other galaxies.

In 1929, the American astronomer Edwin Hubble began to observe and measure these other galaxies. Hubble discovered two very important rules from his observations.

1   The wavelength of light from distant galaxies was longer than expected. Hubble called this the **red-shift** because red light has a longer wavelength than other colours and the wavelengths of light from other galaxies moved towards the red end of the spectrum.

2   The further a galaxy is from the Earth, the greater is its red-shift. This is usually called Hubble's Law.

4.5 The origins of the Universe

During the middle of the twentieth century, two theories were suggested for the origins of the Universe. These were called the **'big bang' theory** and the 'steady state' theory.

The 'big bang' theory suggested that the Universe began with an immense explosion billions of years ago. At that moment, all matter that had been concentrated at one small point exploded violently and started to expand. Dust and gases were forced outwards eventually forming the stars and planets that exist today. Since the 'big bang', the Universe has continued to expand, as stars and galaxies move further apart with increasing speed.

The 'steady state' theory suggested that matter was being created continuously in an expanding Universe.

Any theory about the origin of the Universe must account for Hubble's observations. (See Section 4.4.) Hubble explained his first observation by suggesting that the red-shift occurred because distant galaxies were moving away from our own galaxy at great speed. The light emitted from them appears to have a longer wavelength because the waves are being pulled out.

Hubble explained his second observation by suggesting that galaxies further away must be moving faster.

Hubble's red-shift observations provided evidence for a rapidly expanding Universe and supported the 'big bang' theory better than the 'steady state' theory.

Further evidence for the 'big bang' theory came in 1965 with the discovery of cosmic background radiation. The whole Universe appears to emit radiation, which is thought to be a distant echo of the 'big bang'. Today, most astronomers support the 'big bang' theory.

Science and scientists have come a long way, since the early stargazers, in answering questions about the Universe and its origins. They have answered questions about the Sun and its planets, about galaxies and the way they move. But there are limitations to science and lots of questions about the Universe that scientists still cannot answer. The 'big bang' theory is only a theory – a good idea that helps to explain some important observations. It may or may not be correct. Science cannot explain why the 'big bang' happened or when the Universe will end.

When an object that gives out light is moving away from us, we see a **red-shift** in the light as the wavelength shifts toward the red end of the spectrum. The faster it is moving away from us, the greater the red-shift.

11 Galaxies in the constellation of Ursa Major have a greater red-shift than galaxies in the constellation of Virgo. What can you conclude from this?

The **'big bang' theory** suggests that the Universe was created with an immense explosion of all matter from one small point. At that moment the Universe started to expand and it has continued to do so.

Figure 4.10 This galaxy in the constellation of Ursa Major is moving away from us at a speed of 15 000 kilometres per second.

Activity – Estimating the age of the Universe

Measurements of red-shift allow astronomers to calculate the speed that galaxies are travelling away from us. Table 4.1 shows the speeds of five different galaxies and their distances from Earth.

Galaxy	Speed of galaxy in km per second	Distance of galaxy from Earth in millions of light years
A	6 700	400
B	15 000	900
C	20 000	1 200
D	40 000	2 400
E	60 000	3 600

Table 4.1

❶ What is the range of speeds for the five galaxies?
❷ Is the distance of galaxies from Earth a continuous variable, an ordered variable or a categoric variable?

❸ Table 4.1 does not show clearly any pattern or relationship between the speed of a galaxy and its distance from Earth. Would it be best to draw a bar chart, a line graph or a scattergram to find the relationship between these two variables?
❹ Present the results in Table 4.1 using the method you chose in question **3**.
❺ Another galaxy, F, moves away from Earth at 30 000 km/s.
   a) Use the results in Table 4.1 or your answer to question **4** to estimate the distance of galaxy F from Earth.
   b) How long, in millions of years, would it take light to travel this distance?
   c) Galaxy F is, in fact, moving at one tenth ($\frac{1}{10}$) of the speed of light. So, it has taken 18 000 million years for Galaxy F to get to its present distance from Earth. What is the significance of this value, assuming that *all* matter in the Universe was originally in one place?

Summary

✓ Stars are huge balls of gas in which the nuclei of hydrogen atoms are fusing together to form helium. This nuclear fusion process emits immense amounts of heat, light and other electromagnetic radiations.

✓ People who watch and study the stars are called astronomers.

✓ Careful observations of the stars by early astronomers stimulated further investigations which led to the identification of patterns of bright stars called **constellations**.

✓ Further observation of the Universe with very powerful optical telescopes led to the discovery of **galaxies** (clusters of millions of stars).

✓ The detection of radio waves coming from space led to the development of radio telescopes and the discovery of pulsars and more galaxies.

✓ The distances between stars and galaxies are so large that they are measured in **light years**. One light year is the distance that light travels in one year. This is roughly 10^{13} km.

✓ Space telescopes in orbit above the Earth can identify more distant objects and detect weaker signals than telescopes based on Earth. This is because there is no distortion or interference from the Earth's atmosphere.

✓ The wavelength and frequency of sound waves, light waves and waves from other electromagnetic radiations change when the wave source is moving.

✓ Light and other electromagnetic radiations from distant galaxies have a longer wavelength than expected. This is known as the **red-shift**.

✓ Galaxies further away from the Earth give a greater red-shift than those closer to the Earth.

✓ Observations of red-shift have led astronomers to conclude that all galaxies are moving away from each other and the Universe is expanding.

✓ At present, the most satisfactory explanation for the expanding Universe and its origin is the **'big bang'**

theory. This suggests that the Universe started with an immense explosion millions of years ago. All matter in the Universe exploded from one small point and it is still flying apart.

EXAMQUESTIONS

❶ Match the following questions with answers A, B, C and D below.
a) Which bodies emit light?
b) Which bodies are satellites of stars?
c) Which bodies are satellites of planets?
d) Which bodies are smaller than moons?
e) Which bodies provide evidence for the origin of the Universe?

    A galaxies   **B** meteorites
    C moons   **D** planets   *(5 marks)*

❷ Which of the following statements about the 'big bang' theory are true and which are false?
A It has been proved correct by mathematical calculations.
B It is supported by the fact that distant galaxies are moving away from the Earth.
C It is based on scientific and religious facts.
D It is the most satisfactory explanation of present scientific knowledge.
E It is the only way to explain the origin of the Universe.   *(5 marks)*

❸ a) Radio telescopes are used to investigate distant galaxies. Why are radio telescopes much larger than optical telescopes?
                                  (2 marks)
b) Why are space telescopes usually more sensitive than earthbound telescopes?
                                    (1 mark)
c) The light from distant galaxies shows a red-shift.
  i) Explain the term 'red-shift'.   *(3 marks)*
  ii) What does the red-shift effect tell us about distant galaxies?   *(1 mark)*
  iii) Galaxies further away from the Earth show a larger red shift than galaxies closer to the Earth. What does this tell us about galaxies?   *(1 mark)*

❹ The 'big bang' is one theory about the origin of the Universe.
a) State the main ideas of the 'big bang' theory.   *(3 marks)*
b) How do Hubble's observations of the red-shift of distant galaxies support the 'big bang' theory?   *(1 mark)*
c) How does background radiation from the whole Universe support the 'big bang' theory?   *(1 mark)*
d) Why are some astronomers unsure about the 'big bang' theory?   *(2 marks)*

❺ Figure 4.11 shows a side view of two thin beams of radio waves approaching the dish of a radio telescope.
a) Redraw the figure showing the path of the two thin beams until they reach the receiver.   *(2 marks)*
b) Why is it necessary to use a secondary reflector?   *(1 mark)*

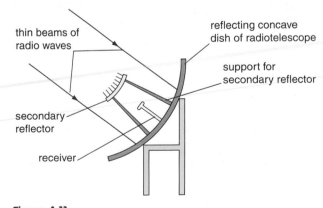

thin beams of radio waves

reflecting concave dish of radiotelescope

support for secondary reflector

secondary reflector

receiver

Figure 4.11

Chapter 5
How can we describe and change the way things move?

At the end of this chapter you should:

✓ be able to describe the movement of a body using a distance–time graph or velocity–time graph;

✓ know that the slope (gradient) of a distance–time graph represents speed;

✓ know that the slope (gradient) of a velocity–time graph represents acceleration;

✓ know that the area under a velocity–time graph represents distance travelled;

✓ understand that if the resultant force acting on a body is not zero, the body accelerates;

✓ know that a falling body initially accelerates due to the force of gravity but reaches a terminal velocity when the resultant force is zero;

✓ be able to describe factors that affect the stopping distance of a vehicle;

✓ understand that when a force transfers energy to, or from, a body, work is done;

✓ know that the kinetic energy of a body depends on both its mass and its speed;

✓ know that momentum is conserved in any collision or explosion, provided no external forces act on the colliding or exploding bodies;

✓ appreciate that safety features are often explained using the idea of momentum;

✓ be able to use and rearrange equations for acceleration, work done, kinetic energy and momentum.

Figure 5.1 In an accident, the crumple zones, seat belt and air bag are all designed to increase the time it takes for you to slow down and stop. This makes the forces on you smaller. The smaller the force, the greater the chance of avoiding serious injury.

What's the difference between speed, velocity and acceleration?

Speed and velocity

If you travel at a fast speed, it takes less time to finish a journey than when you travel at a slow speed. Some passenger trains are so fast they can travel 92 metres in just one second. This is a speed of 92 metres per second (92 m/s) and is the average speed of the train. During a one-hour journey the train will sometimes go faster and sometimes slower.

When you go somewhere it's not just speed that is important – direction also counts. Figure 5.3 shows two routes that Stacey can take to school.

The two routes are the same distance and take Stacey the same time. This means that Stacey goes at the same speed on both routes. But the two routes involve travelling in different directions and each time Stacey changes direction her **velocity** changes. This is because velocity includes speed and direction.

To give the velocity of a body, you need to give both its speed and its direction. Direction can be shown in different ways. You can use:

- an arrow;
- a compass direction;
- a + or − sign.

In Figure 5.4 the two joggers are moving at the same speed but have different velocities.

Figure 5.2 The average speed of a snail is just 0.0005 m/s. How far would a snail go in one hour?

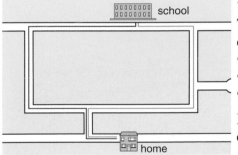

Figure 5.3 Stacey's routes to school

> The **velocity** of a body is its speed in a given direction.

speed   = 3m/s
velocity = 3m/s ←
  or 3m/s west
  or −3m/s

speed   = 3m/s
velocity = 3m/s →
  or 3m/s east
  or +3m/s

Figure 5.4 Where you end up depends on your speed and direction.

> The **acceleration** of an object is the rate at which its velocity changes.

Figure 5.5 Olympic runners accelerating off the blocks

❶ A falcon hovering in the sky sees its prey and dives downwards. The falcon reaches a velocity of 9 m/s in just 1.5 s. Calculate its acceleration.

❷ A motorbike decelerates from 20 m/s to rest (0 m/s) in 4 seconds. Calculate the deceleration of the motorbike.

❸ A cyclist accelerates from rest at 0.9 m/s² for 8 seconds. Calculate the final velocity of the cyclist.

❹ A high-speed train travelling at 36 m/s accelerates at 0.2 m/s². How many seconds will it take the train to reach 50 m/s?

❺ Explain the following statement:
'A model train running at a constant speed around a circular track is accelerating.'

Acceleration

Something is accelerating when its velocity is changing. The bigger the change in velocity, or the shorter the time it takes, the larger the **acceleration**.

Acceleration can be calculated using this equation:

$$\text{acceleration (m/s}^2) = \frac{\text{change in velocity (m/s)}}{\text{time taken for change (s)}}$$

When bodies move in a straight line, 'change in velocity' and 'change in speed' are the same thing.

If velocity is measured in metres per second and time in seconds, the unit of acceleration is metres per second per second, which is usually written as m/s².

Example
At the start of a 100 metre race, an Olympic runner accelerates to 12 m/s in 2 seconds. What is the acceleration of the runner?

starting velocity = 0 m/s

final velocity = 12 m/s

time taken = 2 s

$$\text{acceleration} = \frac{\text{change in velocity}}{\text{time taken}} = \frac{12 - 0}{2} = 6 \text{ m/s}^2$$

Deceleration

A body that is slowing down is decelerating. The body has a negative acceleration. Putting the brakes on makes a car decelerate and slow down. If it decelerates at 3 m/s², then its velocity goes down by 3 m/s every second.

Figure 5.6 On landing, a jet fighter uses its brakes and a parachute to produce a large deceleration.

5.2 Using graphs to describe the motion of a body

Distance–time graphs

A **distance–time graph** can be used to describe and work out the speed of a body.

Figure 5.7 shows the distance–time graph for a short car journey.

The car is travelling the same distance, 600 metres, every minute. So the car is moving at a steady speed of 10 metres per second (m/s). This is the same as the slope (gradient) of the line.

When a distance–time graph gives a straight line the body is moving at a constant (or zero) speed. Calculating the slope (gradient) of the line gives the value of the speed.

Steve and his horse Rocket take part in a long distance ride. Figure 5.8 shows the distance–time graph for the ride. The graph has been divided into three parts.

- Part A – Steve and Rocket move at a constant speed. They travel 16 kilometres in 2 hours. The slope of the line equals 8 km/h, the same as their average speed.
- Part B – Steve and Rocket have stopped to take a rest. The distance moved does not change and the slope of the line is zero.
- Part C – Steve and Rocket move at a steady speed. They travel 24 kilometres in 2 hours. The slope of the line is 12 km/h. This means their speed was the greatest during this part of the ride.

Figure 5.7 A distance–time graph for a short car journey

> The slope of a **distance–time graph** gives the speed of a body.

> When a body is stationary (not moving), the line on a distance–time graph is horizontal.

> A steeper slope means a faster speed.

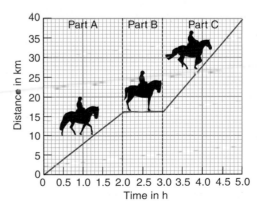

Figure 5.8 Distance–time graph for a horse ride

6 Curtis cycles to school.
Figure 5.9 shows the distance–time graph for his journey.
a) How long did Curtis stop at the traffic lights?
b) During which part of the journey was Curtis cycling the fastest?

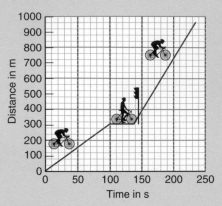

Figure 5.9

7 As Sue and Steve walk down the high street they stop and look in two shop windows. Figure 5.10 shows the distance–time graph for their walk.
a) How long did they spend looking in the windows?
b) How far apart were the two shops they looked in?
c) Between which two times did they walk the slowest? Calculate this speed.
d) Calculate Sue and Steve's average speed as they walked along the high street.

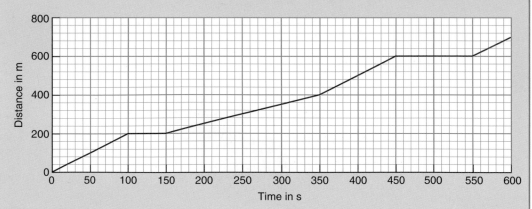

Figure 5.10

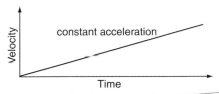

Figure 5.11 The velocity–time graph for something moving with a constant velocity is a horizontal line.

The **slope** (gradient) of a velocity–time graph gives the acceleration of a body.

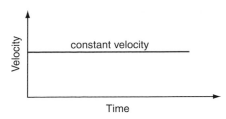

Figure 5.12 The slope of a velocity–time graph gives acceleration. A steeper slope means a greater acceleration.

Velocity–time graphs

A velocity–time graph can be used to describe the velocity and acceleration of a body. Although these graphs may look very similar to distance–time graphs, they mean different things. Always look at the axes.

Figure 5.11 shows the velocity–time graph for a car moving at a constant speed along a straight road. This means the car is moving with a constant velocity.

Figure 5.12 shows the velocity–time graph for a car accelerating along a straight road. The slope of the graph shows how quickly the velocity is changing. This means the slope shows the acceleration of the car. A straight line means the acceleration is constant.

How far does a body travel when it accelerates?

Figure 5.13 shows Ravi's velocity as he cycles downhill on a straight road. How far does Ravi cycle in 10 seconds?

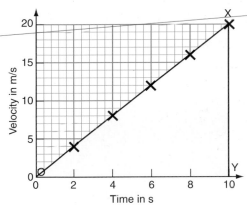

Figure 5.13 The straight line means that Ravi has a constant acceleration.

The area below the graph line in a velocity–time graph represents distance travelled.

distance = average velocity × time

average velocity = ½ × 20

So, the distance cycled = (½ × 20) × 10 = 100 m
= ½ × final velocity × time
= ½ × XY × OY
= shaded area below the graph line

Example

Figure 5.14 shows the velocity–time graph for a lift moving between two floors in a hotel. The graph has been divided into two parts.
● Part A – The velocity is increasing at a constant rate; the lift has a constant acceleration.
● Part B – The velocity is decreasing at a constant rate (negative slope); the lift has a constant deceleration.

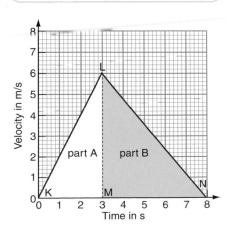

Figure 5.14 Velocity–time graph for a lift

To find the acceleration of the lift in part A we work out the slope of the graph line.

$$\text{slope} = \frac{LM}{KM} = \frac{6}{3} = 2 \text{ m/s}^2$$

You should be able to use the same method to show that the deceleration of the lift in part B is 1.2 m/s².

To find the distance the lift moves while it is accelerating, we work out the area of part A.

$$\text{area} = \frac{1}{2} \times 6 \times 3 = 9 \text{ m}$$

You should be able to use the same method to show that the distance between the two floors in the hotel is 24 m.

⑧ Figure 5.16 shows the velocity–time graph for a cheetah.
a) Calculate the acceleration of the cheetah.
b) Calculate the distance travelled by the cheetah in 10 seconds.

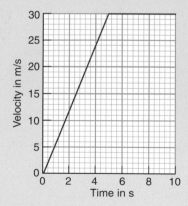

Figure 5.15

Figure 5.16

⑨ Table 5.1 gives some data for a speed skier travelling in a straight line down a steep slope.

Time in s	0	2	4	6	8	10	12	14
Velocity in m/s	0	12	24	32	38	40	40	40

Table 5.1

a) Draw a velocity–time graph for the skier.
b) Describe the motion of the skier.

⑩ Use the data and your velocity–time graph from question **9** to calculate:
a) the acceleration of the skier during the first 4 seconds;
b) the acceleration of the skier during the last 4 seconds.

⑪ A train pulls out from Maidenhead station and accelerates at a constant rate, reaching a velocity of 25 m/s after 90 seconds. The train then travels at this speed for 180 seconds, at which point the brakes are applied and the train comes to a stop at Taplow station 60 seconds later.
Draw a velocity–time graph for the train and use it to calculate:
a) the acceleration of the train;
b) the distance between Maidenhead and Taplow stations.

5.3 How do forces affect the movement of a body?

Forces have size and direction. We use an arrow to show the direction of a force. The length of the arrow represents the size of the force.

To make a supermarket trolley move is simple. You push and the trolley moves forward. You pull and the trolley moves backwards. But whatever the direction of the force you exert, the trolley always exerts an equal sized force on you in the opposite direction. This is because forces always come in pairs. You just can't have one force without another.

Whenever two bodies interact, the forces they exert on each other are always equal in size and opposite in direction.

But the two forces always act on different bodies; this is why they do not cancel out.

Figure 5.17 When you push on the trolley it pushes equally hard on you.

 Josh knows that when he kicks a ball into the air the force of gravity pulls the ball back down. Since forces come in pairs, he thinks that as the ball is pulled down by the Earth, the ball should pull the Earth up. But he has never noticed this. Explain why.

What happens when more than one force acts on the same body?

Each diagram in Figure 5.18 shows two forces. But only one force is shown acting on each different body. This would be unusual. In most situations there will always be more than one force acting on a single body.

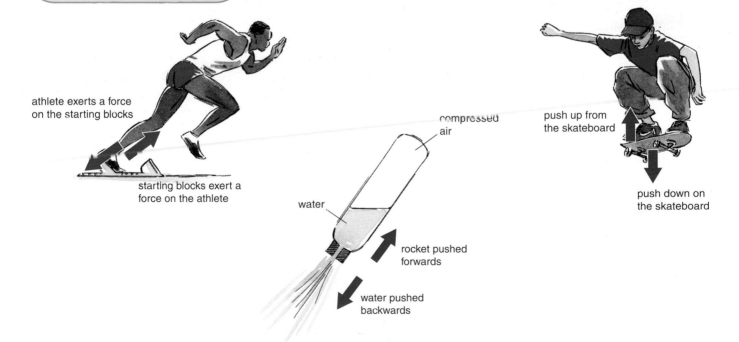

Figure 5.18 Some examples of interacting bodies

athlete exerts a force on the starting blocks

starting blocks exert a force on the athlete

compressed air

water

rocket pushed forwards

water pushed backwards

push up from the skateboard

push down on the skateboard

CHAPTER 5 How can we describe and change the way things move?

The **resultant force** is a single force that has the same effect on a body as all the original forces acting together.

To find out what happens to a body when more than one force acts on it we imagine all the individual forces being replaced by a single force that has the same effect. This single force is called the resultant force. The size and direction of the **resultant force** determines how or even if the body moves.

These forces acting on a body	give this resultant force
2 N ← □ → 2 N	□ 0 N (zero)
2 N → □ → 3 N	□ → 5 N
2 N ← □ → 3 N	□ → 1 N

Table 5.2 Two forces acting in the same direction add to give the resultant force. Two forces acting in opposite directions subtract to give the resultant force.

⑬ Tom and Sam are pulling on the opposite ends of a rope. Tom pulls with a force of 70 N and Sam pulls with a force of 100 N.
a) What is their resultant force?
b) Jim now joins in pulling the rope. The new resultant force is zero. What force does Jim pull with and does he help Tom or Sam?

What happens when the forces are balanced?

Figure 5.19 shows the forces acting on a toy bird. The weight of the toy causes the spring to stretch. The spring stretches until the upward force in the spring (tension) equals the downward weight of the toy. The forces are now **balanced**. In effect the forces have cancelled each other out. So, the resultant force is zero and the toy is stationary (not moving).

If the resultant force acting on a body is zero, the forces are **balanced** and the body does not accelerate. It remains at rest or continues at the same speed and in the same direction.

If the resultant force on a body is zero, the movement of the body does not change. If the body is stationary, it remains stationary. But what if the body is moving? If the forces are balanced so that the resultant force is zero, the body keeps moving at the same speed and in the same direction.

Figure 5.20 shows the forward and backward forces acting on a cyclist. The cyclist is riding along a straight road, keeping the same constant speed. This means that there is no change in the movement of the cyclist. So the two forces must be balanced giving a resultant force of zero.

tension in the spring

weight

Figure 5.19 When the toy bird is stationary, the resultant force on the toy is zero.

backward frictional forces

forward force from cyclist

Figure 5.20 The resultant force on a cyclist with a constant velocity is zero.

What happens when the forces are unbalanced?

In a tug of war, when both teams pull equally hard, the resultant force is zero and the rope does not move. But when one team starts to pull with a larger force the rope moves (Figure 5.22). The resultant force is no longer zero. The rope and both teams start to move in the direction of the resultant force.

weight

upward force from the rope

Figure 5.21 The tightrope walker would have problems if the forces did not balance.

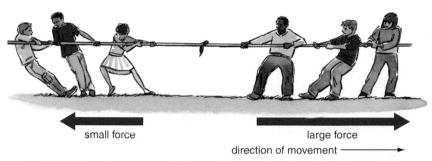

small force

large force

direction of movement ⟶

Figure 5.22 When forces are unbalanced, the resultant force is not zero.

If the resultant force acting on a body is not zero, the forces are **unbalanced** and so the body changes velocity.

When the forces acting on a body are **unbalanced**, the resultant force changes the velocity of the body. Since velocity involves both speed and direction, a resultant force can make a body speed up, slow down or change direction.

An engine produces the driving force needed to move a car forwards. If the car is stationary pushing the accelerator pedal produces a resultant force forwards. The car then accelerates in the direction of the resultant force (Figure 5.23).

Air resistance (or drag) is a force of friction. The direction of air resistance is always opposite to the direction of the moving object.

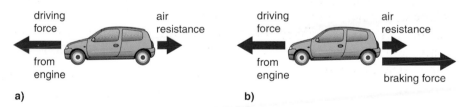

driving force

air resistance

from engine

driving force

air resistance

from engine

braking force

a)

b)

Figure 5.23 a) The car accelerates in the direction of the resultant force. b) The car decelerates in the direction of the resultant force.

When the resultant force on a stationary or moving body is not zero, the body accelerates in the direction of the resultant force.

If the car engine stops or the driver puts the brakes on, the car decelerates (slows down). This happens because the frictional forces backwards are now larger than the force forwards. The resultant force is in the opposite direction to the way the car is moving.

When a body is moving in the opposite direction to the resultant force, it decelerates.

14 Look at the forces acting on a moving boat.

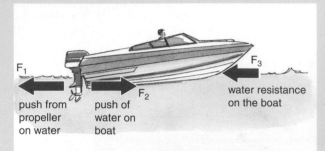

Figure 5.24

a) Which two forces are always equal? Explain the reason for your choice
b) Describe the motion of the boat when:
   i) $F_2 = F_3$;
   ii) F_2 is larger than F_3.

15 Four forces act on a submerged submarine.

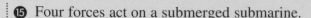
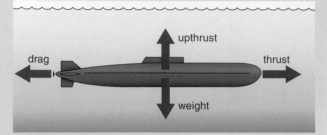

Figure 5.25

a) The submarine is cruising with a constant velocity and at a constant depth. Write down the connection between weight and upthrust; drag and thrust.
b) Explain what happens if the weight of the submarine is increased by filling the buoyancy tanks with water.

Force, mass and acceleration

If you have ever tried to push a broken-down car you will know that it is not easy. If you are the only person pushing, the car accelerates and moves slowly. The more people that push, the greater the resultant force on the car and the greater the acceleration (Figure 5.26).

The greater the resultant force on a body, the greater the acceleration of the body.

Common sense would tell us that it is much more difficult to give a van the same acceleration as a car. A much larger force is needed. This is because the mass of the van is far bigger than the mass of the car. Pushing a larger and larger mass with the same force gives a smaller and smaller acceleration (Figure 5.28).

Figure 5.26 The acceleration of the car depends on the resultant force applied to the car.

The bigger the mass of a body, the bigger the resultant force needed to make it accelerate.

Figure 5.27 A large resultant force acting on the small mass of the drag car gives it massive acceleration.

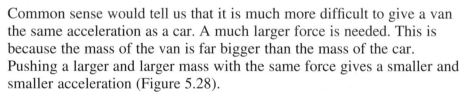

Figure 5.28 More force is needed to give a van the same acceleration as a car.

Figure 5.29 A huge force is needed to accelerate this mass.

The force needed to accelerate a mass can be calculated using this equation:

resultant force	=	mass	×	acceleration
(newton, N)		(kilogram, kg)		(metre/second², m/s²)

or using symbols $F = m \times a$

Example
Calculate the resultant force needed to give a 2 kg ball an acceleration of 6 m/s².

$$F = m \times a$$
$$F = 2 \times 6 = 12\,N$$

5.4 Does a falling body keep on accelerating?

A falling body speeds up or accelerates because of the force of gravity. Gravity is a force of attraction. A ball thrown into the air is pulled back to the ground by gravity. As the ball falls downwards, gravity makes it accelerate. If there were no frictional forces (air resistance) on Earth, the ball would accelerate at 10 m/s². This means that the velocity of a falling object increases by 10 m/s every second – it keeps accelerating.

In a vacuum, there is no air resistance so gravity is the only force acting on the body and all falling objects accelerate at the same rate, 10 m/s².

16. The part of the space shuttle which returns to Earth is called the orbiter. It has a mass of 78 000 kg and lands at a speed of 100 m/s. After touchdown it takes 50 s to decelerate and come to a halt.
   a) Calculate the deceleration of the orbiter.
   b) Calculate the force needed to bring the orbiter to a halt.

17. Gurpal is cycling along a flat road when he stops pedalling. Gurpal's speed drops from 8 m/s to 5 m/s in 6 s.
   a) Calculate Gurpal's deceleration.
   b) The mass of Gurpal and his bicycle is 90 kg. Calculate the resistance force slowing Gurpal down.

18. Explain why the acceleration of a car is reduced when it tows a caravan.

19. Explain why a canoeist slows down when they stop paddling.

Activity – Investigating the acceleration of a falling body

Liam has read about Galileo's famous experiment with falling bodies. Galileo believed that gravity makes all falling bodies accelerate at the same rate. Most people at the time did not believe Galileo. To show that his idea was right, Galileo is supposed to have dropped a small iron ball and a large iron ball from the top of the Leaning Tower of Pisa, in Italy. The two objects are said to have hit the ground at virtually, but not quite, the same time.

1. Most people expected the large iron ball to hit the ground first, and it did. Why did people expect different bodies to fall at different rates?
2. Explain why this result on its own would not disprove Galileo's idea.

Figure 5.30 Galileo planned his famous experiment at the Leaning Tower of Pisa to test whether all falling objects accelerate at the same rate.

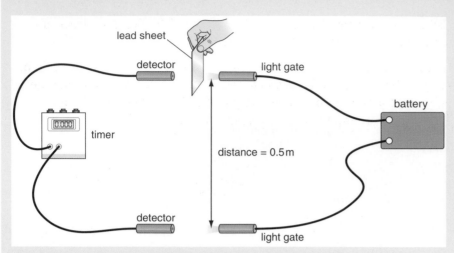

Figure 5.31 The apparatus used by Liam to measure the acceleration of a falling body

Liam decided to investigate the acceleration of falling bodies, to see if Galileo's prediction was right. The apparatus Liam used is shown in Figure 5.31.

Liam started with a small sheet of lead. As soon as he let go, the sheet passed through the top light gate and the electronic timer started. The timer stopped when the sheet passed through the bottom light gate. Liam repeated this four times. The four timer readings are written in Table 5.3.

❸ Why did Liam repeat the time measurement?

❹ Liam left out the third result when he calculated the mean (average) time. Why do you think he did this?

❺ What was the mean time calculated by Liam?

❻ Use the following equation to calculate the acceleration of the lead sheet:

$$\text{acceleration} = \frac{2 \times \text{distance the body falls}}{(\text{mean time taken})^2}$$

By increasing the distance between the light gates Liam was able to get enough information to draw the graph shown in Figure 5.32.

❼ The gradient of the graph line equals the acceleration of the falling lead sheet.
  a) Measure and record the gradient of the line.
  b) Why is the value obtained by measuring the gradient likely to be more accurate than the value worked out by averaging?

Result	Time in s
1	0.326
2	0.330
3	0.465
4	0.319

Table 5.3

❽ When Liam measured the acceleration of a falling polystyrene ball, he got a value considerably less than the value for the lead sheet. Why was this ?

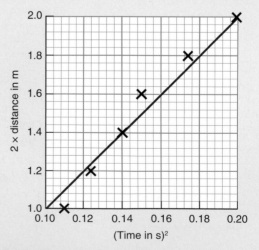

Figure 5.32 The graph drawn using Liam's results

What happens when frictional forces act against gravity?

Usually air resistance acts on a falling body. This has the effect of reducing the resultant force on the body.

Joss is a sky-diver. She understands how important air resistance is in keeping her alive. At the moment when Joss jumps from a plane the only force acting on her is her weight. So she starts to accelerate downwards, as shown in the first part of Figure 5.33.

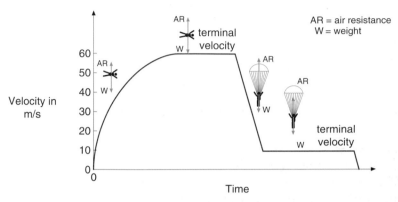

Figure 5.33 The velocity–time graph of a sky-diver

As soon as Joss starts to fall, air resistance begins to act upwards on her. Since her weight is bigger than the air resistance, she still accelerates towards the ground, but her acceleration decreases (the slope of the graph decreases).

> **Terminal velocity** is the constant velocity reached by a moving body when the resultant force acting on it (in the direction it is moving) is zero.

As Joss's speed increases, air resistance increases until it equals her weight. At this point the resultant force on Joss is zero and she stops accelerating. But she doesn't stop falling! She carries on falling but at a constant speed. The velocity–time graph is a straight line. Joss is falling at her **terminal velocity**.

When Joss opens her parachute, the increased surface area causes an increase in the air resistance. This produces a resultant force upwards – the opposite direction to her motion – and so Joss decelerates and slows down. As she slows down, air resistance falls until once again the two forces, weight and air resistance, become balanced. Joss then falls with a new, slower terminal velocity until she lands safely on the ground.

Increasing the surface area of an object increases the air resistance. It then takes less time for the forces to balance to give a resultant force of zero. So, a sky-diver wearing loose clothing and spreading out their arms and legs has a lower terminal velocity than a sky-diver curled up into a ball.

20 The sky-diver in Figure 5.34 is falling at her terminal velocity. Explain why curling up into a ball makes her fall faster and increases her terminal velocity.

21 The velocity–time graph drawn in Figure 5.33 is for a sky-diver weighing 600 N.
  a) How big is the air resistance force when the sky-diver is falling at their terminal velocity? Explain the reason for your answer.
  b) Estimate the size of the air resistance force when the sky-diver first opens the parachute. Explain the reason for your answer.

c) After landing the sky-diver stands still on the ground. Explain why the resultant force on the sky-diver is zero.

Figure 5.34

Figure 5.35 The hull of a hydrofoil lifts out of the water. This reduces the water resistance allowing the hydrofoil to accelerate to a higher velocity.

It's not just sky-divers that have a terminal velocity. All objects falling or moving through a **fluid** have a terminal velocity.

If you have ever paddled a canoe you will know that no matter how hard you paddle, you cannot keep increasing your speed. To start with your speed increases, but as you go faster the water resistance force also increases. Eventually the forward force you produce and the water resistance will be equal. The resultant force is zero and you have reached your terminal velocity.

Substances that flow are **fluids**. Liquids and gases are both fluids.

Activity – Investigating terminal velocity

Figure 5.36 shows a simple model parachute made from a sheet of plastic. When dropped, the plasticine figure soon reaches its terminal velocity.

1 Plan an experiment to find out if the terminal velocity of the plasticine figure depends on the area of the parachute.

2 What measurements would you take?

3 How will you know that the plasticine figure has reached its terminal velocity?

4 Which one of the following is the independent variable in this experiment?
  • distance the parachute falls
  • area of the parachute
  • weight of the plasticine figure
  • time taken to fall

5 What are the control variables in this experiment?

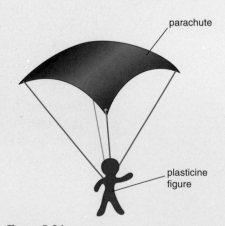

parachute

plasticine figure

Figure 5.36

Figure 5.37 To measure your weight the bathroom scales must measure in newtons.

Mass and weight

If you want to know your weight, you will probably stand on some bathroom scales.

But the units on your bathroom scales are mass units – not weight units. The bathroom scales give your mass in kilograms and not your weight, which is measured in newtons.

Weight is a force, so like all forces it is measured in newtons. Weight is the force which **gravity** exerts on a mass.

More mass does mean more weight, because there is more mass for the force of gravity to pull on. On Earth, gravity pulls on every one kilogram of mass with a force of about 10 newtons. This is called the gravitational field strength (*g*).

$$g = 10\,\text{N/kg}$$

Sakhib, who has a mass of 50 kilograms, will weigh:

$$50 \times 10 = 500 \text{ newtons}$$

You can use the equation below to calculate the weight of an object:

$$\begin{array}{ccc} \text{weight} & = & \text{mass} & \times & \text{gravitational field strength} \\ \text{(newton, N)} & & \text{(kilogram, kg)} & & \text{(newton/kilogram, N/kg)} \end{array}$$

㉒ Explain why a ball-bearing falling through oil has a much lower terminal velocity than an identical ball-bearing falling through the air.

㉓ Kathy, Jon and Cary go on a diet. Table 5.4 shows the mass of each person at the start and end of the month.

Person	Mass at start of the month in kg	Mass at end of the month in kg
Kathy	72.0	70.5
Jon	115.0	110.0
Cary	68.0	66.0

Table 5.4

How much weight did each person lose in 1 month?

㉔ When he was asked his weight, Gorese said it was 45 kg. Why is Gorese wrong?

CHAPTER 5 How can we describe and change the way things move?

 # Stopping safely

> The **thinking distance** is how far a vehicle travels during the driver's reaction time, before the brakes are applied.
>
> The **braking distance** is how far a vehicle travels before stopping, once the brakes have been applied.
>
> **Stopping distance** = thinking distance + braking distance

Friction forces decelerate a moving car and bring it to a stop. In an emergency, for example a dog running out in front of a car, the driver must apply the brakes as soon as possible. But the average driver has a reaction time of about three-quarters of a second. This is the time taken by the driver to react and move their foot from the accelerator pedal to the brake pedal. During this time the car carries on moving at a steady speed. The distance the car moves during the reaction time is called the **thinking distance**. Once the brakes have been applied the car slows down and comes to a stop. The distance the car moves once the brakes are put on is called the **braking distance**.

The total **stopping distance** of a vehicle is made up of the two parts: the thinking distance and the **braking distance**.

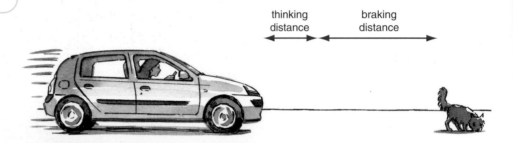

Figure 5.38 Thinking distance + braking distance = stopping distance

Speed affects both the thinking distance and the braking distance. Figure 5.39 shows the stopping distances for a typical car at different speeds. The force applied by the brakes is the same for each of the speeds.

As the vehicle goes faster, a greater braking force is needed to make the vehicle stop in the same distance. But beware – too great a braking force can make a vehicle skid.

The stopping distances given in Figure 5.39 are average values for a family car in good conditions on a dry road. Under different conditions the actual stopping distance can be much longer.

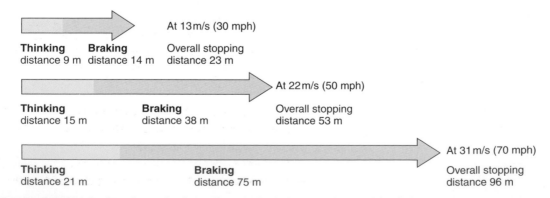

Figure 5.39 For a certain size braking force, the faster the vehicle the greater the stopping distance.

The driver's reactions may be slower than usual. The slower the reaction time, the longer the thinking distance. A driver's reactions are much slower if they:
- have been drinking alcohol;
- have been taking certain types of drug;
- are tired;
- are talking on a mobile phone.

Braking distance can be affected by several factors as well as speed:
- weather conditions – in wet or icy conditions the friction between the car tyres and road is reduced. This increases the braking distance.
- the vehicle being poorly maintained – worn brakes or worn tyres increase the braking distance.
- the road surface – a rough surface increases the friction between the road and the tyres, reducing the braking distance. You may have noticed that high-friction surfaces are often used on the approaches to busy junctions and roundabouts.

25 Explain the effect on the stopping distance of a car when there is ice on the road.

26 Drivers should leave a gap between their vehicle and the one in front. A learner driver said to his instructor, 'If I go twice as fast, I should leave a gap twice as big.' Explain why the learner driver is wrong.

27 A road safety advert had the slogan, 'Only a fool breaks the 2 second rule'. This means that at whatever speed vehicles are being driven, there should be at least a 2 second gap between them.

Copy out Table 5.5. Use the information in Figure 5.39 to complete the table.

Speed in m/s	Distance travelled in 2 s in m	Stopping distance in m
13	26	
22		53
31		

Table 5.5

a) Is a '2 second gap' between cars long enough to stop safely? Give a reason for your answer.
b) Under what conditions would you advise motorists to leave a larger gap than 2 seconds?

28 A policeman caught driving at 160 mph (72 m/s) was found not guilty of dangerous driving. The court was told that the policeman was a trained advanced driver practising his skills.

Do you think that high-speed driving can ever be justified? Give reasons for your answer.

29 Table 5.6 gives the thinking distance and braking distance for a car at different speeds.

Speed in m/s	0	9	13	18	26	36	52
Thinking distance in m	0	6	9	12	18	24	36
Braking distance in m	0	6	14	24	56	96	224

Table 5.6

a) Plot a graph of thinking distance against speed.
b) What pattern links thinking distance and speed?
c) Plot a graph of braking distance against speed.
d) What pattern links braking distance and speed?
e) Use the graphs to find the stopping distance for a car travelling at 72 m/s. (Hint: Extend the graph lines assuming they continue to follow the same pattern. Remember, this is called extrapolating the graph.)

Are you working?

What is work?

Ask people what they think work is and you are likely to get lots of different answers. But the answers usually involve doing something, maybe mowing the lawn, or lifting a box, or even writing an essay.

Figure 5.40 These cranes can do more work than a human.

> **Work** is done when a force makes something move. Work is measured in joules.

In science, **work** has a very specific meaning. Work is done whenever a force makes a body move. A force that causes a body to move is doing work. The bigger the force, and the further the force makes the body move, the more work is done.

Work, like energy, is measured in joules (J).

The work done in moving a body can be calculated using the equation:

work done   =   force applied   ×   distance moved in the direction of the force
 (joule, J)   (newton, N)   (metre, m)

This means that for a force to do work it must make something move. No matter how big the force, if it doesn't make something move it hasn't done any work.

Example
Calculate the work done by a weightlifter when lifting a weight of 750 N to a height of 2.4 m.

$$\text{work done} = \text{force} \times \text{distance moved}$$
$$= 750 \times 2.4 = 1800\,\text{J}$$

30 The Falkirk Wheel (Figure 5.41) is the first ever rotating boat lift. It lifts 600 000 kg of water plus boat through a height of 35 metres.
a) Calculate the weight that the Falkirk Wheel is able to lift.
b) Calculate the work done by the Wheel in one rotation.

Figure 5.41 The Falkirk Wheel in action

Figure 5.42 To lift its own body weight and the rider over the fence, the horse must exert a large force and do a lot of work.

Figure 5.43 Pushing the wheelbarrow involves transferring energy.

Work and energy

It's not easy for a horse to lift itself and the rider over a fence. It needs a large force and a lot of energy. When they are off the ground the horse and rider have gained gravitational potential energy. Since energy is conserved, this energy must have come from somewhere. In this case some of the chemical energy in the horse's muscles has been transferred to the gravitational potential energy of the horse and rider.

Richard works on a building site. One of his jobs is to move sand in a wheelbarrow. When he starts pushing the wheelbarrow, it moves, so work is being done. When it moves, the wheelbarrow gains kinetic energy. This energy has been transferred from Richard. Some of the chemical energy in Richard's muscles has been transferred into the kinetic energy of the wheelbarrow and sand.

Whenever a force makes a body move, work is done and energy must be transferred.

In fact work and energy are linked by the equation:

$$\text{work done} = \text{energy transferred}$$

So if Richard does 1000 J of work to move the wheelbarrow and sand, 1000 J of energy must be transferred.

To keep the wheelbarrow moving at a constant speed Richard must keep pushing with a constant force. This is because there are frictional forces trying to stop the wheelbarrow from moving.

Imagine pushing a heavy crate across the floor. It's hard work! As you push, friction acts with an equal force but in the opposite direction to your push. Since the resultant force on the crate is zero the crate moves across the floor at a constant velocity. Although you are doing work, the kinetic energy of the crate is not changing. The work you do is against the

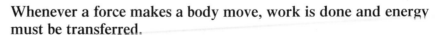

Figure 5.44 When friction tries to stop the movement between two surfaces, energy is transformed into heat.

frictional forces that are trying to stop the crate moving. Where the crate rubs against the floor both the crate and the floor get a little hotter. Chemical energy from your muscles has been transformed into heat.

When work is done against frictional forces, energy is mainly transformed into heat.

Example
Ahmed uses a force of 225 N to drag a heavy box 5 m across a rough floor at a steady speed. Calculate the work done against friction.

$$\text{work done} = \text{force} \times \text{distance moved}$$
$$= 225 \times 5$$
$$= 1125\,\text{J}$$

③① Copy and complete Table 5.7.

Task	Force applied	Distance moved	Work done
Opening a door	12 N	0.8 m	
Pushing a loaded trolley		80 m	2000 J
Lifting a suitcase	180 N		288 J
Stretching a spring	30 N	5 cm	

Table 5.7

③② Explain why falling over and sliding on an artificial astroturf pitch can burn you.

③③ Ray, a survival expert, can light a fire by rubbing two pieces of wood together. Why does this work?

③④ Figure 5.45 shows Matthew pulling a heavy sack up a ramp. The ramp is a simple machine that makes the job of lifting the sack easier to do. Explain why the energy transferred to the sack is less than the work done pulling the sack up the ramp.

Figure 5.45

Elastic potential energy

Figure 5.46 Using a chest expander involves doing work and transferring energy.

Elastic potential energy is the energy stored in an elastic object when work is done to change its shape.

Some objects break easily – a small force is all that is needed to cause permanent damage. If you apply a force to an elastic object it may change shape, but not permanently. When the force is taken away the object goes back to the way it was.

Imagine bending a ruler. As long as the force is not too big, the ruler pings back into shape when the force is removed.

To stretch, squash, twist or bend an elastic object work must be done and energy transferred. The energy stored in an elastic object when work is done to change its shape is called **elastic potential energy**. In Figure 5.46, chemical energy from the person's muscles is transformed into elastic potential energy and stored in the stretched springs. The stored elastic potential energy has the potential to do work.

Figure 5.47 A bungee rope is designed to stretch. The jumper accelerates until the rope becomes tight. The rope then starts to stretch as work is done on the rope. Energy is transferred from the jumper to the rope and the jumper slows down. Some work is also done against air resistance, so some of the jumper's energy is transformed into heat. This is just as well, or the bungee jumper would bounce up and down forever.

Work and kinetic energy

Whenever a force makes a body move, work is done and energy is transferred.

Moving bodies have kinetic energy. The kinetic energy of a body increases when a force makes it speed up and decreases when it slows down.

Kinetic energy is not just to do with the speed of a body; it is also to do with the mass of the body. A lorry with a large mass moving at 20 m/s has more kinetic energy than a car with a small mass moving at 20 m/s. So, the kinetic energy of a moving body depends on:
- its mass;
- its speed.

The kinetic energy of a moving body can be calculated using the equation:

$$\text{kinetic energy} = \tfrac{1}{2} \times \text{mass} \times \text{speed}^2$$
$$\text{(joule, J)} \qquad \text{(kilogram, kg)} \qquad \text{((metre/second)}^2\text{, (m/s)}^2\text{)}$$

Example

A jogger of mass 60 kg runs at 3 m/s. What is the kinetic energy of the jogger?

$$\text{kinetic energy} = \tfrac{1}{2} \times \text{mass} \times \text{speed}^2$$
$$= \tfrac{1}{2} \times 60 \times (3 \times 3) = 270\,\text{J}$$

Braking distance, braking force and kinetic energy

Brakes are used to stop a moving vehicle. The work done by the braking force reduces the vehicle's kinetic energy causing the vehicle to slow down and stop. The kinetic energy is transformed into heat. This is why friction brakes always get hot.

We saw in Section 5.5 that braking distance depends on speed. The greater the speed the longer the braking distance. But they do not increase in direct proportion, i.e. doubling the speed does not double the braking distance. In fact doubling the speed increases the braking distance four times. We can explain this as follows.

To stop a vehicle it must lose all of its kinetic energy. The equation for kinetic energy shows us that kinetic energy depends on speed squared. So, doubling a vehicle's speed increases its kinetic energy four times. If the same braking force is applied but four times as much energy must be transferred, then the vehicle must travel four times further.

You should be able to work out what happens to the braking distance if the speed of a vehicle increases three times.

35 Calculate the kinetic energy of:
a) a motorbike of mass 350 kg travelling at 20 m/s;
b) a 14 kg baby crawling at 0.5 m/s;
c) a 6 kg cat walking at 60 cm/s;
d) a 50 g bird flying at 40 m/s.

36 A ball thrown at 40 m/s has 160 J of kinetic energy. Calculate the mass of the ball.

Kinetic energy also depends on mass. A lorry with a mass ten times the mass of a car must transfer ten times more kinetic energy to stop than a car travelling at the same speed. So, although lorries have powerful brakes, they still take longer to stop than a car because they have a greater mass.

In Section 5.5 we saw that road conditions affect braking distance. For example if the road is icy, braking distances increase. The ice reduces the friction between the tyres and the road. To avoid skidding the driver must use a small braking force. But to transfer the same amount of kinetic energy using only half the braking force would double the braking distance.

37 Why aren't the brakes working as well as usual?

Figure 5.48

5.7 What is momentum?

A moving body has kinetic energy and **momentum**. The greater the mass of the body and the faster it moves, the more kinetic energy and momentum it has. Momentum can be a useful concept in calculations about collisions or explosions – more about these later.

The momentum, mass and velocity of a body are linked by the equation:

momentum	=	mass	×	velocity
(kilogram metre/second, kg m/s)		(kilogram, kg)		(metre/second, m/s)

Momentum is the mass of a body multiplied by the velocity of the body.

There is no short name for the unit of momentum, but you can remember it as the unit of mass (kilogram) multiplied by the unit of velocity (metre/second).

Just like velocity, momentum has a size and a direction. The momentum of a body is always in the same direction as the velocity of the body. If two bodies move in opposite directions, one has a positive momentum and the other negative momentum.

38 Calculate the momentum of:
a) a 60 kg cyclist peddling at 8 m/s;
b) a football of mass 0.4 kg moving at 7 m/s;
c) a bullet of mass 5 g moving at 250 m/s;
d) a 500 kg pony galloping at 16 m/s.

39 A racing car moving at 85 m/s has a momentum of 42 500 kg m/s. Calculate the mass of the racing car.

40 A 1800 kg elephant has a momentum of 10 800 kg m/s. Calculate the velocity of the elephant.

Example
A lorry and a car are travelling in opposite directions. Use the data in the box on page 99 to calculate the momentum of each vehicle.

Since the momentum of the lorry moving to the right has been given as positive, the momentum of the car moving to the left must be given as negative.

Figure 5.49

Lorry	Car
mass = 9000 kg velocity = 14 m/s → momentum = mass × velocity = 9000 × 14 = 126 000 kg m/s momentum of the lorry = +126 000 kg m/s	mass = 900 kg velocity = 25 m/s ← momentum = mass × velocity = 900 × 25 = 22 500 kg m/s momentum of the car = −22 500 kg m/s

How do unbalanced forces affect momentum?

When a resultant force acts on a body, the body accelerates. This means that the velocity of the body changes. If velocity changes, so does momentum. So, a resultant force acting on a body causes a change in momentum.

The size of the resultant force and the change in momentum that occurs are linked by the equation:

$$\text{force} = \frac{\text{change in momentum}}{\text{time taken for the change}}$$

where the force is in newtons (N), time is in second (s) and change in momentum is in kilogram metre/second (kg m/s).

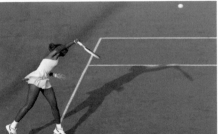

Figure 5.50 A tennis player 'follows through' to give the ball more momentum.

A small force acting for a long time can cause the same change in momentum as a large force acting for a short time.

In lots of sports that involve hitting a ball, the players 'follow through'. In tennis the 'follow through' means that the racquet does not stop the moment it hits the ball. The racquet continues, for a short time, to move with the ball. This action increases the time that the force acts on the ball, which increases the change in momentum of the ball. So the ball gains more speed.

Example

Figure 5.51 shows a golfer about to hit a golf ball of mass 0.045 kg. When the golf club hits the ball it is in contact for 0.001 s and exerts a force of 3600 N on the ball. Calculate the velocity that the ball has when it leaves the club.

$$\text{change in momentum} = \text{force} \times \text{time}$$
$$= 3600 \times 0.001 = 3.6 \text{ kg m/s}$$

Figure 5.51

As the ball started off stationary, its initial momentum = 0. Therefore:

$$\text{change in momentum} = \text{mass} \times \text{final velocity}$$
$$\text{final velocity} = \frac{\text{change in momentum}}{\text{mass}}$$
$$= \frac{3.6}{0.045}$$
$$= 80 \text{ m/s}$$

4 During a crash test, a car of mass 840 kg is driven into a wall at 5 m/s. The car slows down and stops in 1.5 seconds. Calculate the force on the car during the collision.

CHAPTER 5 How can we describe and change the way things move?

Figure 5.52 A cricketer draws his hands back to reduce the force on the ball and the force on his hands.

42 Rafael hits a stationary hockey ball of mass 0.5 kg with a horizontal force of 80 N. The ball leaves Rafael's hockey stick at 12 m/s.
   a) Calculate the momentum of the hockey ball immediately after being hit.
   b) State the change in momentum of the ball.
   c) Calculate the time Rafael's hockey stick was in contact with the ball.

43 A ball and a lump of plasticine of equal mass are thrown at a wall. The ball is in contact with the wall for 0.05 s, then bounces back. The plasticine hits the wall and stops in 0.05 s. It does not bounce back. Explain why the ball exerts a larger force on the wall than the plasticine.

Momentum and saving lives

When two bodies collide, each exerts a force on the other. These forces are equal in size but opposite in direction. The change in momentum of each body is equal in size, but opposite in direction. The longer the time of contact, the smaller is the force needed to change the momentum. This is the principle behind many different types of device aimed at saving lives during collisions.

If you ride a bicycle or go horse riding you should always wear a helmet. Often horse riders also wear a body protector. A helmet and body protector work in the same way. If you fall off your bicycle and hit your head, the padding inside the helmet starts to crush. If you fall off a horse, the padding inside the body protector starts to crush. In both cases the time taken for your body to stop moving increases and the force which could cause an injury is reduced.

Figure 5.53 A horse rider wearing a helmet and body protector

The surface of a child's play area needs to be tough but it also needs to be flexible (Figure 5.54). This is so that if a child falls, the surface squashes a little. The child will slow down more gradually than if they fell on a hard surface. This reduces the force on the child and so reduces the risk of injury.

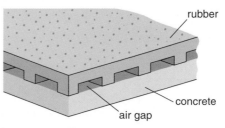

Figure 5.54 A safe surface for a children's area can be made from rubber tiles.

44 Explain the reason for each of the following.

Figure 5.55 This trainer has a gas-filled heel.

Figure 5.56 A climbing rope is designed to stretch a little.

Figure 5.57 The goalkeeper's kit is well padded.

Activity – Safety surfaces

Rakesh has bought a children's slide and swing. Before putting them in his garden he wants to put down a safety surface. The chart in Figure 5.58 shows some data Rakesh found from a manufacturer. The data gives the average height a child can fall onto different surfaces without serious injury.

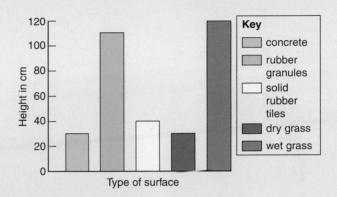

Figure 5.58

1 Are these categoric or continuous variables?
  a) the height the child falls;
  b) the type of surface.
2 The data presented in Figure 5.58 was obtained using a dummy fitted with electronic sensors. Rakesh thinks this makes the data more valid. Do you agree? Explain the reason for your answer.
3 Which type of surface would you recommend Rakesh to use? Explain the reason for your choice.

Car safety

Car design is not all about performance and looks – it is just as much about safety.

A modern car, even in a minor accident is easily damaged. But this is part of the safety design. The car is designed with 'crumple zones' at the front and back. In a collision the crumple zones crush. As they crush, the car slows down and gradually stops. The longer it takes the car to stop, the smaller the force exerted by the car on the occupants and the more likely you are to survive the accident without serious injury.

If you are in a car that suddenly slows down, you keep moving forwards until a force acts to reduce your momentum. Without a seat belt this force may be provided by the impact between your head and the windscreen, often a large and lethal force.

Figure 5.59 This car has been in a serious collision but the important part, where the passengers and driver sit, is undamaged.

Figure 5.60 A seat belt can save a life!

A seat belt is not rigid. In a crash it is designed to stretch slightly. This is very important as it increases the time taken for your momentum to be reduced to zero. So both the force on your body and the risk of injury are reduced.

45 In a crash it takes about 0.04 s for an air bag to inflate. A fraction of a second later the driver's head hits the air bag. The bag, which has tiny holes in it, will start to deflate as the force of impact pushes some of the gas out (Figure 5.61).
a) What happens to the movement of the driver's head when it hits the air bag?
b) Why is it important for an air bag to deflate?
c) Explain how the air bag reduces the risk of serious injury to the driver's head.

Figure 5.61

46 Explain why it would not be a good idea to make cars from thick, rigid steel.

47 John is driving his car at 15 m/s when it is in a collision. John's seat belt slows him down and stops him moving in 0.12 s.
a) Taking John's mass to be 70 kg, calculate:
   i)   John's momentum before the collision;
   ii) the change in John's momentum;
   iii) the average (mean) force exerted by the seat belt on John.
b) Explain why seat belts need to be very strong.

Activity – Investigating the idea of a crumple zone

To investigate the idea of a crumple zone Tracy used the apparatus shown in Figure 5.62. In a collision Tracy expects the trolley and test material to behave in the same way as a car with a crumple zone.

❶ Write down one more way that Tracy made this investigation a fair test.

❷ Suggest another way that Tracy could have produced a constant force on the trolley.

> **Reminder** In a fair test, only the independent variable affects the dependent variable.

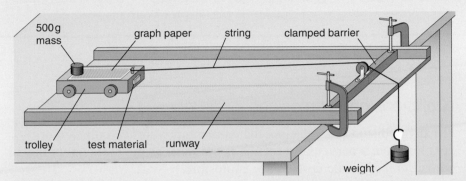

Figure 5.62 Using a trolley and test material to model a car with a crumple zone

A constant force was applied to the trolley by a falling weight. When the trolley hit the barrier it decelerated and stopped. The 500 g mass on top of the trolley slid forwards until it also stopped. Tracy marked the graph paper to show how far the 500 g mass moved. Tracy tested five different types of material for the crumple zone, each of the same area and thickness.

Because a constant force was applied, the trolley always accelerated to hit the barrier at the same speed. This was one factor that made the investigation a fair test.

❸ In Tracy's investigation, what was:
  a) the independent variable;
  b) the dependent variable?

❹ What sort of variable was the 'type of material' used in Tracy's investigation?

Figure 5.63 shows two sets of data obtained using different accelerating forces.

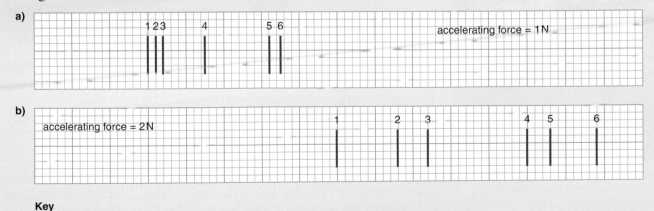

Key
1 = no material; 2 = polystyrene; 3 = foam rubber; 4 = carpet; 5 = fibre wool; 6 = rubber underlay

Figure 5.63 a) Stopping distance using an accelerating force of 1 N. b) Stopping distance using an accelerating force of 2 N.

⑤ Which accelerating force gave the biggest range of results?

> **Remember** The range refers to the maximum and minimum values used or recorded.

⑥ Draw a bar chart for each set of data.
⑦ Why is it more appropriate to draw a bar chart than a line graph?

In her analysis of the investigation Tracy has written:

'Crumple zones do reduce the force on a colliding body by increasing the time taken to stop. Of the five materials that I tested the best was rubber underlay.'

⑧ Do both sets of data support Tracy's analysis? Explain the reasons for your answer.

Collisions and explosions

> Momentum is **conserved** in a collision. The total momentum before a collision is the same as the total momentum after the collision.

In any collision or explosion, the momentum after the collision or explosion in a particular direction is the same as the momentum in that direction before the collision or explosion.

$$\begin{array}{ll}\text{total momentum after} & = \text{total momentum before a} \\ \text{a collision or explosion} & \quad\text{collision or explosion}\end{array}$$

The total momentum is unchanged by the collision or explosion. It doesn't go up and it doesn't go down. The total momentum is **conserved**. This is always true, provided no external forces act on the colliding or exploding bodies.

Look at the white snooker ball in Figure 5.65. It is moving with velocity v directly towards a red snooker ball. Before they collide, the red ball is not moving. The red ball has zero momentum.

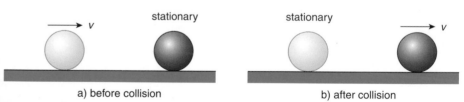

a) before collision   b) after collision

Figure 5.65

Figure 5.64 Understanding forces and momentum can make the difference between winning and losing a game of pool.

During the collision, an equal size force acts on each ball, but in opposite directions. The forces also act for the same time. This means that the momentum of each ball changes by the same amount. (**Remember**, force × time = change in momentum.)

After the collision, the white ball will be stationary. The white ball has zero momentum. The red ball will move with a velocity v in the same direction as the white ball was moving. The total momentum after the collision is the same as the total momentum before the collision.

Although momentum has been transferred from the white ball to the red ball, the total momentum has been conserved.

Figure 5.66 The launch of a rocket

An explosion is the opposite of a collision. Instead of moving together, bodies move apart. But as in a collision, the total momentum of the bodies involved in an explosion remains constant. In an explosion momentum is conserved.

The principle of momentum conservation is used in the launch of a space rocket. Before the launch the total momentum of the rocket and fuel is zero. After lift-off the total momentum must still be zero. The downward momentum of the hot exhaust gases must be equal to the upward momentum of the rocket.

48 A 2 kg trolley, moving at 3 m/s, collides with and sticks to a stationary 1 kg trolley. Calculate:
a) the total momentum before the collision;
b) the speed of the two trolleys after the collision.

49 Explain how the speed of a rocket moving through space can be increased.

50 Explain why, when you step ashore from a rowing boat, the boat moves backwards.

51 Jackie and Jasmin are on roller blades. They stand facing each other, and then give each other a gentle push. Figure 5.67 shows what happens next.
a) Explain why both Jackie and Jasmin roll backwards.
b) What is the total momentum before they push each other?
c) Calculate Jackie's momentum immediately after the push.
d) Calculate Jasmin's velocity immediately after the push.

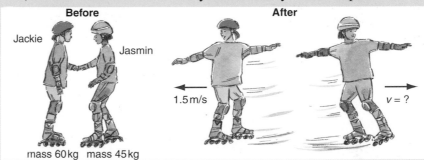

Figure 5.67

Summary

✓ **Velocity** is the speed of a body in a given direction.

✓ **Acceleration** is the rate at which the velocity of a body changes.

✓ **Distance–time graphs** and velocity–time graphs can be used to show the motion of a body.

✓ The slope (gradient) of a distance–time graph gives the speed of a body.

✓ The **slope** (gradient) of a velocity–time graph gives the acceleration of a body.

✓ The area under a velocity–time graph line represents distance travelled.

✓ Two interacting bodies exert forces on each other that are always equal in size and opposite in direction.

✓ The **resultant force** is a single force that has the same effect on a body as all the original forces acting together.

✓ When the resultant force on a body is zero, the movement of the body does not change because the forces are **balanced**. When the resultant force acting on a body is not zero, the forces are **unbalanced** and so the body changes speed.

✓ **Air resistance** (or drag) is a force of friction. The direction of air resistance is always opposite to the direction of the moving object.

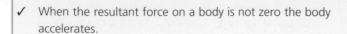

✓ When the resultant force on a body is not zero the body accelerates.

✓ The greater the resultant force, the greater the acceleration of the body.

✓ The bigger the mass of a body, the bigger the resultant force needed to make it accelerate. Force and mass are linked by:

resultant force (N) = mass (kg) × acceleration (m/s²)

✓ **Gravity** is a force of attraction that acts between all bodies.

✓ When the resultant force on a falling body is zero the body falls at its **terminal velocity**.

✓ When a vehicle travels at a steady speed the frictional forces balance the driving force.

✓ **Stopping distance = thinking distance + braking distance**.

✓ The stopping distance of a vehicle depends on the braking force, the driver's reaction time, the condition of the road

and the vehicle, weather conditions, the speed and the mass of the vehicle.

✓ Whenever a force makes a body move, **work** is done and energy is transferred.

✓ When work is done against frictional forces, energy is transformed into heat.

✓ The faster a body moves through a **fluid**, the greater the frictional forces.

✓ **Elastic potential energy** is the energy stored when work has been done to change the shape of a body.

✓ Kinetic energy is the energy of moving bodies.

✓ **Momentum** is defined by the equation:

momentum (kg m/s) = mass (kg) × velocity (m/s)

✓ A resultant force acting on a body causes a change in momentum.

✓ In any collision or explosion, the total momentum is **conserved**, provided no external forces act.

EXAM QUESTIONS

❶ Bill and Veneeta took part in a sponsored run. The distance–time graph for Bill's run is shown in Figure 5.68. Veneeta did not start the run until 500 seconds after Bill. She completed the whole run at a constant speed in 3000 seconds.
a) During which part of the race was Bill running the fastest? (*1 mark*)
b) Copy the distance–time graph for Bill's run. Draw on the same axes a distance–time graph for Veneeta's run. (*2 marks*)
c) How far had Bill run when Veneeta overtook him? (*1 mark*)

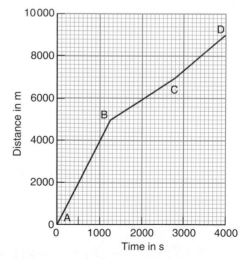

Figure 5.68

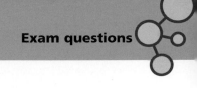

EXAMQUESTIONS

❷ Figure 5.69 shows three racing cars

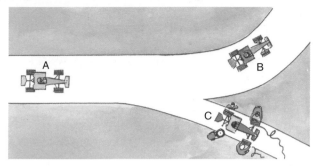

Figure 5.69

Car A has a mass of 500 kg and is moving at 85 m/s along a straight part of the track.
Car B is moving at constant speed around a curved part of the track.
Car C is in the pits and not moving.

a) Which, if any, of the cars has zero momentum? *(1 mark)*
b) Calculate the momentum of car A. *(2 marks)*
c) Which of the following is the unit of momentum?
   N m   kg m/s   J/kg *(1 mark)*
d) The momentum of one of the cars is changing. Which one? Give a reason for your answer. *(2 marks)*

❸ Figure 5.70 shows a space rocket lifting off from the launch pad.

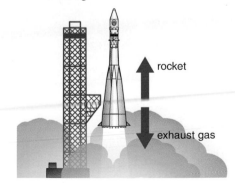

rocket

exhaust gas

Figure 5.70

Use the idea of momentum to explain why the rocket moves off the launch pad.
(3 marks)

❹ To achieve lift-off, the rocket in Figure 5.70 ejects 2500 kg of exhaust gases every second at a speed of 3500 m/s. The mass of the rocket and fuel at launch is 40 000 kg.

a) Calculate the thrust force produced by the rocket. *(3 marks)*
b) Calculate the initial acceleration of the rocket. (Ignore the weight of the rocket and fuel.) *(2 marks)*
c) During the first 10 seconds of flight the rocket maintains the same thrust force. Explain why the acceleration of the rocket increases. *(2 marks)*

❺ Amrita has investigated how different forces stretch a spring. The results of her investigation are given in Table 5.8.

Force in N	Length of spring in cm	Extension of spring in cm
0	5.0	0.0
2	7.5	2.5
4	10.0	
6	11.0	
8	15.0	
10	17.5	12.5

Table 5.8

a) Copy and complete Table 5.8. *(1 mark)*
b) Plot a graph of force against extension. *(3 marks)*
c) Amrita has one anomalous result. What would you expect this result to be? *(1 mark)*
d) What length would the spring be if a 3 N force was used? *(1 mark)*
e) Calculate the mean force exerted on the spring during the investigation. *(1 mark)*
f) Calculate the work done to extend the spring 12.5 cm. *(2 marks)*
g) What is the maximum elastic potential energy stored in the spring? *(1 mark)*

Chapter 6
What is static electricity and how is it used?

At the end of this chapter you should:

✓ know that some insulating materials become electrically charged when they are rubbed against each other;

✓ understand that electrons are transferred from one material to another when materials become charged by friction;

✓ understand that the material that gains electrons becomes negatively charged and the material that loses electrons becomes positively charged;

✓ know that objects with the same type of charge repel one another and objects with different types of charge attract;

✓ understand that an electric current is a flow of charge;

✓ appreciate that static charges are useful in photocopiers, smoke precipitators and electrostatic paint spray guns;

✓ appreciate that static electricity is dangerous in some situations;

✓ understand how electrostatic charge can be discharged safely;

✓ understand that a spark may jump across a gap between a charged body and a nearby earthed conductor if the charge on the body becomes high enough.

Figure 6.1 A flash of lightning is a gigantic spark. Billions and billions of electrons shoot from the bottom of the cloud to Earth. So much heat is produced that it causes a flash of light and the air expands rapidly, causing a clap of thunder.

What is static electricity?

People often call static electricity just 'static' for short. 'Static' results in lightning flashes (Figure 6.1), it makes your hair stand on end and it makes dust stick to TV screens. The word 'static' is normally used to mean 'stationary' and **static electricity** results when materials have stationary charges.

Invisible electrostatic forces

Try this simple experiment. Comb your hair briskly with a plastic comb and then use the comb to pick up tiny pieces of paper. (It only works if your hair is dry and not gelled.) When you comb your hair, the comb becomes **charged** (Figure 6.2), and the charged comb can pick up bits of paper because of electrostatic forces.

You may have noticed some other effects of electric charges.
- When you take off a shirt or top, it tends to cling to your body or your vest.
- A balloon can stick to a wall and possibly the ceiling after you have rubbed it against your sweatshirt or fleece.

These effects show that when certain materials are rubbed against each other or move over each other, they become electrically charged. People sometimes say the materials have 'static electricity' on them. This is how electric charges were first discovered.

Where do the charges come from?

When certain materials are rubbed against each other, friction causes negatively charged electrons to move off one material onto the other – off hair onto the comb, off your body and onto your shirt or top, off your fleece and onto a balloon.

When you comb your hair briskly, the comb removes electrons from some atoms in your hair (Figure 6.2). The comb now has more electrons than protons so it has an overall negative charge. Your hair has lost the electrons. It now has more protons than electrons and so it has an equal positive charge. If you bring the negatively charged comb close to a tiny bit of paper, it repels negative electrons from the area of the paper nearest to it (Figure 6.3a). This part of the paper therefore becomes positive. It is attracted to the comb because objects with different charges **attract**. If the paper is small enough, it can be picked up with the comb (Figure 6.3b).

Have you noticed that your hair sometimes stands up when it is combed – but probably not as much as the hair in Figure 6.2? This is more likely to happen if your hair is clean and dry. It happens because each hair becomes positively charged, and objects with the same charges **repel**.

Static electricity is the formation of stationary positive and negative electric charges on materials when they are rubbed together or move over each other.

The materials become positive or negative and are described as electrically **charged**.

Figure 6.2 A plastic comb gets charged when you comb your hair briskly.

When electrically charged objects are close together, they exert electrostatic forces on each other:
- objects with the same type of charge **repel** each other;
- objects with opposite (different) charges **attract** each other.

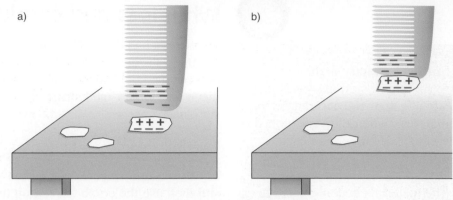

a)

b)

Figure 6.3 A charged comb can pick up bits of paper.

❶ Copy and complete the following sentences using words from the box below.

charge   electrons   friction   neutrons   negative
positive   protons   rubbed   static   transfer

When a polythene rod is _____ with a cloth, the cloth loses _____ to the rod, so the rod gets a _____ charge. The cloth has more _____ than electrons, so it has a _____ charge. This _____ of electrons is caused by _____.

❷ When certain materials are rubbed against each other, electrons move from one material to the other, but protons and neutrons never move. Why is this?

❸ When a Perspex rod is rubbed with a cloth, the Perspex rod becomes positively charged. Explain how the rod gets its charge.

Figure 6.4 A hair-raising experience!

❹ Look at Figure 6.4. The dome on which the boy is resting his hand has a large negative charge and the boy is standing on a rubber mat.
a) What is the charge on the boy's hand?
b) What is the charge on the boy's hair?
c) Why is the boy's hair sticking out?
d) Why is he standing on a rubber mat?

❺ Figure 6.5 shows two identical lightweight plastic balls attached to the same hook by nylon threads. The balls are charged.
a) What can you say about the charges on the balls?
b) Copy Figure 6.5 and show the forces acting on each ball.

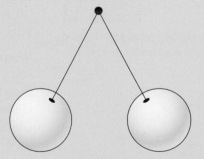

Figure 6.5

6.2

Insulators and conductors

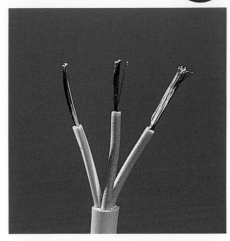

Figure 6.6 Plastics like polythene and PVC are good insulators. They are used to insulate electrical wires and cables.

Insulators are substances that can hold their charge. Electrons cannot flow through them, so they cannot conduct an electric current.

Conductors are substances through which electrons flow easily, so they conduct an electric current.

Materials like plastic, hair, rubber and paper can hold their charge. The charges on them are 'static' (stationary) and electrons do not flow through them. Because of this, these materials are called **insulators**. Plastics like polythene and polyvinylchloride (PVC) are used to insulate electrical wires and cables (Figure 6.6).

In contrast to insulators, electrons flow easily through metals and alloys. These materials are described as **conductors**. The flow of negative charges (i.e. electrons) forms an electric current. An electric current can also be carried by ions, which can have either positive or negative charges.

Table 6.1 shows good conductors, poor conductors and insulators. The best conductors are metals because they contain outer shell, delocalised electrons that are free to move. The outer electrons in insulators are held tightly in covalent bonds.

Conductors			Insulators
Good	**Moderate**	**Poor**	
• Metals, e.g. copper, aluminium, iron • Alloys, e.g. steel, brass	• Carbon (graphite) • Silicon	• Water • Humans	• Plastics, e.g. polythene, PVC • Rubber • Wood • Air

Table 6.1 Some important conductors and insulators

 6.3

How do we use static electricity?

Static electricity is important in the working of smoke precipitators, photocopiers and paint spray guns

Smoke precipitators

When coal is burnt in power stations and factories, a lot of smoke is produced. The smoke consists of tiny particles of soot and ash. A large coal-burning power station can produce up to 40 tonnes of soot and ash every hour. It is important to remove this soot and ash before it gets into the air and causes pollution. In power stations, this is usually done by using an electrostatic smoke precipitator (Figure 6.7).

As the smoke goes up the chimney, it passes through a negatively charged metal grid. The smoke particles pick up electrons from the grid and become negatively charged themselves. The grid now repels the negative smoke particles towards the chimney lining. Here they are attracted by large positively charged collecting plates. The smoke

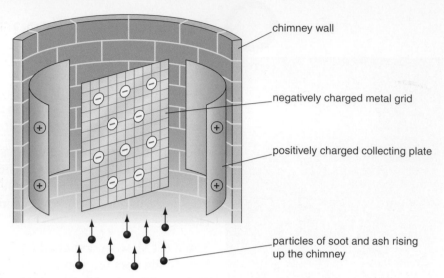

Figure 6.7 An electrostatic smoke precipitator

particles lose their charge on the collecting plates, then fall and collect together (precipitate) at the bottom of the chimney.

Photocopiers

Some substances can act as photoconductors. This means that they conduct electricity in the light, but not in the dark.

- In a photocopier, there is a metal roller coated with a thin layer of photoconductor (Figure 6.8). At the start of the copying process, this photoconducting layer is given a positive charge.

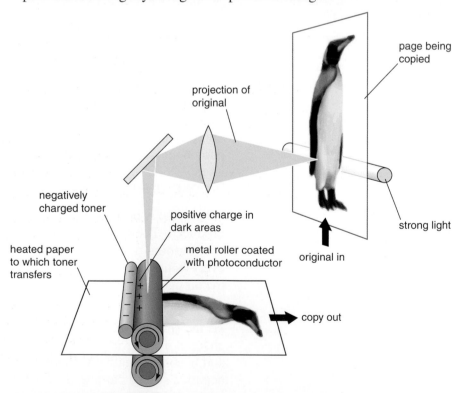

Figure 6.8 The photocopying process

- The page to be copied is then lit with a strong light. This allows an image of the page to be projected onto the charged photoconductor. The bright areas of the photoconductor now lose their charge because it can conduct in the light, but the dark areas keep their charge. So, the places where charge remains on the photoconductor are the same as the dark parts on the page being copied.
- At the same time, the roller moves near a supply of negatively charged black powder called toner. The toner is attracted to and sticks on the positive parts of the photoconductor.
- A blank sheet of paper is then heated and pressed against the roller.
- This melts the toner, which sticks to the paper making a copy of the original page.

---

6 From the list in the box below, name:
  a) one metal;
  b) one alloy;
  c) two non-metals;
  d) two good conductors;
  e) one (moderate) semiconductor;
  f) two insulators.

  brass graphite sulfur titanium wood

7 An electrostatic paint spray gun like the one in Figure 6.9 produces a fine spray of positively charged droplets.
  a) How does the charge on the droplets help to keep the spray fine and evenly spread?
  b) Why is less paint needed if the car bodywork has an opposite charge to the paint?
  c) Why is an opposite charge on the car bodywork beneficial to the workman?
  d) Why is the workman wearing protective head gear?

Figure 6.9 A workman re-spraying parts of a car using an electrostatic paint spray gun

Activity – 'Static' in pipes

Industrial liquids and powders, like flour and custard powder, can be moved from one place to another through pipes. As the liquids and powders flow along a pipe, static electricity is generated. The static electricity is produced by friction as particles in the liquid or powder rub against the wall of the pipe and against one another. Voltages as high as 1000 volts can be produced. These high voltages can result in sparks and start a fire as many of the powders will burn.

Ellie and Jake set up the apparatus in Figure 6.10 to study this problem of 'static' in pipes. They used different sizes of polystyrene beads.

1 The polystyrene beads become negatively charged as they flow down the pipe.
  a) What charge will the pipe have?
  b) What charge will the can and electroscope have when the polystyrene beads start to fill the can?
2 Why does the leaf move to an angle with the vertical part of the metal T-piece as soon as the electroscope is charged?

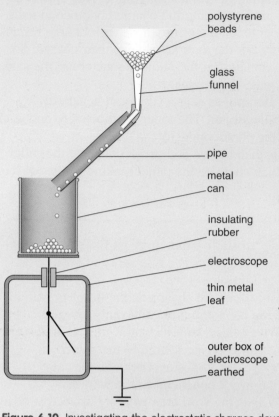

polystyrene beads

1 Polystyrene beads fall through the funnel and flow down the pipe.

glass funnel

pipe

2 Friction produces electrostatic charges on the beads and the pipe.

metal can

3 Beads fall into the metal can and their charge transfers to the can and the electroscope (T-piece and leaf).

insulating rubber

electroscope

thin metal leaf

4 As the charge on the electroscope increases, the metal leaf moves to a greater angle with the vertical bar of the T-piece.

outer box of electroscope earthed

Type of beads used	Estimated angle of thin metal leaf with vertical
Small	15°
Smaller	25°
Very small	45°

Table 6.2

Figure 6.10 Investigating the electrostatic charges developed when polystyrene beads flow down a pipe

❸ Ellie and Jake poured 50 cm³ of small beads down the pipe and then estimated the deflection of the thin metal leaf. Then they repeated their experiment, first with 50 cm³ of smaller beads and finally with 50 cm³ of very small beads (Figure 6.10).

Their results are shown in Table 6.2.
  a) Copy and complete the following sentences.
    i)   As the deflection of the metal leaf increases, the charge on the electroscope _____.
    ii) As the polystyrene beads decrease in size, the charge on the electroscope _____.
  b) Explain why very small beads cause greater deflection of the metal leaf than small beads.

❹ In some industries such as flour milling, very large charges can build up as the powdery flour passes along the pipes. How do you think the problem can be overcome? (Hint: How can you get rid of charges?)

❺ How do you think the following will affect the charge on the electroscope? Explain your answers.
  a) Making the pipe longer.
  b) Increasing the speed of the beads down the pipe.

❻ State three variables that Ellie and Jake controlled to make sure their investigation was fair.

❼ How could Ellie and Jake's results be made more reliable?

❽ Ellie suspects that Jake has measured the angle inaccurately. How could human error like this be reduced in their investigation?

❾ What would you do to get more precise, more quantifiable information about the effect of bead size on the charge on the electroscope?

6.4

What are the dangers of static electricity?

If the static charge on an object is very large, electrons may jump across the gap from the charged object to any nearby conductor, causing a spark. Even a small spark can be dangerous.

Whether or not sparking occurs depends on the potential difference (voltage) between the object and the conductor – the greater the charge on the object, the greater the voltage. If the voltage is too high, electrons will flow as a current from the object to the conductor, and there may be enough current to form a spark.

The problem is usually overcome by **earthing** the object that could become charged. This involves joining the object to a large metal plate in the ground by a conducting wire. If any charge now collects on the object, it just flows harmlessly along the wire to the earth and the object is discharged (loses its charge).

Fuel in pipes

When tankers deliver fuel to petrol stations and aircraft, a charge can build up as fuel flows through the delivery pipe. To prevent charge building up, the petrol storage tank and the aircraft are earthed (Figure 6.11).

> **Earthing** involves connecting a charged body to a metal spike or plate in the ground so that it is discharged, and its potential (voltage) remains close to zero.

❽ Figure 6.11 shows an aircraft being refuelled.
  a) Explain how electrostatic charge can build up on the fuel pipe and on the aircraft during refuelling.
  b) Why is the build-up of charge on the aircraft dangerous?
  c) In order to prevent charge building up, a copper cable is connected between the aircraft and the tanker. Why does this prevent charge building up? (Hint: The fuel pipe is also connected to the tanker.)

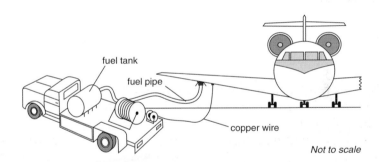

fuel tank
fuel pipe
copper wire
Not to scale

Figure 6.11 An aircraft being refuelled

Conducting 'tails' for cars

Cars are sometimes fitted with conducting 'tails' that touch the ground. This prevents any build-up of charge on the car. As the car moves over the ground and through the air, electrons are transferred from the ground to the car. Discharging reduces the risk of unpleasant sparks when you get out of the car or of a fire caused by sparks when the car is being refuelled.

Aircraft tyres

When an aircraft lands, there is enormous friction between its tyres and the runway. To reduce the build-up of charge, aircraft tyres are made of special rubber that conducts electricity. Any charge that forms on the tyres should then flow straight to earth (Figure 6.12).

Figure 6.12 When an aircraft lands, friction between the tyres and the runway is so great that sparks can fly and the tyres begin to smoke.

Activity – Lightning strikes!

Figure 6.13 shows what happens when lightning strikes the lightning conductor on a church spire.

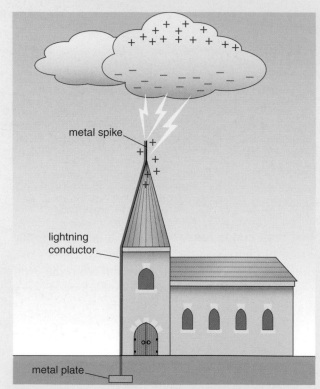

Figure 6.13 Lightning strikes the lightning conductor on a church spire.

❶ Copy and complete the following explanation using the terms in the box.

> cloud   convection currents   copper   earth
> electrons   energy   flash of light   ground
> frictional forces   negative   positive   spire

Large heavy thunderclouds are filled with water vapour and ice crystals moving around in strong _____. As these move around, _____ cause charge to build up and the bottom of the thundercloud has a large _____ charge.

The lightning conductor on the church spire consists of a thick _____ strip down the outside of the building. This is connected to a metal spike at the top of the _____ and a large metal plate in the _____. When the thundercloud passes overhead, the charge on the cloud repels _____ and the top of the lightning conductor becomes _____. If the charge on the cloud is large enough, electrons jump across the gap from the _____ to the spike. In some cases, so much _____ is lost by the electrons that a _____ is produced. Fortunately, the electrons can flow down the conductor to _____ without damaging the church.

❷ Explain why the lightning conductor on the church is:
a) fixed to the ground;
b) made of metal;
c) attached to the highest point on the church.

Summary

✓ **Static electricity** results when materials have stationary charges.

✓ When certain insulating materials are rubbed against each other, friction causes electrons to move off one material onto the other.

✓ The material gaining electrons becomes negatively **charged** and the material losing electrons is left with an equal positive charge.

✓ Two bodies (objects) with the same charge **repel** each other and two bodies with different (opposite) charges **attract**.

✓ **Insulators** are substances that can hold their charge. Electrons cannot flow through them, so they cannot conduct an electric current.

✓ **Conductors** are substances through which electrons flow easily, so they conduct an electric current.

✓ An **electric current** is a flow of charge. The charge may be carried by electrons or by ions.

✓ Electrostatic charges are important in the working of smoke precipitators, photocopiers and paint spray guns.

✓ Static electricity can be dangerous. If the electrostatic charge on an object becomes too large, a spark may result and this can cause a fire.

✓ The flow or movement of charge creates an electric current.

✓ The dangers of static electricity and sparking can usually be overcome by **earthing**.

EXAMQUESTIONS

❶ What is:
 a) an electric current; *(2 marks)*
 b) a conductor, *(1 mark)*
 c) an insulator; *(1 mark)*
 d) a photoconductor? *(2 marks)*

❷ Clingfilm is thin plastic material made of polythene. When clingfilm is peeled off a roll, it tends to stick to itself. Why do you think this happens? *(3 marks)*

❸ a) This question is about photocopiers. Copy and complete the following passage using words from the box below.

> bright   charge   conduct   dark   light
>   metal   photoconductor   same

Photocopiers have a _____ roller coated with photoconductor. Before copying starts, the _____ is given a positive charge. The page to be copied is lit with a strong _____ and an image of the page is projected onto the photoconductor. The _____ areas of the photoconductor now lose their _____ because it can _____ in the light, but the _____ areas keep their charge. So, the places where charge remains on the photoconductor are the _____ as the dark parts on the page being copied.
(8 marks)

 b) Why does a photocopier need toner? *(2 marks)*

 c) Why does the toner need to be charged? *(1 mark)*

 d) Why is the photocopy usually warm when it comes out of the copier? *(2 marks)*

Chapter 7
What affects the current in an electric circuit?

At the end of this chapter you should:

✓ be able to interpret and draw circuit diagrams using standard symbols;

✓ recognise the current–potential difference graph for a resistor at constant temperature, a filament lamp and a diode;

✓ be able to use the equation:

potential difference = current × resistance

✓ know that the current through a component depends on the resistance of the component;

✓ recognise errors in the wiring of a three-pin plug;

✓ understand the difference between direct current (d.c.) and alternating current (a.c.);

✓ be able to explain how mains electricity can be used safely;

✓ understand that an electric current is a flow of charge;

✓ know that the rate at which energy is transformed in a device is called the power;

✓ be able to determine the period and frequency of an electricity supply from the oscilloscope trace it produces.

Figure 7.1 The first Blackpool Illuminations, held in 1879, had just eight electric arc lamps. Today's illuminations, having one million lamps connected by more than 320 kilometres of cables and wiring, stretch out over a distance of 10 kilometres. If one light bulb 'blew', would all the lights go out?

7.1 Circuits – starting out

Remember that current is a flow of electric charge (see Section 6.2). For a current to flow through any **component** in a circuit, there must be a potential difference across the component. This means the circuit must include an energy supply and the circuit must be complete.

> A **component** is a part of an electric circuit.

Each component in a circuit has a standard symbol. Rather than drawing a complicated picture, symbols are used to draw circuit diagrams. This makes life much easier for us and for electricians.

Figure 7.2 shows the symbols you need to know, with the names of the components they represent.

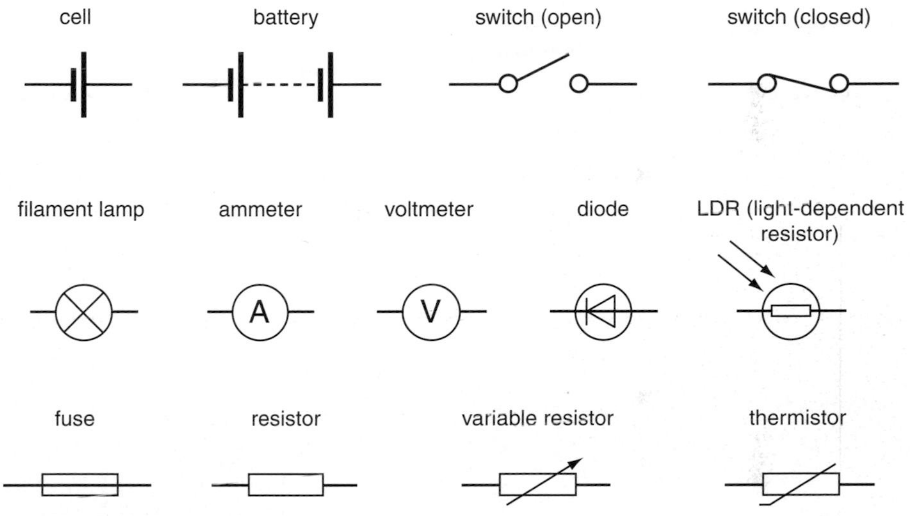

> In a **series** circuit there is only one path for current to follow.
>
> **Potential difference** (or p.d.) is often called voltage. A potential difference causes current to flow.
>
> In a **parallel** circuit each branch is independent of the others. There could be a break in one part of a parallel circuit and the other parts would still have a complete loop for current to flow.

cell	battery	switch (open)	switch (closed)
filament lamp	ammeter	voltmeter	diode	LDR (light-dependent resistor)
fuse	resistor	variable resistor	thermistor

Figure 7.2 Using standard symbols for components makes a circuit easier to understand.

The current in a circuit is measured with an ammeter connected in **series**. This is so that the current flowing around the circuit also flows through the ammeter (Figure 7.3).

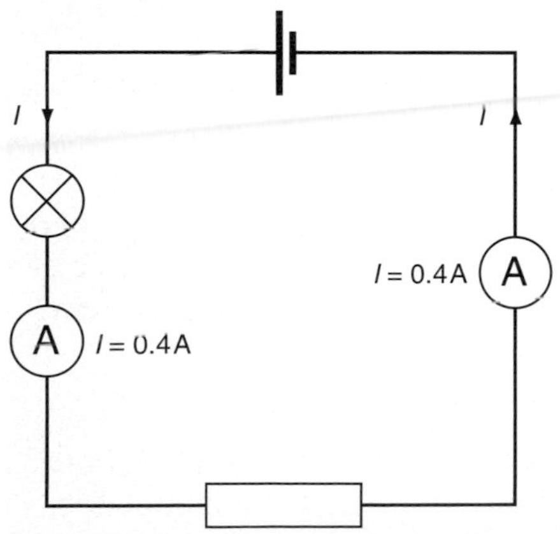

The **potential difference** is measured with a voltmeter connected in **parallel** across a component. Potential difference (or p.d. for short) is measured in volts.

How are series circuits different from parallel circuits?

A series circuit is a single pathway for an electric current through a set of wires and components. A parallel circuit gives more than one pathway for the electric current.

Components joined in series follow each other in one complete loop. The current has only one path it can take. So the same current must flow through each component and wire in the circuit.

$I = 0.4A$ (A)

(A) $I = 0.4A$

Figure 7.3 The same current flows through components joined in series. The arrow shows the direction of current flow from the positive to the negative terminal.

> A **cell** uses chemical reactions to produce a potential difference across its two terminals. A **battery** is two or more cells connected together.

Figure 7.4 A 12 V car battery is six 2 V cells joined together.

The ammeters in Figure 7.3 show the same reading. This is because the current is the same at all points in a series circuit.

Cells and batteries

If you call one **cell** on its own a battery then you are wrong. A **battery** is two or more cells joined together. A cell or battery provides charges with energy that can be transformed into other types of energy as the charges flow around the circuit.

Potential difference – cells in series

For cells joined in series, the total potential difference is worked out by adding the separate potential differences together. This only works if the cells are joined together correctly, positive ($+$) to negative ($-$).

1.5 V   1.5 V   1.5 V

Figure 7.5 The cells are joined correctly. The separate potential differences add to give 4.5 V.

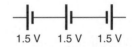

1.5 V   1.5 V   1.5 V

Figure 7.6 One cell is the wrong way round. The p.d. of this cell cancels out the p.d. of one of the other cells. The total p.d. is only 1.5 V.

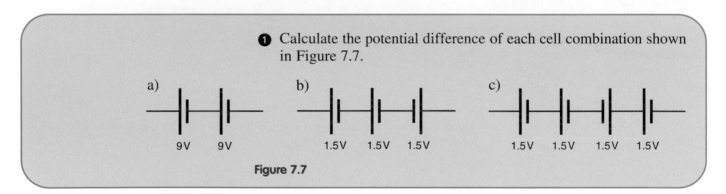

❶ Calculate the potential difference of each cell combination shown in Figure 7.7.

a)

9 V   9 V

b)

1.5 V   1.5 V   1.5 V

c)

1.5 V   1.5 V   1.5 V   1.5 V

Figure 7.7

7.2

What does resistance mean?

All components resist the flow of an electric current through them. The more easily a current flows through a component, the less **resistance** the component has. A high resistance component lets only a small current flow.

> **Resistance** is measured in ohms (Ω). The resistance (R) of a component is defined as potential difference (V) across it divided by the current (I) through it.

Some components change their resistance in response to the environment and resistance changes can be useful in electronics (more about this later). For the same potential difference across a component, changing the resistance changes the current in the circuit: the greater the resistance, the smaller the current.

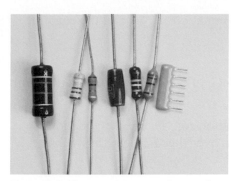

Figure 7.8 These resistors can be used to control the size of the current in a circuit, for example to limit the current in a sensitive electrical component.

Figure 7.10 The resistance of a variable resistor is changed by moving a sliding contact. The variable resistor can be used to control the current and change the potential difference across a component.

Adding resistors in series

Adding more lamps to a circuit (Figure 7.9) makes the current go down, which means the resistance of the circuit has gone up.

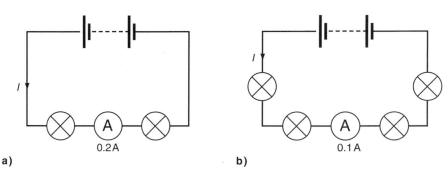

a)   b)

Figure 7.9 Adding components to a series circuit increases the resistance of the circuit.

The total resistance of a series circuit is the sum of the individual resistances.

Example

| 5 Ω | | 10 Ω |

total resistance = 5 + 10 = 15 ohms (Ω)

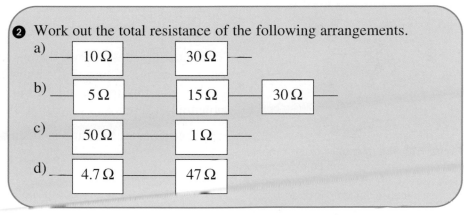

❷ Work out the total resistance of the following arrangements.
a) 10 Ω   30 Ω
b) 5 Ω   15 Ω   30 Ω
c) 50 Ω   1 Ω
d) 4.7 Ω   47 Ω

Linking potential difference, current and resistance

The potential difference across a component, the current through a component and the resistance of a component are linked by the equation:

| **potential difference** | = | **current** | × | **resistance** |
| (volt, V) | | (ampere, A) | | (ohm, Ω) |

You might find the equation easier to use if you remember it like the triangle shown in Figure 7.11.

If you put your finger over the 'R' in the triangle, the equation becomes:

$$R = \frac{V}{I}$$

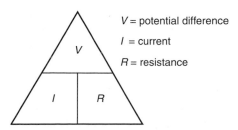

V = potential difference
I = current
R = resistance

Figure 7.11 Equation triangle for potential difference, current and resistance

CHAPTER 7 What affects the current in an electric circuit?

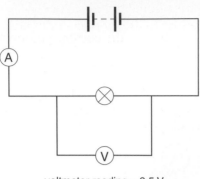

voltmeter reading = 9.5 V
ammeter reading = 1.9 A

Figure 7.12 Knowing the current and potential difference allows the resistance to be calculated.

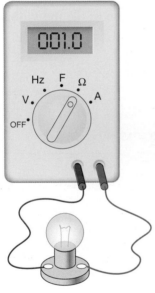

Figure 7.13 The resistance of the lamp, or any other component, can be measured directly using an ohmmeter. The resistance is small because the lamp is cold.

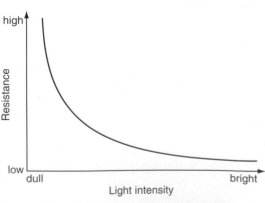

Figure 7.14 The resistance of an LDR changes with light intensity.

You can do the same thing to find the equation for '*I*' and the equation for '*V*'.

Example

A 24 Ω resistor has a potential difference of 12 V across it. What current flows through the resistor?

If you are not sure how to get the equation for '*I*', use the equation triangle in Figure 7.11. Put your finger over the '*I*'. This shows that '*V*' is above '*R*'. So, the equation is:

$$I = \frac{V}{R} = \frac{12}{24} = 0.5 \text{ A}$$

❸ Copy and complete Table 7.1

Device	Potential difference across device in V	Current through device in A	Resistance of device in Ω
Resistor	10		20
Lamp	12	3	
Kettle	230	10	
Motor	415		83
Iron	230		57.5

Table 7.1

How is the resistance of a component measured?

The equation above shows that resistance is defined as *R = V / I*. The circuit drawn in Figure 7.12 shows how the resistance of a component can be found by measuring the current flowing through it (*I*) and the potential difference (*V*) across it. In this case the component is a lamp.

The resistance of the lamp is calculated using the equation:

$$R = \frac{V}{I} = \frac{9.5}{1.9} = 5 \, \Omega$$

The resistance of many components is not fixed – it can change. For example, a lamp has a higher resistance when it is hot than when it is cold (more about this in Section 7.3).

Two special types of resistor

The resistance of a **light-dependent resistor (LDR)** changes as the intensity (brightness) of light shining on it changes. Figure 7.14 and Table 7.2 show that the resistance goes down as the intensity of the light goes up.

Light level	Resistance in Ω
Dark	1 000 000
Bright	2 000

Table 7.2 Resistance of an LDR

A **light-dependent resistor (LDR)** is a component in an electric circuit whose resistance decreases as the intensity of light falling on it increases.

A **thermistor** is a component in an electric circuit whose resistance decreases as the temperature increases.

The LDR can be used as a sensor in light-operated circuits, such as security lighting. The change in resistance of LDRs is used in digital cameras to control the total amount of light that enters the camera.

The resistance of a **thermistor** changes with temperature. As the temperature of the thermistor rises the resistance decreases.

A thermistor can be used as the sensor in a temperature-operated circuit, such as a fire alarm. Some electronic thermometers use a thermistor to detect changes in temperature.

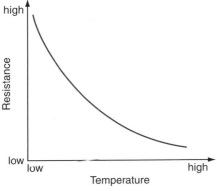

Figure 7.15 The resistance of a thermistor changes with temperature.

Figure 7.16 The change in the resistance of a thermistor can be used to switch on other electrical circuits automatically.

4 Figure 7.17 shows a thermistor in series with a high-power lamp and positioned close to it.
   a) Explain why the lamp only shines dimly when the switch is closed.
   b) Explain why the lamp gets slowly brighter.

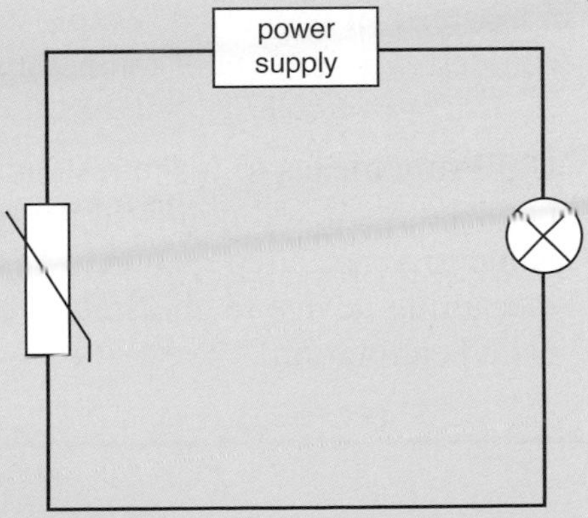

Figure 7.17

5 Ramesh is using the ammeter in Figure 7.18 as a simple light intensity meter.
   a) Explain why the reading on the ammeter changes when the light intensity changes.
   b) Sketch a graph to show how the ammeter reading changes with light intensity.

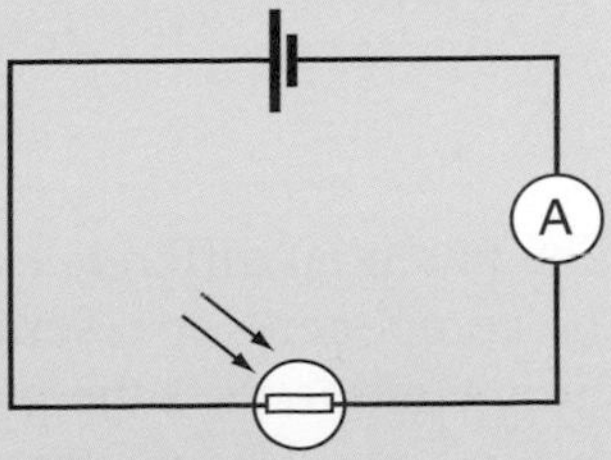

Figure 7.18

Activity – Misti designs an oven thermometer

Misti has designed the circuit shown in Figure 7.19 to replace the broken temperature display on her oven. The thermistor, which Misti is using as a temperature sensor, goes inside the oven. The rest of the circuit is outside the oven.

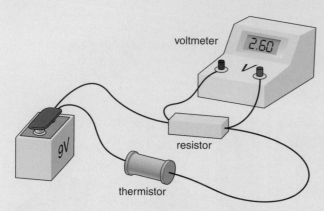

Figure 7.19 Misti's design for an oven thermometer

① Draw a circuit diagram of Misti's oven thermometer design.
② Explain why the voltmeter reading changes as the oven temperature changes.

Before using her oven thermometer Misti must **calibrate** it. She does this by putting the thermistor in a beaker of water and heating the water. She recorded different water temperatures and the

Calibrate means to make a standard scale between two fixed points so that you can give a value to a measured quantity. Testing a measuring device to check its accuracy is also called calibration.

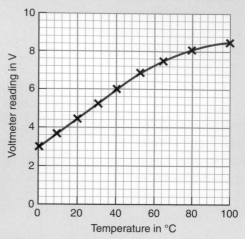

Figure 7.20 Misti's calibration graph

reading on the voltmeter at those temperatures. Misti then drew the calibration graph shown in Figure 7.20.

③ Explain how Misti can use the calibration graph to convert voltmeter readings into temperature values.
④ When Misti tried her thermometer in her oven she obtained voltmeter readings that varied between 7.5 V and 8.0 V. What range of temperatures does this give for the oven?
⑤ Suggest why the voltmeter reading was not constant.
⑥ Misti realises there is a problem with her design. It cannot be used to measure high oven temperatures.
Why can this design not measure temperatures above 100 °C?

More about components in series

The potential differences across the components in a series circuit add to give the potential difference of the power supply.

The current through components joined in series is the same. But the potential difference across the components may be different. The potential differences are the same only if the components have the same resistance.

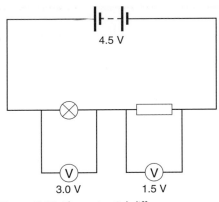

Figure 7.21 The potential difference across a component depends on the resistance of the component.

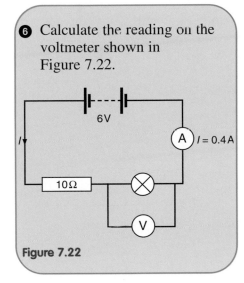

6 Calculate the reading on the voltmeter shown in Figure 7.22.

Figure 7.22

The voltmeters in Figure 7.21 are measuring the potential difference across the lamp and the resistor. The lamp and the resistor cannot have the same resistance, as the voltmeters are giving different readings. The reading across the lamp is the largest, so the lamp must have the largest resistance.

Adding the two voltmeter readings gives the total potential difference across the circuit components. In this case:

$$\text{total potential difference} = 3.0 + 1.5 = 4.5\,V$$

This is the same as the potential difference of the battery. So the potential difference of the battery has been shared between the two components.

More about parallel circuits

When components are joined in parallel, the potential difference across each component is the same.

Joining components in parallel gives the electric current different paths. Some current goes down each path. How much current goes through each component depends on the resistance of the component. The one with the biggest resistance has the smallest current flowing through it.

In Figure 7.23 half the total current flows through each lamp. So the resistance of the lamps must be the same because the current has split into two equal parts. The current joins back together where the parallel paths meet.

In a parallel circuit, the total current flowing through the whole circuit is the sum of the currents flowing through the separate components where the current has split (Figure 7.24).

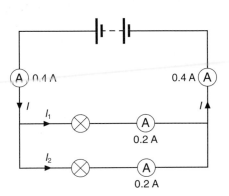

Figure 7.23 The current in a parallel circuit divides between the different paths.

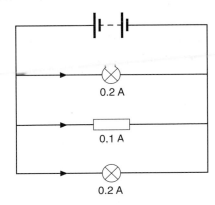

Figure 7.24 Total current = 0.2 + 0.1 + 0.2 = 0.5 A

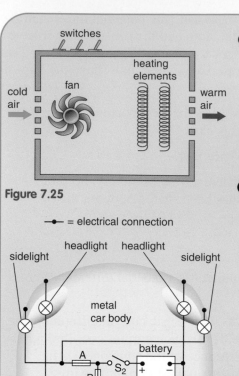

Figure 7.25

—●— = electrical connection

Figure 7.26

❼ Figure 7.25 shows a simplified picture of the inside of a small fan heater. The electrical wiring is not shown.
Draw, using circuit symbols, a diagram to show how the heating elements, fan and switches would be connected together. It is essential that:
- when connected to the mains and switched on the fan comes on;
- both heating elements can be switched on independently;
- on hot days the heater can be used as a fan.

❽ Figure 7.26 shows a simplified circuit diagram for the front lights of a car. The metal car body acts like a wire in the circuit.
a) Which lights would not work if fuse A melted?
b) Which switch operates the headlights?
c) Can the sidelights be switched on without the headlights? Give a reason for your answer.
d) If one headlight breaks, will the other one still work? Give a reason for your answer.
e) How would this circuit need to be changed if the car had a plastic body?

Appliance	Working current in A
Computer	1
Hairdryer	4
Television	2
Stereo	1
Heater	10

Table 7.3 The current drawn from the mains supply by an appliance depends on its power rating.

Figure 7.27 Overloaded circuits can cause fires.

Overloaded circuits

An adaptor lets you plug more than one appliance into a single mains socket. The appliances are in parallel. So the total current taken from the socket is the sum of the currents flowing through each appliance.

If the computer, stereo and television in Table 7.3 are plugged into an adaptor:

total current = 1 + 1 + 2 = 4 A

This is not yet a problem. Up to 13 amps can safely flow through the wire connecting the socket to the mains electricity supply.

However, plugging the hairdryer, television and heater into an adaptor could cause a big problem.

$$\text{total current} = 4 + 2 + 10 = 16\,\text{A}$$

The total current is too large for the connecting wire. The wire could get so hot it causes a fire.

What does a current–potential difference graph show?

The circuit shown in Figure 7.28 can be used to show how the current through a component depends on the potential difference across the component.

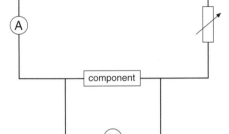

Figure 7.28 A circuit used to investigate the relationship between current and potential difference

If you adjust the variable resistor, this changes the potential difference across the component and the current through the component. Adjusting the variable resistor allows a set of potential difference and current readings to be taken for a component. (You could also change the potential difference by adding more cells.) You can use the readings to draw a graph.

When the component is a resistor

As long as the temperature of the resistor stays the same, the graph is always a straight line going through the origin $(0, 0)$. This shows that as the potential difference increases so does the current.

If you connect the resistor the other way round this does not change its resistance. The graph is still a straight line.

A metal wire has a constant resistance, but only if the temperature of the wire stays the same.

9 Copy Figure 7.29. Label the line A. Draw a second graph line for a resistor with a higher value than A. Label the second line B.

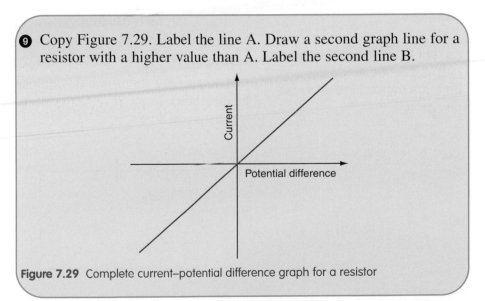

Figure 7.29 Complete current–potential difference graph for a resistor

When the component is a filament lamp

A filament lamp uses a very hot wire (filament) to give out light.

As the potential difference across the lamp increases, the light gets brighter. The light is brighter because more electrical energy is being transformed into light – and heat too. As the filament gets hotter its resistance increases. As a result of the higher resistance, the current does not increase in the same proportion as the potential difference (Figure 7.30). The resistance of a filament lamp is not constant – it depends on its temperature.

Connecting the lamp the other way round makes no difference to the way the resistance of the lamp changes. The resistance always increases when the temperature of the filament increases.

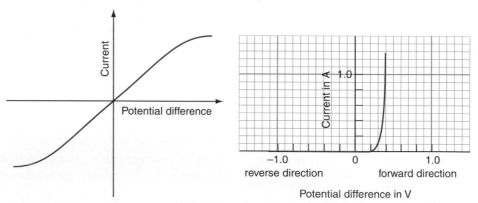

Figure 7.30 Current–potential difference graph for a filament lamp

Figure 7.31 Current–potential difference graph for a diode

When the component is a diode

> A **diode** is a device that allows current to flow in one direction only, since the diode has a very high resistance in the reverse direction.

The graph for a **diode** is different from both a resistor and a filament lamp (Figure 7.31). The resistance of a diode does depend on which way round it is connected in a circuit.

Diodes only let current flow in one direction (called the forward direction). In the reverse direction diodes have a very high resistance so no current flows.

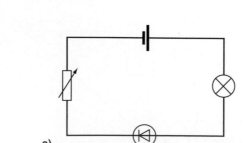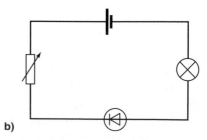

a)   b)

Figure 7.32 a) Lamp is on. b) Lamp is off.

Activity – QTC (Quantum Tunnelling Composite)

Figure 7.33 The outside casing of this prototype drill contains QTC. Squeezing the drill controls its speed.

Figure 7.34 QTC textile switches can be incorporated into 'smart' clothing and bags. Tapping the switches controls your mobile phone and MP3 player. QTC switches are even used in space suits.

Invented in 1997 by David Lussey, QTC is an amazing material. In one form it looks just like a piece of black rubber. But, unlike rubber, when you squash it its electrical resistance falls as it changes from an insulator to a conductor.

The range of potential applications for QTC is huge – from toys to textile switches, robotic sensors to space travel.

❶ Use the internet to investigate at least five different applications for QTC. Start your search by looking at the website www.peratech.co.uk. Write a few sentences about each application.

❷ Which application that you have written about do you think will benefit people most? Give reasons for your choice.

Josh designed a simple experiment to check out what he had read about QTC. The apparatus he used is shown in Figure 7.35. Josh used various weights to squeeze the QTC, which was sandwiched between two metal plates. For each new weight Josh waited 20 seconds before taking the ohmmeter reading. He did this because he had noticed that the reading often changed rapidly in the first few seconds. Even after 20 seconds the reading still changed, but more slowly. For each weight Josh recorded a range of resistance values. These are shown in Figure 7.36.

❸ With a weight of 20 N Josh measured the resistance as 10 Ω. Why has Josh not plotted this value on his results chart?

❹ Josh added another weight to the QTC 'sandwich'. The reading on the ohmmeter was a fairly steady 3 Ω. How many newtons do you think this weight was? Give a reason for your answer.

❺ Josh noticed that there is no overlap between the resistance values produced by two different weights. State with a reason whether this means that QTC could be used as a reliable way to tell one weight from a different one.

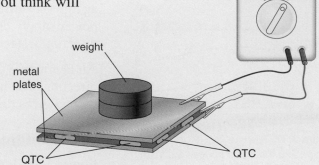

Figure 7.35 Measuring the resistance of QTC with an ohmmeter

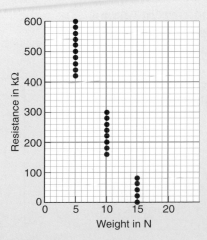

Figure 7.36 For each weight the QTC has a range of resistance.

7.4

What is the difference between direct current and alternating current?

> **Direct current (d.c.)** is electric current that flows in the same direction all the time.

A **direct current (d.c.)** always flows in the same direction around a circuit. It is shown in circuit diagrams by an arrow, usually labelled I, going from the positive terminal to the negative terminal of the power supply. (This is called the conventional current. The current, in terms of electrons, flows in the opposite direction – from the negative terminal of the power supply to the positive terminal.) Cells and batteries produce a constant direct current (d.c.)

> A **cathode ray oscilloscope (CRO)** is a device that displays how a potential difference varies over time.

You can use a **cathode ray oscilloscope (CRO)** to show that the potential difference of a d.c. supply is constant. The display or 'trace' on the CRO screen shows the potential difference in volts across the supply. In Figure 7.37 connecting a cell to the input terminals has made the line on the CRO jump up above the middle line. Connecting the cell the other way around would make the line jump down below the middle line. The bigger the potential difference of the cell, the further the line jumps. The CRO therefore gives us a way of comparing the potential differences of different d.c. supplies.

Alternating current is like having a cell in a circuit but you keep turning the cell around. First the current goes one way, then it goes back again. The current flows backwards and forwards as the terminals of the power supply change from positive to negative. But a.c. changes direction faster and more often than you could turn the cell around.

An alternating current (a.c.) is one that is constantly reversing its direction. The number of times the current changes direction in one second gives the **frequency** of the supply.

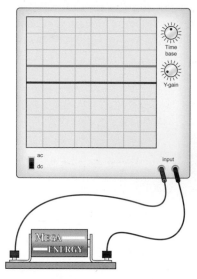

Figure 7.37 The line (trace) on the CRO shows that the cell produces a constant potential difference. The zero value is shown as a red line.

> **Alternating current (a.c.)** is electric current that continually changes its direction.
>
> The **frequency** of an a.c. current is the number of cycles per second.

Comparing CRO traces for two different a.c. supplies

Figure 7.38 shows the CRO traces for two a.c. supplies. The controls on the oscilloscope were the same for both supplies. Each time the trace changes from above to below (or from below to above) the red zero line, the current in the circuit changes direction.

10 Explain the difference between an alternating current and a direct current.

wave trace A

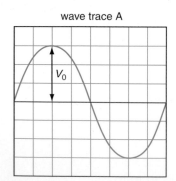

V_0

wave trace B

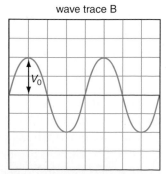

V_0

Figure 7.38 The two a.c. supplies have a different frequency and peak potential difference (V_0).

Trace A is 1½ times taller than trace B. So the peak potential difference (V_0) of supply A is 1½ times bigger than that of supply B.

The CRO trace for supply B shows twice as many waves as supply A. This means the potential difference (and current) of supply B changes direction twice as often as the potential difference (and current) of supply A. So the frequency of supply B is twice the frequency of supply A.

Using the measurements from a CRO trace for an a.c. supply

The screen of a CRO is like a graph. The vertical and horizontal divisions have a scale. Each vertical division represents a certain number of volts. Each horizontal division represents a certain length of time. When you know the scale you can work out three important quantities:

- peak (maximum) potential difference (V_0);
- time to complete one cycle (called the **time period**);
- frequency of the supply.

Look back at trace A in Figure 7.38. If each vertical division on the CRO represents 2 volts and each horizontal division represents 0.005 seconds, then:

$$\text{peak potential difference} = 3 \text{ divisions} \times 2 \text{ volts per division} = 6\text{ V}$$

$$\text{time period} = 8 \text{ divisions} \times 0.005 = 0.04\text{ s}$$

$$\text{frequency} = \frac{1}{\text{time period}} = \frac{1}{0.04} = 25\text{ Hz}$$

The mains electricity supply

The UK mains electricity is an a.c. supply of about 230 V. It has a frequency of 50 Hz. This means the current flows one way, then back again, 50 times in each second.

The mains electricity supply cable to a house has two wires   a live wire and a neutral wire. The current comes into the house on one wire and returns on the other.

Electricity is supplied through the live wire. The potential (voltage) at the live terminal alternates between positive and negative with respect to the neutral wire with a mean (average) potential of 230 V. The live wire is a dangerous wire.

The neutral wire is kept at a potential (voltage) close to zero. This is done by connecting it to a huge metal plate in the earth at the local electricity sub-station.

⑪ Figure 7.39 shows the CRO traces for different a.c. supplies. Which of the supplies has the:
 a) largest peak voltage;
 b) highest frequency;
 c) lowest frequency;
 d) smallest peak voltage?

⑫ Each horizontal division on the CRO screen in Figure 7.39 represents 0.002 s. Calculate the frequency of each trace.

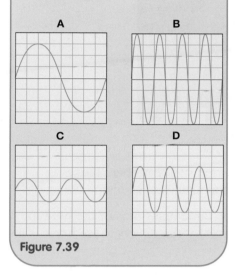

Figure 7.39

The **time period** is the time taken for a.c. current to complete one cycle. Time period is related to frequency.

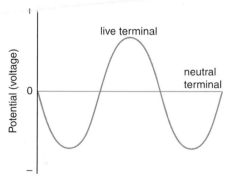

Figure 7.40 The alternating potential at the live terminal makes the current flow backwards and forwards (a.c.).

How can the mains electricity supply be used safely?

Many electrical appliances are designed to work from the mains electricity supply. Most of these appliances are connected to the mains using a cable and three-pin plug. Both the cable and plug are designed to make the appliance safe to use.

Inside the cable are either two or three copper wires (the inner cores). Copper is used because it is a good electrical conductor. A layer of plastic covers each wire and another layer forms the outside of the cable. Plastic is used because it is a good insulator and is flexible.

Figure 7.41 Three-core and two-core cables

The outside case of the plug is made of plastic or rubber. These materials are used because they are good electrical insulators.

Pushing the plug into a socket joins the three brass pins of the plug to the terminals of the socket. Brass is used for the pins because brass is a good electrical conductor.

Inside the plug there is a cable grip and a fuse. The cable grip is there to hold the cable firmly in place. If the cable is pulled the cable grip stops the copper wires inside the plug being pulled loose.

Figure 7.42 A three-pin plug and its wall socket

Fuses

A **fuse** is a thin piece of wire that lets a current of up to a certain value flow through it. Above this value the fuse overheats and melt. We often say that the fuse has 'blown'.

The fuse joins the live pin to the live wire inside the plug. If a fault causes the fuse to melt the live wire is disconnected. This protects the appliance from taking a current that might damage it or cause its wiring to overheat and start a fire.

> A **fuse** is a thin wire that is designed to melt and break the circuit when the current through it exceeds the rating on the fuse.

Most plugs are fitted with a 3 A or 13 A fuse. Appliances like table lamps and TVs take small currents (well below 3 A), so they should have plugs with 3 A fuses. Kettles, irons and hairdryers usually take currents greater than 3 A, so they should have plugs with a 13 A fuse.

Figure 7.43 Electricity is useful but also dangerous. Many household fires are caused by electrical faults.

Connecting an appliance to a three-pin plug

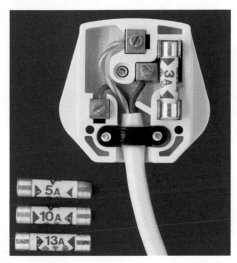

Figure 7.44 A correctly wired three-pin plug:
- the brown wire (live wire) is joined to the fuse, which is joined to the live pin;
- the blue wire (neutral wire) is joined to the neutral pin;
- the green/yellow wire (earth wire) is joined to the earth pin.

All new electrical appliances come with a plug already fitted. But at some time you may need to fit a new plug to an older appliance. When you do this you must connect the correct wire from the appliance to the correct pin in the plug. The wires are colour coded to help you connect them in the right place.

🔺 An electric coffee maker takes a current of 2 A from the mains supply. Explain why the plug of the coffee maker should not be fitted with a 13 A fuse.

🔺 Why would it be dangerous to connect the fuse inside a plug to the neutral wire rather than the live wire?

🔺 Say why each of the plugs drawn in Figure 7.45 is not safe to use.

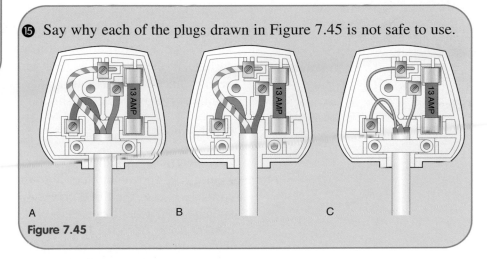

A   B   C

Figure 7.45

Circuit breakers

The mains supply to a house starts at a consumer unit. Often this is called the 'fuse box'. In the consumer unit are several separate fuses. Each fuse leads to a different circuit supplying electricity to a different part of the house.

Many consumer units now contain **circuit breakers** rather than fuses. The circuit breaker is a fast acting switch that automatically turns off

A **circuit breaker** is a resettable fuse.

Figure 7.46 An RCCB plugged into a socket ready for use

('trips') when the current through it goes above a set value. Having mended the fault that caused the current to rise you press a button to reset the circuit breaker.

A second type of circuit breaker, a **residual current circuit breaker (RCCB)**, should be used with certain types of appliance, particularly those used outside. It is a circuit breaker that disconnects the circuit when it detects current leaking out of the circuit to earth due to a fault.

An RCCB works by detecting any difference between the currents in the live and neutral wires of the supply cable. If everything is working properly the two currents are the same. If something happens to make the current in the wires different, the RCCB automatically switches the circuit off.

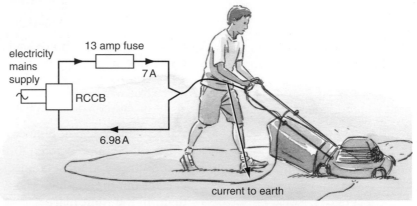

Figure 7.47 Using an RCCB saves Vince from a nasty experience.

16 Give two ways that a circuit breaker is a better safety device than a fuse.

17 Why should electric hedge trimmers always be plugged into an RCCB?

For extra safety Vince plugs his lawn mower into an RCCB. Just as well, because Vince has been careless and cut into the cable insulation. This causes a current to flow through Vince to earth. This means the currents in the live and neutral wires are now different. The RCCB detects this difference and rapidly switches the circuit off saving Vince from a very nasty electric shock.

Earthing

Any electrical appliance with an outside metal case is usually earthed. Figure 7.48 shows an electric toaster. It has been earthed by joining the earth wire from the three-core cable to the metal casing. If while it's switched on, a fault causes the live wire to touch the metal case, a large current flows from the live wire to the earth wire. This large current in the circuit causes the fuse to melt, which switches the toaster off.

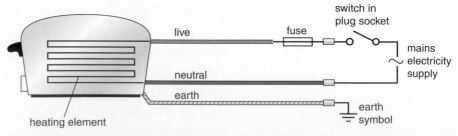

Figure 7.48 The earth wire is an important safety feature of appliances with outer metal parts.

Without the earth wire the toaster would become live. Anyone who touches the metal case would get an electric shock as the current flows through them to earth.

Activity – Using electricity safely

We use electrical appliances and gadgets to make our lives more comfortable and enjoyable. Yet electricity is dangerous, it can and does kill. We not only run the risk of electrocution, but also the risk of fires caused by electrical faults.

Write a short, lively article for a gadget or fashion magazine. The article should start by saying why the discovery of electricity was so important to individuals and society. It should go on to warn readers about the potential risks of using electricity and also give advice on how to reduce these risks.

18 The pictures drawn in Figure 7.49 show electricity being used dangerously. Explain the danger in each picture.

wires individually wrapped
in insulating tape

Figure 7.49

19 Zafran leans against his washing machine. Unfortunately the live wire inside the machine has become loose and is touching the metal casing. Explain how the earth wire, which is correctly connected, protects Zafran from a serious electric shock.

7.6 What links current, charge, energy and power?

Current and charge

An electric current is a flow of charge. In a metal wire, an electric current is a flow of negatively charged electrons. A larger current means there is a greater rate of flow of charge.

The amount of charge transferred by a circuit depends on two factors:
- the size of the current;
- how long the circuit is switched on.

> 1 **coulomb** is the charge that passes a point when a current of 1 **ampere** flows for 1 second.

Charge is measured in **coulombs** (C) and current is measured in **amperes** or **amps** (A). The link between charge and current is given by the equation:

$$\underset{\text{(coulomb, C)}}{\text{charge}} = \underset{\text{(ampere, A)}}{\text{current}} \times \underset{\text{(second, s)}}{\text{time}}$$

Example

To boil water a current of 10 A flows through the heating element of an electric kettle for 2 minutes. How much charge passes through the heating element?

$$
\begin{aligned}
\text{charge} &= \text{current} \times \text{time} \\
&= 10 \times 120 \\
&= 1200 \text{ coulombs}
\end{aligned}
$$

> [20] A horse got an electric shock from touching an electrified fence. Calculate how much charge passed through the horse if a current of 0.020 A flowed for 0.1 s.

Energy and charge

In any circuit, the battery or mains supply is an energy source that provides energy to charges. Energy is transformed into other forms of energy as the charges flow around the circuit.

How much total energy is transformed by a component in a circuit depends on two factors:
- the potential difference across the component;
- how much charge flows through the component.

The link between energy transformed, potential difference and charge is given by the equation:

$$\underset{\text{(joule, J)}}{\text{energy transformed}} = \underset{\text{(volt, V)}}{\text{potential difference}} \times \underset{\text{(coulomb, C)}}{\text{charge}}$$

This equation also applies to the electrical energy transferred from a power supply to an appliance.

Power and energy

Sometimes knowing how quickly energy is transferred or transformed is as important as, or more important than, knowing how much energy is transferred or transformed.

> **Power** is the rate at which a device transforms energy, in J/s or W.

For example, an electric kettle transfers heat energy to the water inside the kettle. But if the transfer takes a long time the water warms up slowly. To know how quickly the water warms up you need to know how much energy the kettle transfers to the water every second. What you need to know is the **power** of the kettle.

$$\text{power (watt, W)} = \frac{\text{energy transferred (joule, J)}}{\text{time (second, s)}}$$

A kettle with a high power rating of 2000 W (2 kW) transfers 2000 joules of electrical energy every second. This is a rapid transfer, so the kettle heats the water quickly.

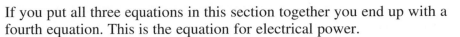

If you put all three equations in this section together you end up with a fourth equation. This is the equation for electrical power.

$$\underset{\text{(watt, W)}}{\text{power}} \quad = \quad \underset{\text{(ampere, A)}}{\text{current}} \quad \times \quad \underset{\text{(volt, V)}}{\text{potential difference}}$$

Most appliances have their power and the p.d. of the supply they need printed on them. From this you can work out the current they use and the fuse they need.

Activity – Using the information on an information plate

All electrical appliances used at home have an information plate somewhere on the outside. Find the information plates on three different types of appliance.

❶ For each appliance write down the technical information from the plate.

❷ Calculate the normal operating current of each appliance.

❸ Suggest the correct fuse rating to use with each appliance.

㉑ Table 7.4 shows how long it takes three different electric kettles to boil some water. The starting temperature of the water in each kettle is the same.

Kettle	Mass of water in the kettle	Time to boil the water
X	1.0 kg	4 minutes
Y	500 g	2½ minutes
Z	1.2 kg	4 minutes

Table 7.4

Assuming the kettles are equally efficient, which one has the highest power? Explain your choice.

㉒ Calculate the power rating in watts of:
a) a car starter motor operating from a 12 V supply, taking a 100 A current;
b) a torch bulb operating from a 4.5 V supply, taking a 0.3 A current;
c) a pocket calculator operating from a 3 V supply, taking a 0.0001 A current.

㉓ A 24 W set of Christmas lights has 20 identical lamps in series worked from a 120 V supply. Calculate:
a) the current through each lamp;
b) the potential difference across one lamp;
c) the resistance of the lighting circuit.

㉔ A 12 V battery drives a motor taking a current of 2 A for 20 seconds. Calculate the electrical energy transferred to the motor.

㉕ Usually a 3 A or 13 A fuse is fitted to the plug of a 230 V household appliance.
a) Calculate the current each of the appliances in Table 7.5 draws from the mains.
b) State the correct fuse to use with each appliance.

Appliance	Power rating
Microwave	750 W
Oven	2.5 kW
Toaster	350 W
Radio	15 W

Table 7.5

㉖ Figure 7.50 shows the circuit diagram for a 'flame effect' electric fire.

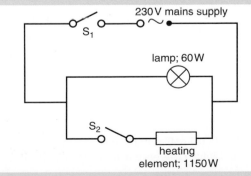

Figure 7.50

a) Explain why you cannot switch only the heating element on.
b) With both switches closed calculate:
   i)   the current taken by the heating element;
   ii) the current taken by the lamp (give your answer to the nearest whole number);
   iii) the total current taken from the supply;
   iv) the resistance of the heating element.
c) What size fuse should be fitted to the fire, 3 A or 13 A? Give a reason for your choice.

Summary

✓ A **component** is a part of an electric circuit.

✓ **Potential difference** (or p.d.) is often called voltage. A potential difference causes current to flow.

✓ A **cell** uses chemical reactions to produce a potential difference across its two terminals. A **battery** is a number of cells connected together.

✓ The **resistance** of a component in ohms is defined as the potential difference across it divided by the current through it.

✓ The **resistance** of a **light-dependent resistor (LDR)** decreases as the intensity of the light increases.

✓ The resistance of a **thermistor** increases as its temperature decreases.

✓ A resistor at constant temperature has a constant resistance – the current is directly proportional to the potential difference.

✓ The resistance of a filament lamp increases as the temperature of the filament increases.

✓ **Calibrate** means to make a standard scale between two fixed points so that you can give a value to a measured quantity. Testing a measuring device to check its accuracy is also called calibration.

✓ A **diode** lets current flow in only one direction.

✓ For components joined in **series:**
   – the same current flows through each component;
   – the total resistance is the sum of the individual resistances;
   – the potential differences across the components add to give the potential difference of the power supply.

✓ For components joined in **parallel:**
   – the potential difference across each component is the same;

   – the total current flowing through the whole circuit is the sum of the currents flowing through the separate components.

✓ **Direct current (d.c.)** flows in one direction only but **alternating current (a.c.)** changes direction.

✓ In the UK the mains supply is at 230 V a.c. with a **frequency** of 50 hertz.

✓ Traces on a **cathode ray oscilloscope (CRO)** can be used to compare potential differences of a.c. and d.c. supplies.

✓ The **time period** is the time taken for a.c. current to complete one cycle. Time period is related to frequency.

✓ The period, and therefore the frequency, of a supply can be found from its CRO trace.

✓ A correctly wired three-pin plug contains a **fuse** and an earth wire.

✓ A **circuit breaker** is a resettable fuse. A **residual current circuit breaker** (**RCCB**) is a circuit breaker that disconnects the circuit when it detects current leaking out of the circuit to earth due to a fault.

✓ Any appliance with a metal case should be earthed.

✓ Important equations that you should be able to use:

potential difference = current × resistance

$$\text{power} = \frac{\text{energy transferred}}{\text{time}}$$

power = current × potential difference

charge = current × time

energy transformed = potential difference × charge

✓ 1 **coulomb** is the charge that passes a point when a current of 1 **ampere** flows for 1 second.

EXAMQUESTIONS

1 Tasmin wants to find out how the current through component 'X' varies with potential difference. To do this she sets up the circuit shown in Figure 7.51. Tasmin's one set of results are recorded in Table 7.6.

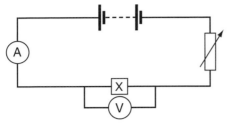

Figure 7.51 The circuit set up by Tasmin

Potential difference in V	0.0	3.0	5.0	7.0	9.0	11.0
Current in A	0.0	1.0	1.4	1.7	1.9	2.1

Table 7.6 Tasmin's results

a) i) What did Tasmin do to vary the potential difference across component 'X'? *(1 mark)*

   ii) What range of potential difference values did Tasmin use? *(1 mark)*

   iii) Suggest why Tasmin should have included some values of potential difference below 3 volts. *(1 mark)*

b) i) Plot a graph of potential difference (horizontal axis) against current (vertical axis). *(3 marks)*

   ii) Use your graph to calculate the resistance of component 'X' when the potential difference is 10 V. *(3 marks)*

c) What is component 'X'? Explain the reason for your answer. *(2 marks)*

2 Figure 7.52 shows Sulaman using a 12 V heater to warm a block of metal. He is using a joulemeter to measure the energy transferred to the heater.

Before starting the experiment Sulaman reset the joulemeter to zero. After switching on and leaving for 5 minutes the reading was 7200.

a) i) Calculate the energy transferred each second to the heater. *(1 mark)*

   ii) State the power of the heater. *(1 mark)*

b) Sulaman correctly calculated that the temperature of the metal block should go up by 18 °C. But, when he measured the temperature he found it had increased by only 15 °C. Give two reasons why the temperature of the block did not increase by 18 °C. *(2 marks)*

3 For the heater in question **2**:

a) calculate the charge that flowed through the heater in 5 minutes. Give the units for your answer. *(3 marks)*

b) calculate the current, in amps, through the heater during the 5 minutes. *(2 marks)*

4 The ammeters in Figure 7.53 are identical.

a) i) What are the readings on the ammeters A_1 and A_2? *(2 marks)*

   ii) Is the resistance of 'K', larger, smaller or equal to 30 Ω? Give a reason for your choice of answer. *(2 marks)*

b) i) Calculate the reading on the voltmeter. *(2 marks)*

   ii) State the potential difference of the power supply. Give a reason for your choice of value. *(2 marks)*

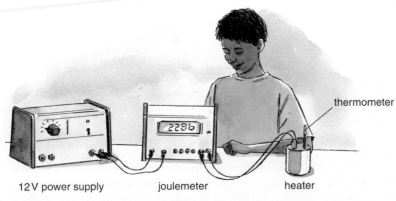

12 V power supply   joulemeter   heater

Figure 7.52 Sulaman investigates heating

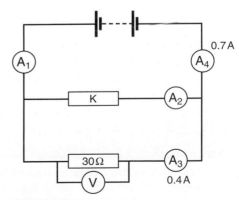

Figure 7.53

Chapter 8
What happens during radioactive decay, nuclear fission and nuclear fusion?

At the end of this chapter you should:

✓ know the relative masses and relative charges of protons, neutrons and electrons;

✓ know that atoms have a very small nucleus containing protons and neutrons surrounded by a much larger region of empty space in which there are electrons;

✓ understand how atoms can lose or gain electrons to form ions;

✓ know that alpha, beta and gamma radiations are emitted when the nuclei of radioactive substances decay;

✓ understand the changes in atomic number and mass number as a result of alpha and beta decay;

✓ know what causes background radiation;

✓ know that nuclear fission releases large amounts of energy which can be used in nuclear reactors to generate electricity;

✓ understand that the neutrons released by nuclear fission can start a chain reaction;

✓ know that nuclear fusion involves the joining together of two nuclei with the release of vast amounts of energy.

✓ be able to explain from the experimental evidence why the nuclear model of atomic structure replaced the 'plum pudding' model;

Figure 8.1 A small nuclear reactor on board this submarine provides sufficient energy for it to remain submerged in the ocean for months or even years without refuelling. The energy comes from the break-up (fission) of uranium nuclei. The heat and light emitted from stars also come from nuclear processes. In this case, the energy comes from the joining together (fusion) of hydrogen nuclei.

Where do radioactivity and atomic energy come from?

Radioactive substances such as uranium give out (emit) energy naturally. When radioactivity was discovered in 1896, no one could explain where this energy came from. Marie Curie soon discovered that the intensity of the radiation emitted depended only on the amount of uranium in her sample. Nothing she did to the uranium – such as heating it up – affected the rays. This, she said, 'shows that radioactivity is an atomic property'.

What do we know about the structure of atoms?

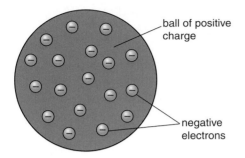

Figure 8.2 Thomson's 'plum pudding' model for the structure of atoms

In 1897, J. J. Thomson discovered tiny negative particles that were about 2000 times lighter than hydrogen atoms. He called these particles electrons. When Thomson put very high voltages across terminals made of different metals in different gases, the particles that he obtained all had the same mass and charge. This led him to suggest that all substances and all atoms must contain electrons.

Thomson knew that atoms had no electrical charge overall. So, the rest of the atom must have a positive charge to balance the negative charge of the electrons.

In Thomson's **'plum pudding' model**, each atom was thought to be a positively charged sphere with electrons embedded in it.

In 1904, Thomson suggested a model for the structure of atoms. This became known as the **'plum pudding' model** of atomic structure. Thomson suggested that atoms were tiny balls of positive material with electrons embedded in it, like currants scattered throughout a cake, or chocolate chips in a chocolate chip cookie (Figure 8.2).

Activity – Rutherford and his colleagues find the positive nucleus

In 1898, Ernest Rutherford showed that there were at least two types of radiation given out by radioactive materials. He called these alpha 'rays' and beta 'rays'.

At this time, Rutherford and his colleagues didn't know exactly what alpha rays were. But they did know that alpha rays contained particles. These alpha particles were small, heavy and positively charged. Rutherford and his colleagues used the alpha particles from radioactive substances as tiny 'bullets' to fire at atoms.

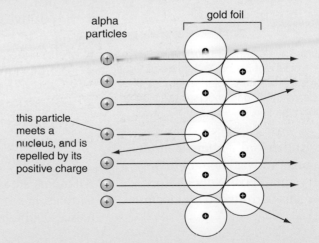

Figure 8.3 When positive alpha particles are directed at a very thin sheet of gold foil, they emerge at different angles. Most pass straight through the foil, some are deflected and a few appear to rebound from the foil.

In 1909, Rutherford designed an experiment in which his colleagues Hans Geiger and Ernest Marsden directed narrow beams of positive alpha particles at very thin gold foil only a few atoms thick (Figure 8.3). They expected the particles to pass straight through the foil or to be deflected slightly.

The results showed that:
* most of the alpha particles went straight through the foil;
* some of the alpha particles were scattered or deflected by the foil;
* a few alpha particles rebounded from the foil.

❶ Why did most of the alpha particles pass straight through the foil? (Hint: Most of an atom is empty space.)

❷ What conclusions can you draw about the size of any positive and negative particles in the gold atoms if most alpha particles pass straight through the foil?

❸ Why were some alpha particles deflected? (Remember that alpha particles are positive.)

❹ How did these results cast doubts on Thomson's plum pudding model for atomic structure?

❺ Why did a few alpha particles seem to rebound from the foil? (Hint: What will happen if an alpha particle approaches another positive charge head-on?)

❻ In 1911, Rutherford interpreted these results and put forward a new model for the structure of atoms. How do you think Rutherford described atoms?

Rutherford's nuclear model

Rutherford summarised the results of Geiger and Marsden's experiment by saying that atoms have a very small positive nucleus surrounded by a much larger region of empty space in which electrons orbit the nucleus like planets orbiting the Sun (Figure 8.4).

Rutherford's model of atomic structure was called the **nuclear model**. His nuclear model quickly replaced Thomson's plum pudding model and is still the basic model of atomic structure that we use today.

Through the work of Thomson, Rutherford and their colleagues we now know that:
* the positive charge of the nucleus is due to positive particles called protons;
* protons are about 2000 times heavier than electrons;
* electrons have a relative charge of -1 and protons have a relative charge of $+1$;
* atoms have equal numbers of protons and electrons, so that atoms have no overall electrical charge;
* the nuclei of atoms contain neutrons as well as protons. Neutrons have no charge and their mass is the same as that of protons.

All atoms are made up from protons, neutrons and electrons. These particles are sometimes called sub-atomic particles. Their relative masses and relative electric charges are summarised in Table 8.1.

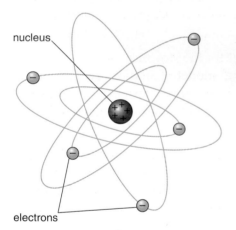

nucleus

electrons

Figure 8.4 Rutherford's nuclear model for the structure of atoms. Rutherford pictured atoms as miniature solar systems with electrons orbiting the nucleus like planets around the Sun.

In Rutherford's **nuclear model**, each atom was thought to have a very small positively charged nucleus surrounded by electrons.

Particle	Relative mass	Relative charge
Proton	1	+1
Neutron	1	0
Electron	$\dfrac{1}{2000}$	−1

Table 8.1 The relative masses and relative charges of protons, neutrons and electrons

The **atomic number** is the number of protons in an atom.

The **mass number** is the total number of protons plus neutrons in an atom.

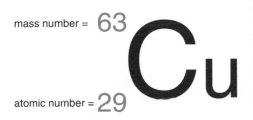

mass number = 63

atomic number = 29

Figure 8.5 We can write the symbol $^{63}_{29}Cu$ to show the mass number and atomic number for a copper nucleus.

Isotopes are atoms of an element with the same atomic number, but different mass numbers.

8.2 Atoms of different elements

Atoms of different elements have different numbers of protons. Hydrogen atoms are the only atoms with one proton. Helium atoms are the only atoms with two protons, lithium atoms are the only atoms with three protons, and so on. This means that the number of protons in an atom tells you straight away which element it is. Scientists call this number the **atomic number** (Section 3.7). So, hydrogen has an atomic number of one, helium has an atomic number of two, and so on.

The atomic number of an atom can tell you which element it is, but it cannot tell you its mass. The mass of an atom depends on the total number of protons and neutrons in its nucleus. Scientists call this number the **mass number** of an atom.

Hydrogen atoms (with one proton and no neutrons) have a mass number of 1, lithium atoms (with three protons and four neutrons) have a mass number of 7 and copper atoms (with 29 protons and 34 neutrons) have a mass number of 63.

All the atoms of a particular element have the same atomic number and therefore the same number of protons. But they don't all have the same number of neutrons. These atoms of the same element with different numbers of neutrons and therefore different mass numbers are called **isotopes** (Section 3.7).

From atoms to ions

When gamma rays and fast moving beta particles (electrons) hit atoms, they sometimes cause the atoms to become ions. These ionising radiations have so much energy that they can remove outer electrons from the atoms to form positively charged particles called ions (Figure 8.6).

CHAPTER 8 What happens during radioactive decay, nuclear fission and nuclear fusion?

$$\text{gamma rays} \quad\quad Na \rightarrow Na^+ + e^-$$

gamma rays   sodium   sodium   electron knocked
              atom   ion   out of Na

$$e^- + Cl \rightarrow Cl^+ + e^- + e^-$$

fast-moving   chlorine   chlorine   beta particle   electron
beta particle   atom   ion   retreating   knocked
                                                       out of Cl

Figure 8.6 The formation of ions when sodium and chlorine atoms are hit by ionising radiations

1 Copy and complete the following sentences.

Uranium has two isotopes. Each isotope has 92 protons and _____ electrons and therefore an _____ number of 92. But one of these isotopes has 143 neutrons and the other has 146 neutrons. Their mass numbers are therefore _____ and _____. They are sometimes called uranium-235 and _____.

2 Copy and complete Table 8.2 using words from the box below.

> atomic   chemical   neutrons   physical   protons

Isotopes have the same:	Isotopes have different:
• number of _____ • number of electrons • _____ number • _____ properties	• numbers of _____ • _____ properties

Table 8.2

3 Because there are different isotopes, chlorine gas can exist as $^{35}_{17}Cl_2$ and $^{37}_{17}Cl_2$. These two forms have the same chemical properties but different physical properties.
   a) Which particles determine the chemical properties of substances – protons, neutrons or electrons?
   b) Why do $^{35}_{17}Cl_2$ and $^{37}_{17}Cl_2$ have the same chemical properties?
   c) Why do $^{35}_{17}Cl_2$ and $^{37}_{17}Cl_2$ have different boiling points?
   d) Which has the higher boiling point, $^{35}_{17}Cl_2$ or $^{37}_{17}Cl_2$?

4 How many protons, neutrons and electrons are there in:
   a) $^{19}_{9}F$ and $^{19}_{9}F^-$;
   b) $^{27}_{13}Al$ and $^{27}_{13}Al^{3+}$?

 8.3

What causes background radiation?

Background radiation is the nuclear radiation that is present all around us. It comes mainly from natural sources.

Nuclear radiation is all around us. This is because there are naturally occurring radioactive elements in low concentrations in many materials. There is also nuclear radiation from space and from medical examinations, such as X-rays. This **background radiation** (Section 3.10) gives all living things a dose of nuclear radiation. Fortunately, the level of background radiation is normally low and this is not a health risk for most people. However, people who work with radioactive

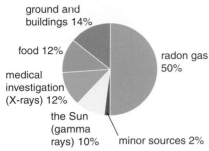

ground and
buildings 14%

food 12%

medical
investigation
(X-rays) 12%

the Sun
(gamma
rays) 10%

radon gas
50%

minor sources 2%

Figure 8.7 The main sources of background radiation in the UK

materials, such as radiographers and radiotherapists, must take special precautions to reduce their exposure to nuclear radiations (see Section 3.4).

Figure 8.7 shows the main sources of background radiation for people living in the UK.

- Various rocks in the Earth, particularly granite, contain small percentages of radioactive uranium. As the uranium decays it emits radioactive radon gas, which can accumulate to dangerous levels inside buildings.
- Rocks and soils, as well as building materials, contain small amounts of radioactive elements that give out radiation as they decay.
- Our food contains traces of radioactive materials.
- The Sun and other stars in the Universe emit gamma radiation, some of which reaches the Earth.
- X-rays used for diagnosis by doctors and dentists are ionising radiations.

 8.4

What happens during radioactive decay?

Radioactive materials emit ionising radiation all the time. During **radioactive decay**, the unstable nuclei of radioactive atoms break up. The break-up is random. When the nuclei break up, they emit **alpha particles**, **beta particles** and **gamma rays**. But what exactly happens during these radioactive decay processes?

Alpha decay

Unstable isotopes with atomic numbers above 83 often decay (break up) by losing an alpha particle. This is called alpha decay. Isotopes that break up by alpha decay include radium-226, uranium-238 and plutonium-238. These isotopes tend to decay because their nuclei are just too heavy – they contain lots of protons and neutrons. Their nuclei become more stable by losing mass in the form of an alpha particle.

For example, when an atom of $^{226}_{88}Ra$ loses an alpha particle, it loses two protons and two neutrons from its nucleus. The atom left behind has a mass number of 222 (four less than $^{226}_{88}Ra$) and an atomic number of 86 (two less than $^{226}_{88}Ra$).

All atoms of atomic number 86 are those of radon, Rn. So we can summarise the alpha decay of radium-226 in a nuclear equation as:

$$^{226}_{88}Ra \rightarrow\ ^{222}_{86}Rn + ^{4}_{2}He$$

Radioactive decay is the random emission of radiation from the unstable nuclei of radioactive atoms as alpha particles, beta particles and gamma rays.

Alpha particles are helium nuclei, $^{4}_{2}He^{2+}$.

Beta particles are electrons with negligible (almost zero) mass and a charge of -1, so they are written as $^{0}_{-1}e$.

Gamma rays are very penetrating electromagnetic rays.

Beta decay

Radioactive isotopes with atomic numbers below 83 tend to undergo beta decay by losing an electron ($_{-1}^{0}e$). During beta decay, a neutron in the nucleus splits up into a proton and an electron. The proton stays in the nucleus, but the electron is ejected as a beta particle. Thus, the mass number of the remaining nucleus stays the same, but its atomic number increases by one (Table 8.3).

For example, when carbon-14 ($_{6}^{14}C$) loses a beta particle ($_{-1}^{0}e$), the product nucleus has an atomic number one more than $_{6}^{14}C$. This is $_{7}^{14}N$. The nuclear equation for the process is

$$_{6}^{14}C \rightarrow {}_{7}^{14}N + {}_{-1}^{0}e$$

The nuclei left behind after radioactive decay are called decay products.

	Alpha decay	Beta decay
Isotopes involved	Atomic number > 83	Atomic number < 83
Particle lost	$_{2}^{4}He^{2+}$	$_{-1}^{0}e$
Change in mass number	-4	0
Change in atomic number	-2	$+1$

Table 8.3 Comparing alpha decay and beta decay. In both cases, the atomic number changes so one element is converted to another element.

Remember that:
- Nuclear equations only show changes in the nuclei of radioactive elements. They do not involve electrons in the shells of the atom.
- The electrons ejected in beta decay come from the nucleus and not, as you might expect, from the shells of the decaying atoms.
- The total mass and total charge of the decay products are the same as those of the initial nucleus.

5 Uranium 238 ($_{92}^{238}U$) decays by losing an alpha particle to form thorium (Th).
  a) What is the mass number of the thorium produced?
  b) What is the atomic number of the thorium?
  c) Write a nuclear equation for the decay process.

6 Write nuclear equations for the beta decay of:

  a) $_{19}^{43}K$ to calcium;

  b) $_{11}^{24}Na$ to magnesium.

7 Explain the following terms:
  a) radioactivity;
  b) nuclear reaction;
  c) alpha decay.

 8.5 # Nuclear fission and atomic energy

Chemical reactions and nuclear reactions

Chemical reactions involve changes in the electrons in the outer parts of atoms. During chemical reactions, electrons are either:
- transferred from one atom to another; or
- shared between two atoms.

Nuclear reactions, on the other hand, involve changes to nuclei in the centre of atoms. During nuclear reactions, one element is converted to another element by:
- radioactive decay;
- nuclear fission; or
- nuclear fusion.

Activity – From Dalton to the atom smashers

Figure 8.8 John Dalton was born in Cumbria in 1766. For most of his life, he was a teacher in Manchester. John Dalton put forward his atomic theory in 1807.

Dalton's ideas about atoms are still helpful to scientists. But modern knowledge about elements and atomic structure has shown that some of his ideas were incorrect. Dalton said that:

- all matter is made up of tiny particles, called atoms;
- atoms cannot be made;
- atoms cannot be broken apart;
- all the atoms of one element are exactly alike;
- atoms of one element are different from those of all other elements.

The first scientists to convert one element into another were Rutherford and his colleagues in the 1920s. They turned sodium into magnesium and aluminium into silicon. In 1940, chemists in the USA managed to make (synthesise) new elements from uranium, the heaviest natural element. They did this by bombarding heavy elements like uranium with neutrons. For example, neptunium-239 and plutonium-239 were obtained by bombarding uranium-238 with neutrons.

1. We now know that matter is composed of smaller particles than atoms. What are these smaller particles called?
2. Atoms of new elements were first made by chemists in the 1940s.
   a) Name two elements synthesised by chemists.
   b) Where do these synthesised elements lie in the Periodic Table?
   c) Why do you think that neutrons were better 'bullets' than protons and alpha particles for synthesising new elements?
3. a) What type of element breaks apart naturally?
   b) What happens when elements break apart?
4. a) What name is given to atoms of the same element which are not exactly alike?
   b) How do these atoms differ?
5. How do atoms of one particular element always differ in atomic structure from those of all other elements?
6. In 1938, German scientists discovered that bombarding uranium-235 with neutrons could produce enormous amounts of energy. This process split uranium atoms in two and was called atomic fission.
   What were the consequences of the discovery of atomic fission, or 'splitting the atom'?

Nuclear fission

Nuclear fission is the splitting of an atomic nucleus, resulting in the release of large amounts of energy.

In 1938, the German scientist Otto Hahn discovered that enormous amounts of energy could be obtained from **nuclear fission**. His discovery happened almost by chance. Hahn and his colleagues were trying to make a new element by bombarding uranium with neutrons. Instead of producing just one new element with a slightly different atomic number, the neutrons caused the uranium nuclei to break up violently, forming two smaller nuclei. More neutrons were also released plus vast quantities of energy (Figure 8.10).

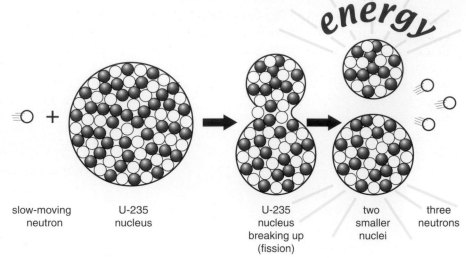

Figure 8.10 Fission of a nucleus of uranium-235

Figure 8.9 Lise Meitner was born in Austria and worked with Otto Hahn in Germany for several years. Lise was Jewish and had to flee from Germany in 1938. It was Hahn who first split the atom, but Lise Meitner who explained the process and gave it the name nuclear fission.

A **chain reaction** occurs when the neutrons released by splitting one nucleus go on to split more nuclei. The reaction needs no further input.

Nuclear fission differs from radioactive decay in two important ways.
- Nuclear fission does not happen spontaneously like radioactive decay. It only happens when unstable nuclei like uranium-235 absorb neutrons.
- Nuclear fission involves the break-up of one large nucleus into two fragments of roughly the same size. During radioactive decay, the products are one large fragment and one very small fragment (either an alpha particle or a beta particle).

Natural uranium contains two isotopes, $^{235}_{92}U$ and $^{238}_{92}U$. Only 0.7% is uranium-235. Experiments show that only uranium-235 takes part in nuclear fission. This has led scientists to realise that if natural uranium is enriched with more uranium-235, the neutrons released during fission can go on to split more uranium nuclei and start a **chain reaction**.

In an atomic bomb, the fission of enriched U-235 atoms releases three neutrons. These three neutrons collide with three more U-235 atoms, releasing nine neutrons; these nine release 27, then 81, and so on. Each time, more and more energy is produced in an uncontrolled reaction resulting in vast amounts of energy.

In a nuclear reactor, a lower concentration of U-235 is used to produce a controlled chain reaction. In this case, only one of the three neutrons released at each fission goes on to cause another fission and a steady chain reaction occurs.

Activity – How do nuclear reactors work?

Figure 8.11 shows a simplified diagram of a gas-cooled nuclear reactor. At the centre of the reactor, rods of 'enriched' uranium containing 3% of uranium-235 are stacked inside a large block of graphite. Neutrons released by the fission of uranium-235 are slowed down by collision with carbon atoms in the graphite. A slow-moving neutron splits a nucleus more easily.

The energy released by nuclear fission in the fuel

rods heats up the reactor. The temperature of the reactor is controlled by moveable rods of boron that absorb neutrons. A controlled chain reaction can be obtained by carefully adjusting these neutron-absorbing rods. Heat is produced steadily and taken away by carbon dioxide circulating through the reactor. The heat is used to turn water into steam, which drives a turbine to generate electricity.

Reactors have also been developed that use plutonium-239 as the fuel in place of uranium-235. Plutonium-239 can use fast neutrons, unlike uranium-235, which undergoes fission more readily with slow neutrons. This means that a plutonium reactor does not need a graphite block to slow down neutrons. These reactors are called fast reactors. The first atomic power station to use a fast reactor for generating electricity was built at Dounreay in Scotland.

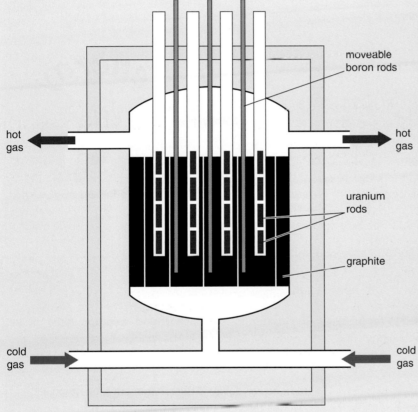

moveable boron rods

hot gas

hot gas

uranium rods

graphite

cold gas

cold gas

Figure 0.11 A simplified diagram of a gas-cooled nuclear reactor

❶ Why are the uranium rods sunk in graphite?

❷ How do the boron rods control the temperature of the reactor?

❸ What should a technician do if the reactor core suddenly gets too hot?

❹ Why is the reactor inside thick concrete?

❺ How is the energy from nuclear fission converted into electricity?

❻ Which two fissionable isotopes are used in nuclear reactors?

❼ Why is the symbol for a neutron $_0^1n$?

❽ What numbers should replace the letters **A–E** in the following equation for the possible fission of uranium-235?

$$_A^1n + _{92}^BU \rightarrow _{56}^CBa + _D^{88}Kr + E\,_0^1n$$

❾ Draw a labelled diagram to show:
  a) how a controlled, steady chain reaction can occur in a nuclear reactor;
  b) how an uncontrolled explosive chain reaction can occur in an atomic bomb.

8.6 Nuclear fusion

Nuclear fusion is the joining together of two atomic nuclei, resulting in the release of large amounts of energy.

The energy that is released by our Sun and other stars comes from **nuclear fusion**. Fusion means 'joining together'. During nuclear fusion, two nuclei are joined together to form just one larger nucleus and energy is released.

Temperatures get to about 15 000 000 K (fifteen million kelvin) at the centre of the Sun. At these temperatures, the nuclei of atoms are stripped of their electrons. The nuclei collide at high speed with each other and with individual protons and neutrons. Some of the collisions result in fusion. The particles stick together to form larger nuclei. One of the major fusion processes in stars involves hydrogen nuclei fusing to form helium (Figure 8.12).

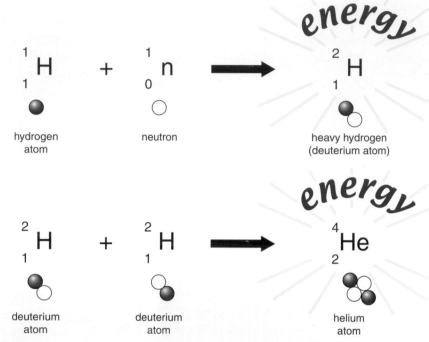

Figure 8.12 The fusion processes which produce helium from hydrogen inside a star

Summary

✓ Experiments by Rutherford and his colleagues led to the idea that atoms have a tiny positive nucleus containing protons and neutrons surrounded by a much larger region of empty space in which there are electrons.

✓ This idea became known as the '**nuclear model**' of atomic structure, which rapidly replaced the '**plum pudding model**' suggested by Thomson.

✓ All the atoms of a particular element have the same number of protons. The number of protons in an atom is known as the **atomic number**.

✓ The total number of protons + neutrons in an atom is known as the **mass number**.

✓ **Isotopes** are atoms of an element with the same atomic number, but different mass numbers.

✓ The main sources of **background radiation** in the UK are rocks in the Earth, bricks, building materials, our food, the Sun and medical uses.

✓ **Radioactive decay** is the random emission of radiation from the unstable nuclei of radioactive atoms as alpha particles, beta particles and gamma rays.

Alpha particles are helium nuclei, $^4_2He^{2+}$.
Beta particles are electrons.
Gamma rays are very penetrating electromagnetic rays.

✓ During alpha decay, the mass number of a nucleus decreases by four and its atomic number decreases by two.

✓ During beta decay, the mass number of a nucleus remains unchanged, but the atomic number increases by one.

✓ During **nuclear fission**, a nucleus first absorbs a neutron and then splits into two smaller nuclei, releasing two or three neutrons and large amounts of energy. The neutrons released in the process can start a **chain reaction**.

✓ There are two fissionable nuclei in common use in nuclear reactors – uranium-235 and plutonium-239.

✓ During **nuclear fusion**, two nuclei join together to form one larger nucleus, releasing vast amounts of energy.

EXAMQUESTIONS

1 What do 24, 12, Mg and 2+ mean in the symbol $^{24}_{12}Mg^{2+}$? *(5 marks)*

2 Match the processes labelled **A**, **B**, **C** and **D** to the statements numbered **1**, **2**, **3** and **4** below:

A alpha decay	**1** nuclei join together
B beta decay	**2** nucleus absorbs a neutron
C nuclear fission	**3** nucleus loses an electron
D nuclear fusion	**4** nucleus loses two protons

(4 marks)

3 Some patients who suffer from cancer are given an injection of boron, which is absorbed by cancer cells. The cancerous tissue is then irradiated with neutrons. After this, the reaction which occurs is:

$$^{11}_{5}B \rightarrow {}^{7}_{x}Li + {}^{y}_{z}He$$

a) Copy the equation and write numbers in place of *x*, *y* and *z*. *(3 marks)*
b) What is the special name for this type of reaction? *(1 mark)*
c) Why do the lithium and helium nuclei repel each other? *(1 mark)*
d) Why can this treatment kill cancer cells? *(1 mark)*

4 Copy and complete the following sentences.

In a nuclear reactor, the fuel rods are made of _____ 'enriched' with about 3% of uranium-235. For _____ to occur, the uranium-235 atoms must first absorb a _____. The process releases energy in a controlled _____ reaction and can be used to generate _____. Some reactors use _____ as the fissionable material in place of uranium-235. *(6 marks)*

5 a) What is nuclear fission? Say what happens and what is produced. *(5 marks)*
b) State one way in which nuclear fission is similar to radioactive decay. *(1 mark)*
c) State two ways in which nuclear fission is different from radioactive decay. *(2 marks)*
d) What numbers or symbols replace the letters **A–E** in the following nuclear equation?

$$^{A}_{92}B \rightarrow {}^{234}_{C}Th + {}^{D}_{2}E$$ *(5 marks)*

6 Many people are concerned about our use of nuclear energy. Their worries can be summed up in three words 'cost', 'disposal' and 'security'.
a) Suggest two major costs involved in providing electricity from nuclear energy. *(2 marks)*
b) Explain the concerns that people have about 'disposal'. *(2 marks)*
c) What are people's concerns about security? *(1 mark)*
d) Suggest two benefits or advantages of using nuclear energy to generate electricity. *(2 marks)*

7 In Geiger and Marsden's experiment, about one in every 10 000 alpha particles appeared to bounce back from the gold foil.

Explain how you think the number of alpha particles bouncing back would change if:
a) thicker gold foil was used; *(2 marks)*
b) aluminium foil of the same thickness was used. *(3 marks)*

Chapter 9
When does a force cause rotation?

Figure 9.1 Staying balanced can be a matter of life or death. The tightrope walker uses a pole to adjust his centre of mass and remain stable.

9.1 Why do some forces have a turning effect?

Look closely at Figure 9.2. Notice that all three pictures show forces that can make a body turn.

Figure 9.2 All these pictures show a force that can make a body turn.

> An **axis of rotation** is an imaginary line about which a body can rotate.

A body that can turn has an **axis of rotation**. A single point at the centre of the axis of rotation is often called the pivot. A force that acts on a body but does not go though the axis of rotation will have a turning effect.

Have you ever tried undoing a tight nut with just your fingers? It's not easy. The job is much easier if you use a spanner. The same force then has a much larger turning effect. The longer the spanner, the larger the turning effect because the force will be further from the axis of rotation (or pivot).

The size of the turning effect about the axis of rotation (or pivot) is called the **moment** of the force. The size of a moment can be calculated using the equation:

moment = force × perpendicular distance from the line of action of the force to the axis of rotation

The line of action of a force is a line drawn in the same direction as the force.

Figure 9.3 Using the right tool makes it easy to undo the wheel nuts. A small force applied at the end of the long wheel wrench has a large turning effect.

The units of a moment are newton metres (N m), because the units of a force are newtons (N) and the units of distance are metres (m).

Figure 9.4 shows how the perpendicular distance between the line of action of the force exerted by a cyclist on the pedal of a bicycle and the axis of rotation depends on the position of the pedal.

> The **moment** of a force is the turning effect of the force.

Perpendicular means 'at right angles'. So the distance must be measured along a line that goes from the axis of rotation and hits the line of action of the force at right angles.

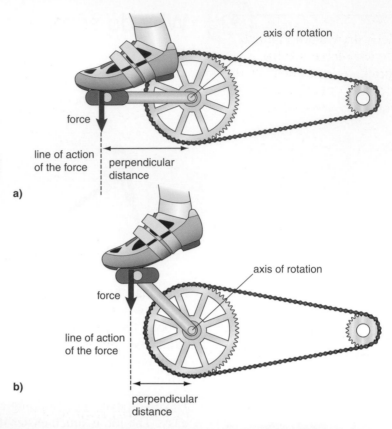

axis of rotation

force

line of action
of the force

perpendicular
distance

a)

axis of rotation

force

line of action
of the force

b)

perpendicular
distance

Figure 9.4 The size of the moment exerted depends on the perpendicular distance from the axis of rotation. The turning effect of the force is bigger in a) even though the force is the same.

The person in Figure 9.5 is pushing the door as hard as they can, but the door is hardly moving. This is because the person is pushing near the hinge and the hinge is on the axis of rotation. The distance between the force and the axis of rotation is close to zero, so the moment is very small. For this reason, door handles are always put as far away from door hinges as possible to give the biggest turning effect (moment).

Figure 9.5 Where is the best place to push open a door – near the hinge or far away from it?

❶ Curtis wants to remove a tree stump from his garden. He tries to lever the stump out of the ground using a strong but short steel bar. Explain why the tree stump would come out more easily if Curtis were to use a longer steel bar.

Figure 9.6 A length of strong steel makes a good lever.

❷ Each drawing in Figure 9.7 shows a force that has a turning effect. Calculate the moment of each force about the axis of rotation (labelled P).

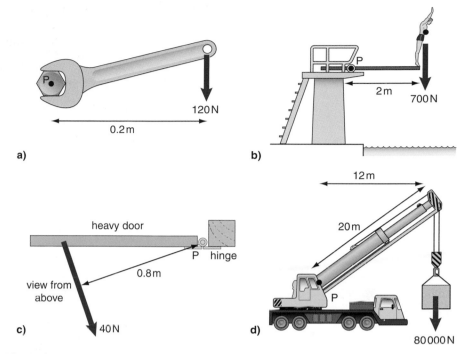

a)

b)

c)

d)

Figure 9.7

Balancing moments

Figure 9.8 shows Josh and Simran on a playground see-saw.

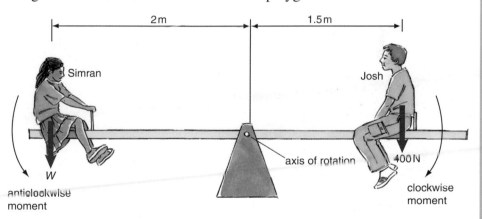

Figure 9.8 The see-saw is balanced horizontally.

If Josh were sitting on the see-saw on his own, his weight would make the see-saw rotate clockwise. Josh is causing a clockwise moment. If Simran were sitting on the see-saw on her own, her weight would make the see-saw rotate anticlockwise. Simran is causing an anticlockwise moment. But the see-saw is not turning. We say 'it is balanced' or it is 'in equilibrium'. This means that the size of the clockwise moment caused by Josh must be exactly the same as the size of the anticlockwise moment caused by Simran. This is called the **principle of moments**.

The **principle of moments** says that if a body is not turning, the total clockwise moment must be exactly balanced by the total anticlockwise moment about any axis of rotation.

We can use this idea to calculate Simran's weight.

clockwise moment caused by Josh $= 400 \times 1.5 = 600\,\text{N m}$
clockwise moment caused by Josh = anticlockwise moment caused by Simran
$$600 = W \times 2$$
Simran's weight $(W) = 300\,\text{N}$

Sometimes we want a force to have a turning effect, like using a force to turn on a tap or unscrew a nut. At other times, we need the turning forces to be balanced. For example, if the turning forces on a crane were not balanced the crane might topple over. Using the principle of moments, we can calculate the size of a force, or the distance the force must act from an axis of rotation, to keep a body balanced.

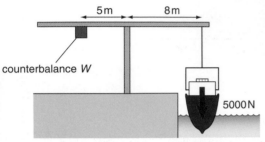

5 m   8 m

counterbalance *W*

5000 N

Figure 9.9

Example
The crane in Figure 9.9 is being used to lift a container off a ship. Calculate the weight of the counterbalance needed to stop the crane from toppling over.

clockwise moment produced by the container $= 5000 \times 8 = 40\,000\,\text{N m}$

anticlockwise moment caused by the counterbalance $= W \times 5$

total clockwise moment = total anticlockwise moment
$$40\,000 = W \times 5$$
$$W = \frac{40\,000}{5} = 8000\,\text{N}$$

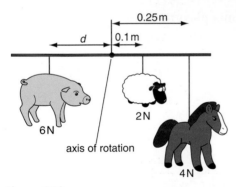

0.25 m
0.1 m
d

6 N
2 N
4 N
axis of rotation

Figure 9.10

Example
Figure 9.10 shows a mobile which hangs from a ceiling. The soft toys are arranged so that the mobile balances horizontally. Calculate the distance *d* between the toy pig and the axis of rotation.

In this example there are two forces causing a clockwise moment: the weight of the toy sheep and the weight of the toy horse. The only force causing an anticlockwise moment is the weight of the toy pig.

total clockwise moment = moment caused by the sheep + moment caused by the horse

$$= 2 \times 0.1 + 4 \times 0.25$$
$$= 0.2 + 1.0 = 1.2\,\text{N m}$$

total anticlockwise moment = moment caused by the pig
$$= 6 \times d$$

total clockwise moment = total anticlockwise moment
$$1.2 = 6 \times d$$
$$d = \frac{1.2}{6} = 0.2\,\text{m}$$

3 To keep a racing yacht balanced the crew lean over the side of the boat. Look at Figure 9.11 and explain why leaning out over the side stops the boat from capsizing.

Figure 9.11 Racing a yacht takes a lot of skill to keep the boat stable.

4 Figure 9.12 shows how Ted used a simple 'see-saw' to weigh his holiday luggage. Calculate the weight of Ted's luggage.

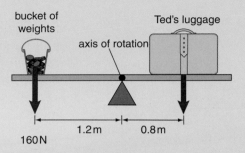

Figure 9.12

5 Figure 9.13 shows three children on a see-saw. Show, using calculations, that the see-saw is balanced.

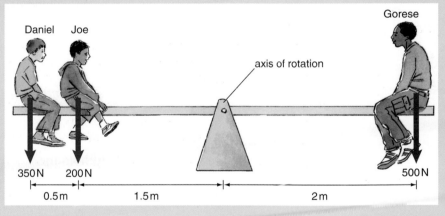

Figure 9.13

Moments and the human body

Most of the joints in the human body have an axis of rotation passing through them. This is why you can rotate, twist and lift different parts of your body. For example, the axis of rotation passing through your elbow lets you rotate your lower arm up towards your shoulder and down towards the ground.

If you hold your lower arm horizontal your biceps muscle will soon ache. This is because the moment produced by the weight of your lower arm must be balanced by a moment in the opposite direction from your biceps muscle. Figure 9.14 shows the forces acting on your lower arm when you hold it horizontally. The distances and forces are average values.

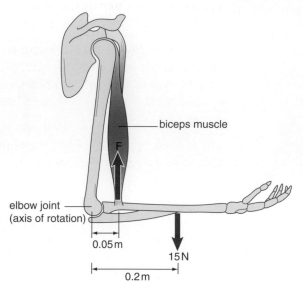

Figure 9.14 When you move your arm you use turning forces.

6 Figure 9.15 shows two acrobats holding a perfectly balanced position. Explain how the acrobats manage to stay balanced.

Figure 9.15

The force in the biceps muscle can be calculated using the principle of moments.

moment produced by the weight of the lower arm = 15 × 0.2 = 3 N m

opposing moment produced by the biceps muscle = F × 0.05

total clockwise moment = total anticlockwise moment

3 = F × 0.05

F = force in the biceps muscle = 60 N

So, the force exerted by the muscle to hold the lower arm horizontal is four times larger than the weight of the lower arm itself. This is because the muscle is attached so close to the axis of rotation.

9.2

Centre of mass

It's easy to balance a ruler on the tip of your finger, but it only works if the centre of the ruler rests on your finger tip.

This balance point on the ruler is called its **centre of mass**. Although every part of the ruler has mass, the centre of mass is the point where we can think of the whole mass of the ruler as being concentrated. The centre of mass is also the point through which the weight of the ruler acts – its centre of gravity. So if your finger tip is at the centre of mass, the weight of the ruler will produce no resultant clockwise or anticlockwise moment. The ruler is therefore balanced.

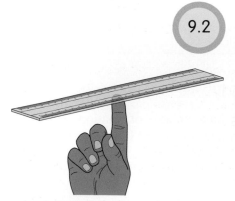

Figure 9.16 Find the right place for your finger and the ruler will balance.

The **centre of mass** of a body is the point at which we can think of its mass as being concentrated.

A tightrope walker will stay balanced if he keeps his centre of mass directly above the rope (see Figure 9.1). The long pole helps the tightrope walker to keep his balance. If he starts to topple to one side of the rope he just moves the pole to the other side. This brings the centre of mass of the walker and the pole back over the rope.

The ruler in Figure 9.16 is symmetrical. The centre of mass of the ruler is at the centre of the ruler, along an axis of symmetry. An axis of symmetry is a line about which an object or shape is symmetrical.

Figure 9.17 shows three common symmetrical shapes. The dotted lines are axes of symmetry. For all symmetrical bodies, the centre of mass (M) is on an axis of symmetry.

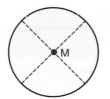 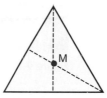 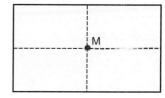

Figure 9.17 What is the same for each of these centres of mass?

When a body is suspended, it comes to rest with its centre of mass directly below the point of suspension.

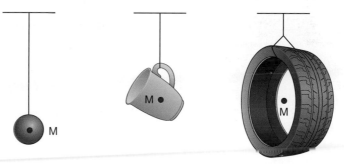

Figure 9.18 For stable objects, the centre of mass is always below the point of suspension.

The centre of mass of a body is not always inside the body itself. For example, the centre of mass of the tyre in Figure 9.18 is in the air at the centre of its circular shape. But its centre of mass is still below the point of suspension and the tyre is balanced.

Physics is important in the sport of pole-vaulting. First there is energy transformation. The kinetic energy gained by athletes in the run up is converted to gravitational potential energy as they lift themselves up from the ground. Then, as they go over the bar, pole vaulters arch their back. This action moves the athlete's centre of mass from inside to outside their body. The energy they use to lift themselves off the ground raises their centre of mass, which goes under the bar. But their body

Figure 9.19 Sergey Bubka set the men's world pole-vault record of 6.14 metres in 1994.

goes over the bar. So, for the same energy transformation, their body goes higher and they achieve a higher pole vault.

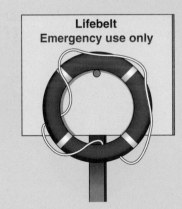

Figure 9.20

❼ The lifebelt shown in Figure 9.20 is hanging from a metal bar.
  a) Draw a lifebelt and mark on your picture the centre of mass of the lifebelt.
  b) Explain why you think the centre of mass is at the point you have marked.

❽ Figure 9.21 shows an athlete using the 'Fosbury-flop' technique. Explain how the 'Fosbury-flop' can allow athletes to jump higher in the high jump event.

Figure 9.21

Finding the centre of mass of a sheet of material

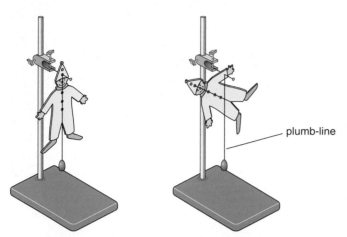

The centre of mass of an irregularly shaped piece of card can be found using a plumb-line.

- Make a small hole in the card.
- Suspend the card from a long pin. Make sure the card can swing freely.
- Suspend a plumb-line from the same pin.
- When the card and plumb-line stop swinging, mark the position of the plumb-line on the card.
- Now suspend the card and plumb-line from a different point.
- Draw a second vertical line on the card.
- Where the two lines cross is the centre of mass of the card.

Figure 9.22 The centre of mass is always directly below the point of suspension. Since the centre of mass is somewhere on each line and there is only one centre of mass, it must be where the two lines cross over.

If the position of the centre of mass is found accurately, the card will balance at this point on the tip of a finger.

9 Figure 9.23 shows an irregular piece of card suspended from two points K and L. Copy one of the diagrams.
a) Mark with an 'X' the centre of mass of the card.
b) Suppose both the card and a plumb-line are now suspended at point M. Draw on your diagram a line to show the position of the plumb-line.

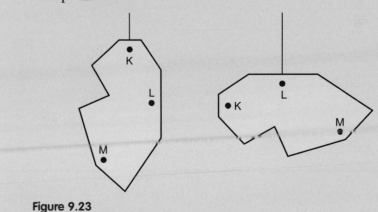

Figure 9.23

9.3 Moments and the centre of mass

The weight of a body always acts vertically downwards through its centre of mass. This means that a body suspended from a point other than its centre of mass will always try to turn so that its centre of mass comes directly below its suspension point. However, a body can be balanced by an additional force. Imagine a window cleaner walking along carrying a ladder on his shoulder (Figure 9.24). A bucket of water

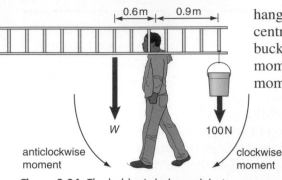

0.6 m   0.9 m

W   100 N

anticlockwise moment   clockwise moment

Figure 9.24 The ladder is balanced, but where is the axis of rotation?

hangs from one end of the ladder. The weight of the ladder (acting at its centre of mass) causes an anticlockwise moment. But the ladder and bucket of water are balanced so there must be an equal clockwise moment. The weight of the bucket of water creates this clockwise moment.

clockwise moment due to the bucket of water = $100 \times 0.9 = 90 \, N \, m$

anticlockwise moment due to the ladder = $W \times 0.6$

total clockwise moment = total anticlockwise moment
$$90 = W \times 0.6$$
$$W = 150 \, N$$

⑩ Jerry the builder, needs to weigh a plank of wood. The maximum weight that Jerry's spring balance can measure is 50 N, which is less than the weight of the plank. Figure 9.25 shows how Jerry overcame the problem. Calculate the weight of the plank.

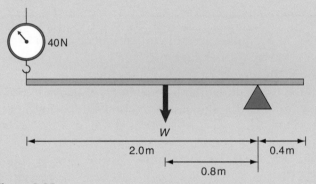

40 N

W

2.0 m

0.8 m

0.4 m

Figure 9.25

⑪ Figure 9.26 shows a simple balancing toy. Explain why, when the toy is given a small push,

it will rock backwards and forwards without falling off the bar.

Figure 9.26

⑫ Use the principle of moments to find the weight of the ruler in Figure 9.27.

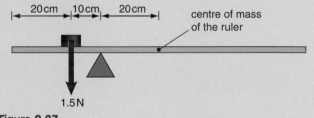

20 cm   10 cm   20 cm   centre of mass of the ruler

1.5 N

Figure 9.27

Activity – Measuring weight without a balance

Figure 9.28 shows an irregularly shaped piece of wood, a ruler, a 1 N weight and a small triangular block of wood.

❶ Describe how you could use the apparatus in Figure 9.28 to measure the weight of the irregularly shaped piece of wood. Make use of the following hints:
  • The centre of mass of the wood needs to be

found. You can use the triangular block to do this.
  • You can use the 1 N weight to balance the wood on the triangle.
  • Once balanced, careful measurements and the principle of moments will enable you to calculate the weight of the wood.

❷ If you have the apparatus, try out your method and see if it works. Use a balance to compare the weight you calculate with the weight given by a balance.

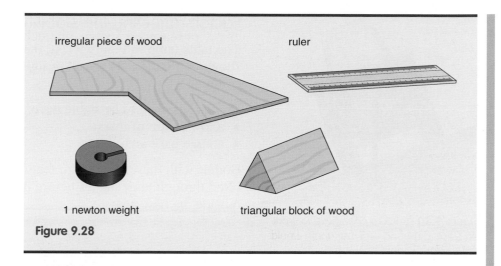

irregular piece of wood

ruler

1 newton weight

triangular block of wood

Figure 9.28

9.4 Stability

Many household objects are designed to be stable. This means that if they are tilted slightly and then released they won't fall over. They just fall back to their original position. If objects are tilted too much, they will become unstable and fall over. So, how much can a body be tilted and remain stable?

Figure 9.29 shows two different table lamps tilted on one edge. A vertical line from the centre of mass M shows the line of action of each lamp's weight, *W*. In Figure 9.29a, the line of action of the weight falls inside the base of the lamp. The moment (turning effect) caused by the lamp's weight about the pivot will make the lamp fall back to its original position. This lamp is stable. In Figure 9.29b, the line of action of the weight falls outside the base of the lamp. This time the moment caused by the lamp's weight will make the lamp topple over. This lamp is unstable.

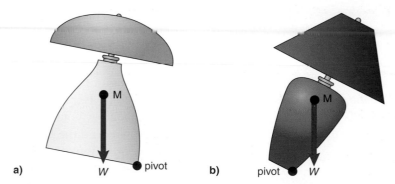

a)   *W*   pivot   b)   pivot   *W*

Figure 9.29 How does the design of a table lamp affect its stability?

> If the line of action of the weight of a body falls outside its base, the body will start to topple over.

Tractors are often used on steep slopes, so they need to be designed to be stable. Figure 9.30 shows that even on very steep sloping ground, the line of action of the tractor's weight falls inside its wheel base, so the tractor is stable.

Factors affecting the stability of a body

The table lamp in Figure 9.29a, the tractor in Figure 9.30 and the bodies shown in Figure 9.31 are all designed to be stable. What do they have in common?

Bodies designed to be stable have:
- a low centre of mass;
- a large base area.

Bodies with these two design features tend to be stable. They need to be tilted through large angles before the line of action of their weight falls outside the base area.

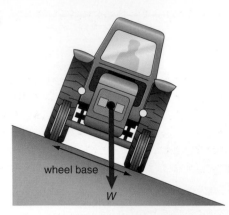

Figure 9.32

Figure 9.33

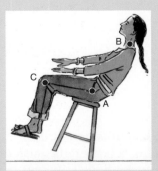

Figure 9.34

Figure 9.30 Tractors often have to work on sloping ground. At what angle would the tractor become unstable?

Figure 9.31 The only thing these bodies have in common is stability.

⑬ Look at the three glasses in Figure 9.32. Which glass will be the hardest to knock over? Explain the reason for your answer.

⑭ Why do you think passengers are not allowed to remain standing on the top deck of a double decker bus?

⑮ The two sumo wrestlers in Figure 9.33 are trying to push each other over. How do they use the idea of stability to their advantage?

⑯ Figure 9.34 shows a student leaning back on her stool. The stool and student are in danger of toppling over.
  a) Which one of the dots, A, B or C, marks the centre of mass of the stool and student? Explain the reason for your answer.
  b) How could the stool have been designed to make it more stable?

Activity – Investigating the stability of toy vehicles

Imran used the apparatus in Figure 9.35 to investigate the stability of three different toy vehicles.

Imran increased the tilt of the ramp until the toy started to topple over. He then measured the angle of the ramp with the horizontal. Imran's results are given in Table 9.1.

Toy	Angle of the ramp
A	15°
B	40°
C	28°

Table 9.1 The results of Imran's investigation

1. What type of variable is the toy vehicle?
2. What type of variable is the angle of the ramp?
3. Which toy, A, B or C, is the:
   a) racing car;
   b) double decker bus;
   c) family car?
   Explain the reason for each of your answers.
4. How could Imran improve the accuracy of his results?
5. Imran would like to find out how changing the weight of a vehicle affects its stability. Describe how he could carry out this new investigation. You can assume that Imran is able to use other simple laboratory equipment.

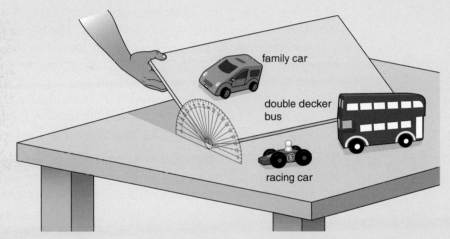

Figure 9.35 The bigger the angle that the ramp can be tilted before the object topples, the more stable the object is.

9.5 Moving in a circle

In Section 5.1 you learned that the velocity of a body is given in terms of both its speed and its direction. A body going round in a circle is continually changing direction. This means that its velocity is continually changing, even if its speed stays the same. You also learned that acceleration is equal to the rate of change of velocity. This means that a body moving in a circle must be accelerating, and for acceleration to happen, an unbalanced force is needed (see Section 5.3).

In Figure 9.36 a ball tied to a string is being whirled around in a horizontal circle.

Figure 9.36 The force in the string keeps the ball going round in a circle.

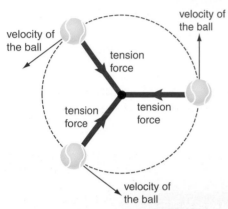

Figure 9.37 The force and velocity are always at 90°.

Although the speed of the ball stays the same, its direction is constantly changing. This means that its velocity is changing and the ball is accelerating. Just because the ball is accelerating does not mean it is getting faster. The acceleration changes the direction in which the ball is moving, not its speed.

The force causing the acceleration is the inward pull on the ball through the string. This is called the tension force. The acceleration of the ball and the force on the ball are towards the centre of the circle. But remember, although the ball is accelerating, this does not mean it is getting faster. The force on the ball and the velocity of the ball are always at 90° to each other, no matter where the ball is in the circle (Figure 9.37). If the string breaks and the tension force disappears, the ball will fly off in a straight line at a tangent to the circle.

This idea is used in the sport of hammer throwing. Hammer throwers make the hammer move in a circle by using the pull of their arms. At the right moment, the thrower lets go and the hammer flies off into the air in a straight line.

Figure 9.38 A hammer thrower in action

A **centripetal force** is a force that makes an object move in a circle.

The force that makes a body move in a circle is called the **centripetal force**. This force always acts inwards, towards the centre of the circle. Although a centripetal force can be provided in different ways, the size of the centripetal force always depends upon the same three factors.

The centripetal force needed to keep a body moving in a circle is greater if:
- the mass of the body is greater;
- the speed of the body is greater;
- the radius of the circle is smaller.

The speed of the body has the greatest effect on the size of the centripetal force. Doubling the speed of a body increases the centripetal force four times.

Centripetal force in action

The hammer thrower, motorcyclist, and fairground ride shown in Figures 9.38 to 9.40 all have one thing in common. Their motions involve centripetal forces.

Figure 9.39 Friction between the tyres and the ground provides the centripetal force needed to take the corner at high speed.

The centripetal force needed to make a motorbike change direction is provided by the friction between the road and the motorbike's tyres. The faster the motorbike and the tighter the bend, the larger the centripetal force. Ice, oil or loose gravel on the road will reduce the friction. On a poor or slippery road surface motorcyclists must reduce their speed and corner less severely if they want to stay in control and not skid off the road.

Tension, gravity and electrostatic attraction forces can also provide a centripetal force. In all these cases, it is the resultant force that must act towards the centre of the circle, and be large enough to hold the body moving in a circle.

Figure 9.40 What provides the centripetal force in this fairground ride?

⑰ Explain how a body can move at constant speed and at the same time be accelerating.

⑱ a) Explain why the roads that join or leave a motorway are usually built as curves with a wide radius.
   b) What must drivers do if the curve of a bend in the road has a small radius? Explain your answer.

⑲ Explain why a car may skid going round a bend on an icy road.

9.6 Gravitational forces in space

Gravity is a force which tries to pull bodies together. It is a force of attraction. Gravity acts between all bodies, no matter how big or how small. The bigger the masses of the bodies, the bigger the gravitational force between them.

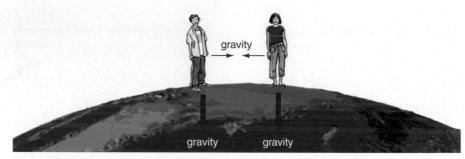

Figure 9.41 We only notice the force of gravity when one of the objects has a very large mass. We feel the pull of the Earth because it has a large mass.

As the distance between bodies increases, the gravitational force between them decreases. The Earth's gravitational force on a rocket gets smaller and smaller as the rocket gets further and further away from the Earth. Doubling the distance between a rocket and the Earth reduces the gravitational force by more than half. In fact the gravitational force goes down to only a quarter in this case.

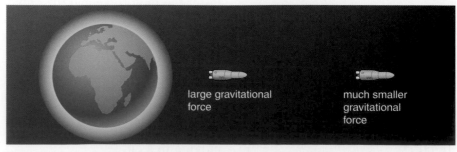

Figure 9.42 The gravitational force between bodies decreases as distance increases.

The gravitational forces between planets are very weak. However, the gravitational force between a planet and the Sun is much stronger because the Sun has such a huge mass.

Although the orbits of the planets are not completely circular, the gravitational force on the planet always acts towards the Sun. This gravitational force provides the centripetal force on the planet and keeps it in orbit (Figure 9.43a).

The further a planet is from the Sun, the weaker the gravitational force. This means to stay in orbit at a particular distance, the planet must move at a particular speed. Planets far from the Sun must move more slowly, so the planet takes longer to complete one orbit. Similarly, planets near to the Sun must have a high velocity, so their orbital periods are short.

The time for each complete orbit is longer the further out the planet is because:

- the speed is less
- the circumference of the orbit is bigger.

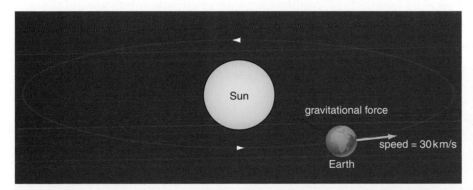 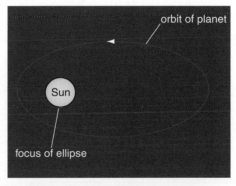

Figure 9.43 a) The gravitational pull of the Sun provides the centripetal force on the planet. b) The orbits of the planets are elliptical.

An **ellipse** is the shape of a squashed circle or oval. The **focus** is a point to one side of the centre of the ellipse.

All the planets move in **elliptical** orbits around the Sun with the Sun at one **focus** of the ellipse (Figure 9.43b). Because the orbits are elliptical, the distance between a planet and the Sun changes during the planet's orbit. As the planet moves closer to the Sun it will speed up, and as the orbit takes it further from the Sun the planet will slow down.

20 Table 9.2 gives some information about five planets.

Planet	Average distance from the Sun in millions of km	Average time to complete one orbit in Earth years
Earth	150	1
Mars	230	2
Jupiter	780	12
Saturn	1400	29
Uranus	2900	84

Table 9.2

a) Draw a graph of average distance from the Sun against average time to complete one orbit for the planets in Table 9.2.
b) What is the connection (pattern) between the average distance from the Sun and the average orbital time?
c) An asteroid is in orbit 500 million km from the Sun. Use your graph to estimate how long it takes the asteroid to complete one orbit.
d) Why is your estimate in part c) much more accurate than it would have been for an asteroid 5000 million km from the Sun?

9.7 Artificial satellites

There are hundreds of satellites moving in circular orbits around the Earth. The centripetal force for these satellites is provided by the gravitational pull of the Earth. To stay in orbit a satellite must have a forward speed at right angles to the direction of the force of gravity. As the gravitational force pulls the satellite towards the Earth, its forward speed makes it move in a circle.

Figure 9.44 One of the hundreds of satellites in orbit around the Earth.

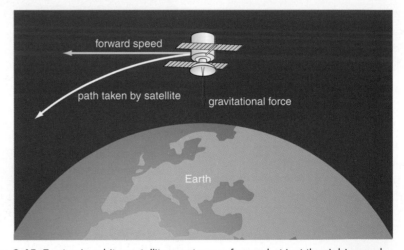

forward speed

path taken by satellite

gravitational force

Earth

Figure 9.45 To stay in orbit a satellite must move forward at just the right speed.

To stay in orbit at a particular distance from the Earth, a satellite must move at the right speed (Figure 9.45). If the forward speed is too low, the gravitational force will make the satellite fall out of its orbit and drop towards Earth. If the forward speed is too high, the gravitational force will be too small to hold the satellite in its orbit and the satellite will shoot off into space.

A satellite in **polar orbit** is in a low, fast orbit that passes near or over the North and South Poles.

Using satellites for monitoring

Satellites that monitor and observe the Earth are usually put into low orbits that pass over the North and South Poles, called polar orbits. As they pass over the Earth, they scan the surface, sending back detailed pictures. Such things as the position of an oil slick, the path of a hurricane or the eruption of a volcano can all be watched and monitored.

As the Earth spins on its axis, the satellite passes over a different part of the Earth's surface on each orbit. If the satellite is carefully programmed, the whole surface of the Earth can be scanned every day – and compared, days or months later.

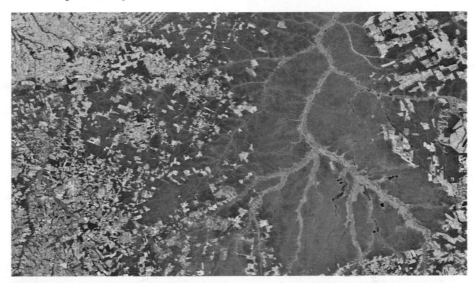

Figure 9.46 A satellite image of part of the Amazon Basin in Brazil showing deforestation

Communication satellites

A satellite in **geostationary orbit** stays in the same position directly above a point on the equator and has an orbital period of 24 hours.

Satellites used for communications are usually put into **geostationary** orbits high above the equator. A geostationary orbit takes the satellite 24 hours to orbit the Earth once. This means that the satellite moves round the Earth at the same rate as the Earth spins. The satellite will always be above the same point on the Earth's surface.

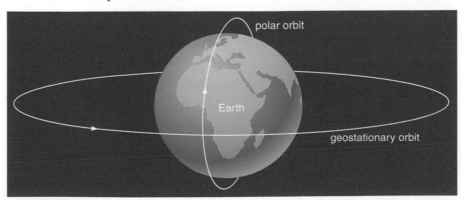

Figure 9.47 Satellites in a geostationary orbit take longer to orbit the Earth than satellites in a polar orbit. This is because they are further from the Earth.

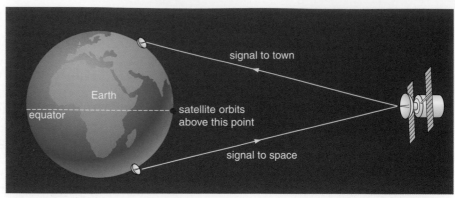

Figure 9.48 Communications satellites must be geostationary so that ground-based receiving dishes can point in fixed directions.

Figure 9.49 Geostationary satellites can be used to transmit telephone signals when local telephone networks have been disrupted, for example following an earthquake.

㉑ Explain how a satellite can appear to be stationary above the Earth.

㉒ Describe the differences between a polar orbit and a geostationary orbit.

㉓ A global positioning system (GPS) uses signals from several satellites to pinpoint your position. What type of satellite does GPS use?

Summary

✓ An **axis of rotation** is a line about which a body can rotate.

✓ The turning effect of a force about an axis of rotation is called the **moment**.

✓ The size of a moment can be calculated using the equation:

moment = force × perpendicular distance from the line of action of the force to the axis of rotation

✓ If a body, balancing at one point, is not turning, the total clockwise moment is equal to the total anticlockwise moment. This is called the **principle of moments**.

✓ The **centre of mass** of a body is the point at which the mass of the body can be considered to be concentrated.

✓ For all symmetrical bodies, the centre of mass is along an axis of symmetry.

✓ The weight of a body always acts vertically downwards through its centre of mass.

✓ A stable body is one which, when tilted slightly and then released, does not fall over.

✓ Bodies designed to be stable have a low centre of mass and a large base area.

✓ A **centripetal force** is a force acting on a body moving in a circle. The centripetal force acts towards the centre of the circle.

✓ Tension, friction, gravity and electrostatic attraction can all provide a centripetal force.

✓ The centripetal force on a body is greater if:
  – the mass of the body is greater;
  – the speed of the body is greater;
  – the radius of the circle in which it moves is smaller.

✓ Gravity is a force of attraction between all bodies.

✓ The bigger the masses of the bodies, the bigger the gravitational force between them.

✓ If the distance between bodies increases the gravitational force between them decreases.

✓ Gravity provides the centripetal force that keeps satellites in circular orbits and planets in **elliptical** orbits with the Sun at one **focus**.

✓ At closer distances an orbiting body feels a stronger gravitational pull, so it has to move faster to stay in orbit. This means the orbital period is shorter.

✓ Satellites are put into either a **polar orbit** or a **geostationary orbit**.

✓ A satellite in a geostationary orbit takes 24 hours to orbit the Earth once.

❶ Figure 9.50 shows a playground roundabout.

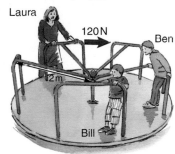

Figure 9.50

a) In which direction does the centripetal force act on the children? *(1 mark)*
b) Ben weighs 200 N, his brother Bill weighs 150 N. Explain why the centripetal force on Ben is larger than the centripetal force on Bill. *(2 marks)*
c) Each time Laura pushes on one of the bars the roundabout goes a little faster. How does the centripetal force on the children change each time Laura pushes? *(1 mark)*
d) Laura pushes with a force of 120 N at right angles to the bar. Use the following equation to calculate the moment of Laura's force. Show how you work out your answer and give the unit.

moment = force × perpendicular distance from the line of action of the force to the axis of rotation

(3 marks)

❷ a) Figure 9.51 shows three regular shapes cut from a thin sheet of card.

Figure 9.51

a) Copy each of the shapes. Mark with an 'X' the position of the centre of mass, for each shape. *(3 marks)*
b) Describe with the aid of a diagram the method you would use to find the centre of mass of one of these shapes. *(3 marks)*

❸ Figure 9.52 shows a satellite in orbit around the Earth. The satellite takes 83 minutes to orbit the Earth once.

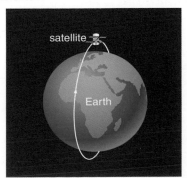

Figure 9.52

a) Is the satellite in a geostationary orbit? Give two reasons for your answer. *(2 marks)*

EXAMQUESTIONS

b) Give one use for this type of satellite.
(*1 mark*)

c) After orbiting the Earth for several years, small rockets on the satellite are fired to send it deep into space. Explain how this change in position affects the gravitational pull of the Earth on the satellite. (*2 marks*)

④ Figure 9.53 shows a forklift truck lifting a heavy crate.

Figure 9.53

Which point A, B or C marks the most likely position for the centre of mass of the forklift truck, driver and crate? Explain the reason for your answer. (*3 marks*)

⑤ Figure 9.54 shows a student who weighs 500 N about to do 'press ups'. Use the equation below to calculate the upward force *F* needed to keep his body in a stationary horizontal position.

moment = force × perpendicular distance from the line of action of the force to the axis of rotation

(*4 marks*)

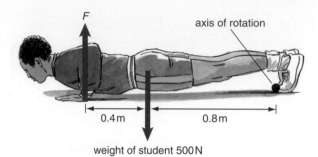

Figure 9.54

Chapter 10
What do mirrors and lenses do to light?

At the end of this chapter you should:

✓ know that when light is reflected the angle of incidence equals the angle of reflection;

✓ be able to construct ray diagrams to show how images are formed by plane and curved mirrors;

✓ know that light can be refracted (change direction) when it passes from one medium (material) into another;

✓ be able to construct ray diagrams to show how images are formed by lenses;

✓ understand how to define images as real or virtual and know that the size and 'way up' of the image depends on the type of mirror or lens and its distance from the object;

✓ be able to calculate the magnification produced by a mirror or lens;

✓ understand how converging lenses are used in cameras.

Figure 10.1 The image that you see when light is reflected depends on the reflecting surface.

Reflections in a mirror

I bet you use a mirror at least once a day, even if it's only to comb your hair. What you see is called your image. The image you see depends on whether the surface of the mirror is flat or curved. If you look into a curved shaving mirror or make-up mirror your image is enlarged and slightly distorted.

Figure 10.2 The size and shape of your image depends on the surface of the mirror.

Mirrors are not used just to see reflections but are also useful to reflect light in the direction that we want. Every time you play a CD, light is reflected from a laser to a detector. Laser light can even be reflected from the Moon by a mirror left by the Apollo 11 mission.

Mirrors work by reflecting light. A mirror with a flat surface is called a plane mirror. Figure 10.3 shows what happens when a ray of light, called the incident ray, hits a plane mirror.

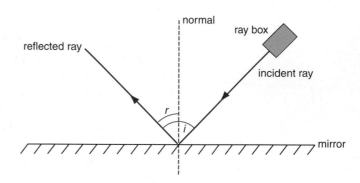

Figure 10.3 Reflection in a plane mirror showing the angle of incidence (i) and the angle of reflection (r)

The line drawn at 90° to the mirror surface is called the **normal**. The angle between the incident ray and the normal is called the **angle of**

A **normal** is a construction line drawn at 90° to a surface.

The **angle of incidence** is the angle between the incident ray and the normal.

The **angle of reflection** is the angle between the reflected ray and the normal.

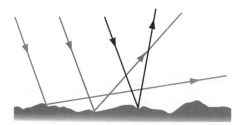

Figure 10.4 A rough surface reflects light in all directions with each individual ray of light obeying the reflection rule.

A **virtual image** is an image that cannot be projected onto a screen.

Figure 10.6 Part of this picture is an image – go behind the person and you would see what they are doing.

incidence. The angle between the reflected ray and the normal is called the **angle of reflection**.

Whenever light is reflected, the light rays obey the following rule:

the angle of incidence = the angle of reflection

It's not just mirrors that reflect light – all surfaces do. While a smooth flat surface gives a clear image, a rough surface reflects but does not give a clear image. The early fuzzy images produced by the Hubble Space Telescope were due to the mirror not being perfectly smooth.

The image in a plane mirror

Figure 10.5 shows that the image of an object seen in a plane mirror appears to be behind the mirror. The image in the mirror also appears to be the same distance behind the mirror as the object is in front of the mirror.

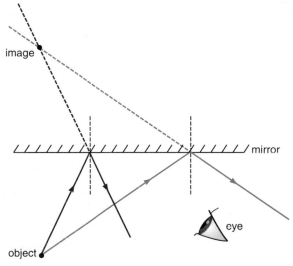

Figure 10.5 When you look into a mirror the image you see appears to be behind the mirror.

Rays of light from the object are reflected by the mirror and enter your eye. Since light travels in straight lines your brain thinks that these light rays have come from behind the mirror. Someone looking behind the mirror would not see the image. The image is not really there, so you would not be able to form a picture on a screen at that point. The only way to see the image is to look into the mirror and pick up the reflected rays with your eye. This type of image is called a **virtual image**. A plane mirror always produces a virtual image.

Cameras and projectors could not work if there were only virtual images. These and many other optical instruments produce images that can be projected onto a screen or a light sensor. This type of image is called a **real image**. Light rays actually converge at the image.

A **real image** is an image that can be projected onto a screen.

Whether an image is real or virtual helps us to describe the nature of the image (what the image is like). The other features used to describe an image are:

- its size compared to the object;
- whether it is upright or inverted (upside down) compared to the object.

The nature of the image produced by a plane mirror is:

- virtual
- same size
- upright

Figure 10.7 A periscope is useful for seeing over a crowd.

❶ Figure 10.8 shows two plane mirrors used as a periscope.

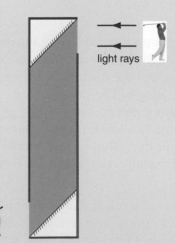

light rays

eye

Figure 10.8

a) Copy and complete Figure 10.8 to show the path taken by the two light rays from the object to the eye.
b) Describe the nature of the image obtained using the periscope.

❷ a) Jane walks slowly towards a tall plane mirror. Describe what happens to Jane's image.
b) How far is Jane from the mirror when her image is 2.4 metres away from her?

10.2 Why are reflections in curved mirrors so strange?

There are two types of curved mirror:
- concave mirrors in which the reflecting surface curves inwards;
- convex mirrors in which the reflecting surface curves outwards.

Light rays incident on either type of mirror obey the reflection rule. But the image produced depends on the type of mirror and the position of the object.

Concave mirrors

Figure 10.9 shows how a concave mirror reflects a narrow beam of parallel light rays. The rays are parallel because they are travelling from a distant object. After reflection from a concave mirror the rays converge and pass through a single point. This point is called the **focus** (F) of the mirror. The distance between the focus and the mirror is called the **focal length** of the mirror. The point labelled C is the centre of curvature of the mirror. The distance between the mirror and point C is always twice the focal length of the mirror. The line joining point C to the centre of the mirror is called the principal axis.

> The **focus** of a concave mirror is the point through which light rays parallel to the principal axis converge after reflection.
>
> The **focal length** is the distance from the centre of the mirror to the focus.

Images formed by a concave mirror

The nature of the image in a concave mirror depends on how far the object is from the mirror. A ray diagram with any two of the three rays shown in Figure 10.10 will show the position and nature of the image. If the reflected rays cross over in front of the mirror, the image is real. If the reflected rays seem to come from behind the mirror, the image is virtual.

The ray diagrams drawn in Figures 10.11 to 10.14 show how the nature of an image formed by a concave mirror can vary, depending on the distance of the object from the mirror.

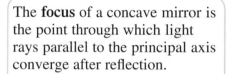
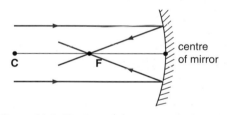

Figure 10.9 The focus of a concave mirror is always in front of its reflecting surface.

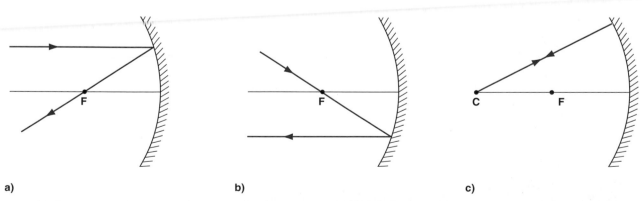

a)   b)   c)

Figure 10.10 a) A ray of light parallel to the principal axis is reflected through the focus (F). b) A ray of light passing through the focus (F) is reflected parallel to the principal axis. c) A ray of light passing through the centre of curvature (C) is reflected back through the centre of curvature (C).

In Figure 10.11 the object is further from the mirror than the centre of curvature (C). This is how a concave mirror reflects the rays from a distant object such as the Sun. The image formed is real – the rays really do converge at a point. Solar cookers are just concave mirrors. The image at the focus is definitely smaller than the Sun and therefore has an intense brightness. Anything you place at this point gets very hot.

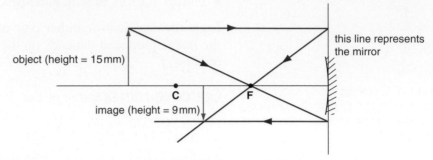

Figure 10.11 When the object is beyond the centre of curvature, image is real, smaller and inverted.

In Figure 10.12 the object is at the centre of curvature (C).

In Figure 10.13 the object is between the centre of curvature (C) and the focus (F).

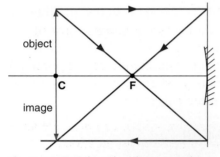

Figure 10.12 When the object is at the centre of curvature, the image is real, the same size and inverted.

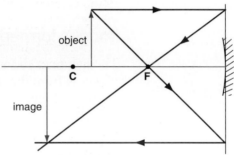

Figure 10.13 When the object is between the centre of curvature and the focus, the image is real, bigger and inverted.

In Figure 10.14 the object is between the focus (F) and the mirror.

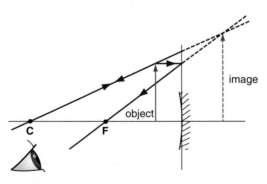

Figure 10.14 When the object is between the focus and the mirror, the image is virtual, bigger and upright.

The **magnification** tells us the size of the image compared with the size of the object.

The **magnification** produced by a mirror gives the size of the image compared to the object. It can be calculated using the equation:

$$\text{magnification} = \frac{\text{image height}}{\text{object height}}$$

Figure 10.15 A concave mirror can be used to give an upright magnified image, as long as the object is close to the mirror as in Figure 10.14.

Example

Look at Figure 10.11. Here the height of the object is 15 cm and the height of the image is 9 cm:

$$\text{magnification} = \frac{9}{15} = 0.6$$

If the magnification is less than 1.0 the image is smaller than the object. A magnification of 1.0 means the image and object are the same size.

❸ Calculate the magnification produced by the mirrors in Figures 10.12, 10.13 and 10.14.

❹ An object 2 cm tall is placed 10 cm in front of a concave mirror of focal length 6 cm. Draw a ray diagram to find:
a) the position of the image;
b) the nature of the image;
c) the magnification produced by the mirror.

❺ An object 2 cm tall is placed 3 cm in front of a concave mirror of focal length 4 cm.
a) Draw a ray diagram to find the position of the image.
b) Is the image real or virtual? Explain your answer.
c) Calculate the magnification produced by the mirror.

❻ Draw a ray diagram to show how a concave mirror can produce an image the same size as the object. What is the magnification produced by the mirror?

Images formed by a convex mirror

Figure 10.16 shows that the light rays reflected by a convex mirror spread out. Looking into the mirror it seems as if the rays have come from a focus (F) behind the mirror. This means it is a **virtual focus**.

A **virtual focus** is the point from which light rays parallel to the principal axis seem to come after reflection by a convex mirror.

Unlike a concave mirror, the nature of the image formed by a convex mirror (Figure 10.17) does not change with the position of the object. The image is always:
• virtual
• smaller than the object
• upright

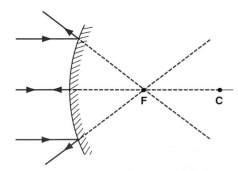

Figure 10.16 The focus of a convex mirror is always behind its reflecting surface.

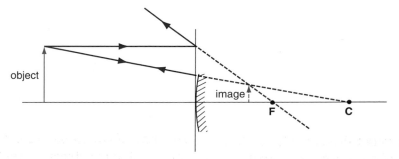

Figure 10.17 The image produced by a convex mirror is always virtual, upright and smaller than the object.

7 Explain why convex mirrors are not used as shaving mirrors.

8 An object 3 cm tall is placed 6 cm in front of a convex mirror of focal length 4 cm. Draw a ray diagram to find:
   a) the position of the image;
   b) the nature of the image;
   c) the magnification produced by the mirror.

9 The image of an object 4 cm in front of a convex mirror is 3 cm behind the mirror. The mirror produces a magnification of 0.75. Draw a ray diagram to find the focal length of the mirror.

10 Some of the following statements are true and some are false. Copy out the true statements. Rewrite the false statements so that they are true.
   a) A convex mirror always produces a real image.
   b) A concave mirror produces a virtual image when the object is between the mirror and the focus.
   c) The image produced by a convex mirror is always smaller than the object.
   d) A concave mirror can never produce an image that is larger than the object.
   e) A real image cannot be projected onto a screen.

10.3 Refraction by lenses

When a ray of light crosses the boundary between two different transparent materials it usually changes direction. This change in direction is called **refraction**.

> **Refraction** is the change in direction of a ray of light as it travels across the boundary from one medium (material) to another.

Figure 10.18 shows the path of a light ray through a glass block. As it enters the glass block from the air the light ray is refracted towards the normal. As it leaves the glass block and goes back into the air the light ray is refracted away from the normal.

Light is not refracted when the ray travels along a normal and hits the boundary at 90° (Figure 10.19).

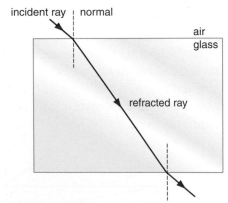

Figure 10.18 Refraction of light by a glass block

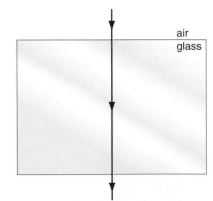

Figure 10.19 Light is not refracted when it travels at 90° to a boundary.

Figure 10.20 Raindrops refract and disperse sunlight to give a rainbow showing all the colours of the spectrum.

Refraction by a triangular prism

When white light is refracted by a prism, it splits into the seven colours of the spectrum. This effect is called dispersion. It happens because white light is a mixture of colours. The prism refracts each colour by a slightly different amount. Violet light is refracted the most and red light the least. This means the colours go into the prism together but they come out separated.

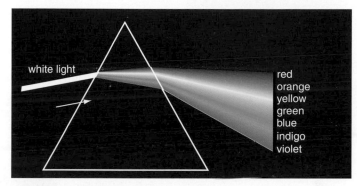

white light

red
orange
yellow
green
blue
indigo
violet

Figure 10.21 Dispersion of light produces a spectrum.

> A **converging** lens is a lens that is thicker in the middle than at the edges. A **diverging** lens is thinner in the middle than at the edges.

Refraction by a lens

Lenses refract light to produce images. Many optical devices, including cameras, magnifying glasses, binoculars, spectacles (glasses) and microscopes, use lenses. There are even lenses in your eyes.

There are two types of lens:
- **converging** lenses (also called convex lenses) – thicker in the middle than at the edges;
- **diverging** lenses (also called concave lenses) – thinner in the middle than at the edges.

Converging lenses

Notice in Figure 10.23 that light entering a converging lens is refracted towards the normal and light leaving the lens is refracted away from the normal. As a result of these refractions, parallel rays of light entering the lens converge and meet at a point. This point is called the **focus** of the lens (Figure 10.24).

> **⑪** Look at the lenses in Figure 10.22. Which of the lenses are converging?
>
>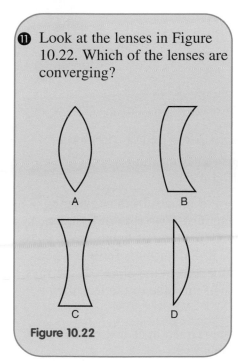
>
> A   B
>
> C   D
>
> **Figure 10.22**

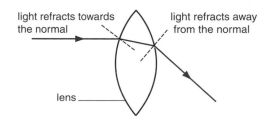

light refracts towards the normal

light refracts away from the normal

lens

Figure 10.23 Light refracted by a converging lens

> The **focus** of a converging lens is the point through which light rays, parallel to the principal axis, pass after refraction.

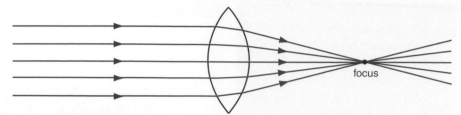

Figure 10.24 Parallel rays of light converge at the focus of a converging lens.

Light can pass through the lens in either direction. So, parallel rays of light from the right would converge at a focus an equal distance from the lens on the left.

A converging lens can be used to focus the light from a distant object onto a sheet of paper or onto a screen. The image is sharpest when the paper or screen is at the focus of the lens.

Figure 10.25 This is the earliest known picture of a person wearing spectacles. It was painted by Tommaso da Modena in 1352.

Figure 10.26 A converging lens can, but does not always, produce a real image.

Images formed by a converging lens

As with mirrors, the position and nature of images from converging lenses can be found by drawing ray diagrams. Two rays of light are drawn from the same point on an object. Each ray of light always takes a fixed path (Figures 10.27 and 10.28). A real image is formed where two rays cross on the opposite side of the lens to the object. If the rays only appear to come from a point on the same side of the lens then a virtual image is formed.

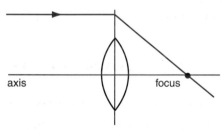

Figure 10.27 A ray of light parallel to the principal axis of the lens is refracted through the focus.

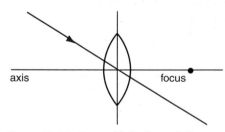

Figure 10.28 A ray of light through the centre of the lens continues in a straight line.

In ray diagrams it is simpler to show the refraction as if it happens at a straight line through the centre of the lens.

With a converging lens the position of the object affects the nature of the image.

When the object is a long way from a converging lens, the image is real, smaller than the object and inverted (Figure 10.29). When the object is close to the focus, the image is real, larger than the object and inverted (Figure 10.30).

⓬ Simon has found an old converging lens. Describe a simple method that Simon could use to find the approximate distance between the lens and its focus.

⓭ James has written: 'Moving an object closer to a converging lens makes the image move further away from the lens.'
  a) Draw three ray diagrams to support what James has written.
  b) How does the size of the image change as the object moves towards the lens?
  c) Dianne says that what James has written is not always true. Draw a ray diagram to show why Dianne is right.

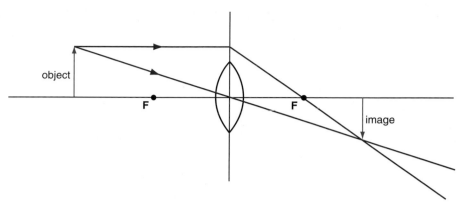

Figure 10.29 The image produced when the object is a long way from a converging lens is real, smaller than the object and inverted.

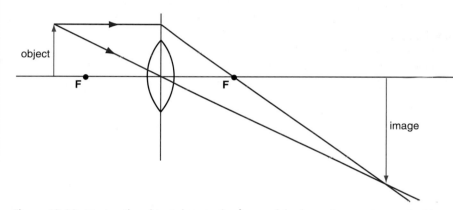

Figure 10.30 Moving the object close to the focus of the lens gives an image that is real, larger than the object and inverted.

Remember

$$\text{magnification} = \frac{\text{image height}}{\text{object height}}$$

The equation for the magnification produced by a lens is the same as the equation for a mirror.

Activity – Investigating the images produced by a converging lens

Figure 10.31 shows the apparatus used by Amir to obtain real images using a converging lens.

Height of object in mm	Height of image in mm	Distance between object and lens in mm	Distance between image and lens in mm
10	11	100	100
10	6	160	80
10	3	60	300
10	18	80	140
10	8	120	90

Table 10.1

By moving the object and the screen, Amir is able to obtain the results given in Table 10.1.

❶ Why is Amir unable to use this method to measure the height of a virtual image?

❷ Use each set of results in Table 10.1 to calculate:
  a) the magnification produced by the lens;
  b) $\dfrac{\text{distance between image and lens}}{\text{distance between object and lens}}$

❸ Draw a new table and record the results of your calculations in question 2. Record the results in order of increasing magnification.

❹ Which set of results in Table 10.1 seems to contain an anomalous measurement? Give a reason for your answer.

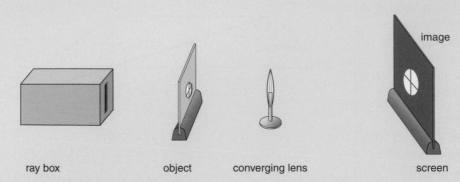

Figure 10.31 The lens produces a real image on the screen.

❺ Amir concludes that he has found another way to calculate the magnification produced by a converging lens. He writes the equation as:

$$\text{magnification} = \frac{\text{distance between image and lens}}{\text{distance between object and lens}}$$

Do the results of Amir's investigation support this conclusion? Give a reason for your answer.

❻ Does Amir have enough evidence to say that this equation applies to all lenses? Give a reason for your answer.

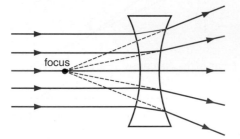

Figure 10.32 A diverging lens has a virtual focus from which rays of light that are parallel when they enter the lens will appear to diverge.

Diverging lenses

As a result of refraction, parallel rays of light entering a diverging lens spread out as they leave the lens (Figure 10.32). The rays do not meet at a single point but look as though they spread out or diverge from a single point. This point is the focus of the lens. It is a virtual focus.

Images formed by a diverging lens

Ray diagrams can be drawn for diverging lenses in the same way as those for converging lenses. A ray of light incident on the centre of the lens continues in a straight line. A ray of light parallel to the principal axis is refracted so that it seems to have come from a virtual focus. An image is formed where the two rays seem to cross.

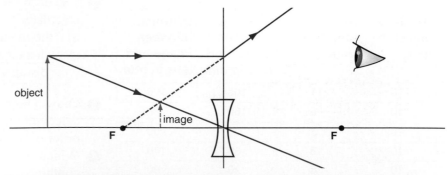

Figure 10.33 A diverging lens always produces a virtual, upright image that is smaller than the object.

⑭ How is the virtual image produced by a diverging lens different from the virtual image that can be produced by a converging lens?

⑮ An object 15 mm tall is placed 60 mm from a diverging lens. The distance between the centre of the lens and the focus is 45 mm.
   a) Draw a ray diagram to find the position and nature of the image formed.

   b) Calculate the magnification produced by the lens.
   c) The object is now moved so that it is only 30 mm from the lens. Draw another ray diagram to show how the position and size of the image changes. Calculate the new magnification produced by the lens.

⑯ Copy and complete each of the ray diagrams drawn in Figure 10.34. 'F' marks the focus of the lens.

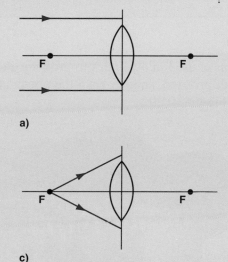

a)

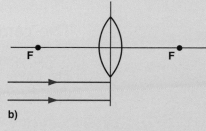

b)

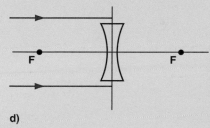

d)

c)

Figure 10.34

(10.4)

How are lenses used?

Using a converging lens as a magnifying glass

A single converging lens can be used as a magnifying glass (Figures 10.35 and 10.36). The most powerful magnifying glasses use very thick lenses.

The most powerful Magnifying glasses use very thick lenses

Figure 10.35 When you look through a converging lens at a close object you see a magnified image of the object.

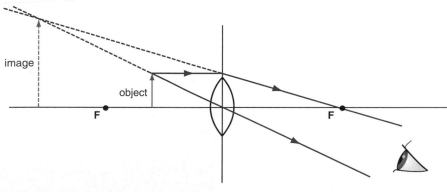

Figure 10.36 A converging lens produces a magnified image of a close-up object.

When the object is between the lens and its focus, the rays of light which pass through the lens from the object do not meet. The only way to see the image is to look through the lens. The image is virtual, upright and magnified.

> **17** A converging lens is used as a magnifying glass. The distance between the centre of the lens and its focus is 5 cm. An object 2 cm tall is placed 3 cm from the lens.
> a) Draw a ray diagram to find the position and nature of the image.
> b) Calculate the magnification produced by the lens.

The camera

A converging lens is used in a camera to produce an image of an object. The image is real, inverted, smaller than the object and nearer to the lens than the object (Figure 10.29).

Figure 10.37 A traditional camera produces a real image on photographic film.

The basic difference between a traditional camera and a digital camera is the way in which the image is processed. In a digital camera an image sensor takes the place of photographic film. This sensor converts the incoming light into electrical charges. A microprocessor inside the camera then produces the image that you see.

> **18** Copy and complete the following sentences:
>
> A _____ lens is thinner in the middle than at the _____.
>
> Parallel rays of light _____ by a convex lens pass through the _____.
>
> **19** In a traditional camera, a lens is used to produce an image on photographic paper.
> a) What type of lens is used to produce the image?
> b) State two ways in which the image produced on the film is different from the object.

Summary

✓ A **normal** is a construction line drawn at 90° to a surface.

✓ The **angle of incidence** is the angle between an incident ray of light and the normal.

✓ The **angle of reflection** is the angle between a reflected ray of light and the normal.

✓ The angle of incidence equals the angle of reflection.

✓ A **real image** can be projected onto a screen.

✓ A **virtual image** cannot be projected onto a screen.

✓ A plane mirror always produces a virtual, upright image that is the same size as the object.

✓ The nature of the image in a concave mirror depends on the distance of the object from the mirror.

✓ A convex mirror always produces a virtual, upright image that is smaller than the object.

✓ The **magnification** produced by a mirror or a lens can be calculated using the equation:

$$\text{magnification} = \frac{\text{image height}}{\text{object height}}$$

✓ The **focus** is the point through which light rays parallel to the principal axis pass after reflection by a concave mirror or refraction by a converging lens.

✓ A **virtual focus** is the point from which light rays parallel to the principal axis seem to come after reflection by a convex mirror or refraction by a diverging lens.

✓ The **focal length** of a mirror or lens is the distance between the centre of the mirror or lens and the focus.

✓ **Refraction** is the change in direction that happens when light rays travel across the boundary from one medium (material) to another.

✓ The image produced by a **converging** lens depends on the focal length of the lens and the distance between the object and the lens.

✓ A **diverging** lens always produces a virtual, upright image that is smaller than the object.

✓ When a beam of white light is refracted by a prism it splits into the colours of the spectrum. This is called **dispersion**.

EXAMQUESTIONS

❶ Figure 10.38 shows five pieces of glass.

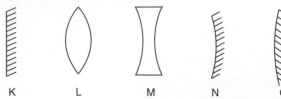

K   L   M   N   O

Figure 10.38

a) Which one of the pieces of glass K, L, M, N or O is
   i)   a plane mirror;
   ii) a converging lens;
   iii) a convex mirror?   (*3 marks*)
b) Which of the pieces of glass always form a virtual image?   (*2 marks*)

❷ An object 2 cm tall is placed 9 cm in front of a concave mirror of focal length 3 cm.
a) Draw a ray diagram to show the position and size of the image.   (*4 marks*)
b) State two ways in which the image is different from the object.   (*2 marks*)
c) Calculate the magnification produced by the mirror.   (*2 marks*)
d) State one use for a concave mirror. (*1 mark*)

❸ The converging lens in a camera produces a real image. The converging lens in a magnifying glass produces a virtual image.
a) Explain the difference between a real and a virtual image.   (*2 marks*)
b) Why is it important that the lens in a camera produces a real image?   (*1 mark*)
c) Copy and complete Figure 10.39 to show how a converging lens produces a virtual image. Put an **F** on the diagram to label the focus of the lens.   (*3 marks*)

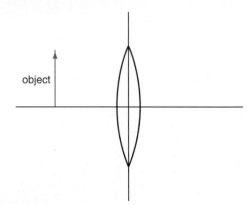

object

Figure 10.39

Chapter 11
What are sound and ultrasound?

At the end of this chapter you should:

✓ know that sound is caused by mechanical vibrations and travels as a wave;
✓ understand why sound cannot travel through a vacuum;
✓ know that sound waves can be reflected and refracted;
✓ be able to compare the amplitudes and frequencies of sounds from oscilloscope traces;
✓ understand what affects the pitch, loudness and quality of a musical note;
✓ appreciate that only sounds within a certain range of frequencies can be detected by humans;

✓ know that ultrasound has a frequency above the maximum frequency humans can hear;
✓ explain some of the industrial and medical uses for ultrasound;
✓ know how ultrasound is used to measure the distance to the boundary between two different materials;
✓ be able to use the diagram of an oscilloscope trace to determine the distance to the boundary between two different materials.

Figure 11.1 Razorlight in concert. The singer, the instruments and the loudspeakers produce vibrations in the air, which we hear as sound.

11.1 Sound waves

Sound waves are produced when an object vibrates. The object could be the skin of a drum, the string of a guitar or the vocal chords in your throat. It doesn't really matter what the vibrating object is. The important thing is that when the object vibrates, it makes the air next to it vibrate.

Figure 11.2 Vibrating objects create sounds.

Figure 11.3 The small polystyrene balls move up and down with the vibration of the loudspeaker cone.

Look at the loudspeaker in Figure 11.3. As the cone vibrates up and down it makes the air above it vibrate up and down. As the cone moves upwards, it pushes gas molecules in the air together causing an increase in air pressure. When the cone moves downwards the gas molecules in the air move further apart causing a decrease in air pressure. The changes in pressure spread out through the air away from the loudspeaker cone. These are the sound waves. When the waves reach your ears the changes in air pressure cause your ear drum to vibrate and the sound is 'heard'.

In fact we only hear sounds if their frequencies (see Section 3.1) are between 20 Hz and 20 000 Hz. In general, any sound with a vibration frequency outside this range cannot be detected by our ears.

Although gas molecules transmit sound, they do not travel along with the sound wave. As the molecules vibrate backwards and forwards, it is the energy of the wave and the pattern of vibration that moves through the air away from the vibrating object.

In a similar way, energy can be transferred through a slinky spring by continually moving the ends of the spring backwards and forwards (Figure 11.4). This makes the coils of the spring alternately compress then stretch out. It takes energy to compress and stretch the spring so energy is transferred along the length of the spring in the same direction as the vibration of the coils. This type of wave is called a **longitudinal wave**. Sound waves are also longitudinal waves. The particles in the material that a sound wave travels through are alternately compressed and then move apart, like the coils of the slinky spring.

> A **longitudinal wave** is a wave in which energy is transferred in the same direction as the vibrations producing the wave.

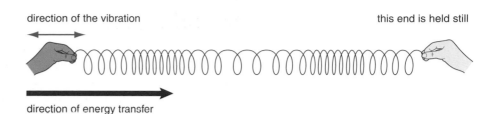

direction of the vibration

this end is held still

direction of energy transfer

Figure 11.4 A slinky spring can model a sound wave. We can't see what's happening in a sound wave because the gas molecules in air are too small and vibrate too fast, but we can see what's happening with the slinky.

Sound waves cannot travel through a vacuum. This is because a vacuum is totally empty. There is nothing in it, not even a few particles. Without particles the energy from a vibrating object cannot be transferred because there is nothing to vibrate.

Figure 11.6 Sound can be reflected off different surfaces to produce multiple echoes.

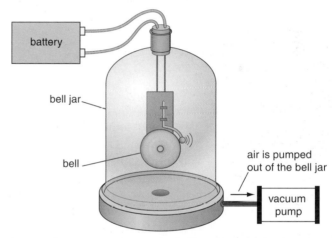

battery

bell jar

bell

air is pumped out of the bell jar

vacuum pump

Figure 11.5 As long as there is air in the jar, the bell can be heard. When the air is removed, we no longer hear the bell. But it's still working, and we can see the hammer hitting the metal gong.

11.2 Reflection and refraction of sound

Reflection

All surfaces reflect and absorb the energy transferred by a sound wave to some extent. A hard surface will reflect more sound and absorb less sound than a softer surface. When sound waves are reflected, they obey the same rule of reflection as light rays (Section 10.1).

An echo is a reflected sound wave. The sound reflects off a surface and is heard a short time after the original sound.

Figure 11.7 The curved discs hanging from the ceiling of the Royal Albert Hall reduce echoes, making the sounds we hear clearer and easier to understand.

❶ Draw a diagram to show why an echo takes longer to reach the listener than the original sound.

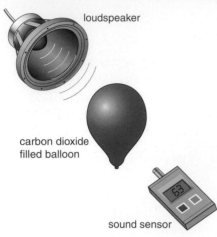

loudspeaker

carbon dioxide
filled balloon

sound sensor

Figure 11.8 The carbon dioxide inside the balloon is denser than the air outside. So, the balloon refracts sound just like a converging lens refracts light. The sound detected by the sensor is loudest at the focus of the 'lens'.

Refraction

Like light, sound can be refracted. This usually happens when sound moves from one substance into another. However, it can sometimes happen as sound travels through different layers of air. If layers of air are at different temperatures they have slightly different densities. Sound waves travelling from one layer of air to another are refracted. At night, differences in air temperature cause sound waves to be refracted towards the ground. This is one reason why distant sounds sometimes seem louder and clearer at night.

❷ Explain why sound waves cannot travel through space.

❸ Describe how you could demonstrate that sound can be refracted.

Activity – Measuring the speed of sound in air

Phil and Rowena decided to use the echoes from a tall building to measure the speed of sound. Phil stands in front of the building and bangs two blocks of wood together. Each time he hears an echo he bangs the pieces of wood together again. Rowena uses a stopwatch to time how long it takes to hear 10 echoes (Figure 11.9).

Figure 11.9 Using echoes to measure the speed of sound

The results of their experiment are written in Table 11.1.

Experiment number	Time in seconds
1	3.4
2	3.8
3	3.0

Table 11.1 The time for 10 echoes

❶ What problem would there have been if Phil had stood:
   a)   too close to the wall;
   b)   too far from the wall?

❷ Rowena measured the distance between Phil and the wall as 50 m.
   a)   Which of the following instruments should Rowena have used to measure the distance?

   30 cm ruler   metre ruler   25 metre tape measure

   Give a reason for your choice.
   b)   Calculate the mean value of the time for 10 echoes.
   c)   How long does it take the sound to travel 100 m?
   d)   Use the equation below to calculate Phil and Rowena's value for the speed of sound.

   speed = distance ÷ time

   e)   What could Phil and Rowena do to improve the accuracy of their value for the speed of sound?

❸ To check their results, Phil and Rowena repeated the experiment on another day. There is a strong wind blowing but Phil says that it doesn't matter. Rowena disagrees and thinks the wind will stop it being a fair test.
   Who do you agree with? Give a reason for your answer.

11.3 Looking at sound waves

We cannot really look at sound waves, but we can detect them with a microphone. A microphone transforms sound energy to electrical energy. So, if the microphone is connected to an oscilloscope (CRO, Section 7.4), a wave trace can be obtained on the screen (Figure 11.10). The oscilloscope trace is really a graph showing how the air pressure in front of the microphone changes with time. It is not a picture of a sound wave but it does represent the sound wave.

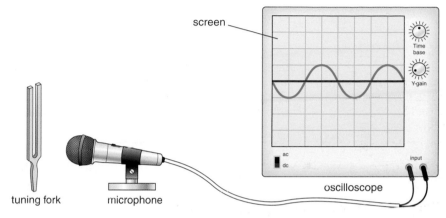

Figure 11.10 Displaying sound waves on an oscilloscope screen

Amplitude and loudness

If you shout, the sound is louder than if you whisper. Louder sound waves have bigger vibrations. As you should remember from Section 3.1, the size of the vibration in a wave is called the amplitude. The amplitude of a vibration affects the loudness of the sound produced. The bigger the amplitude, the louder the sound. Loud sounds transfer more energy than quiet sounds, so shouting all day would be very tiring.

Pitch and frequency

Most musicians will describe notes in terms of **pitch**. A guitarist would say the bass string produces a low pitch note. We could also describe this as a low frequency note. The thinnest string produces the note with the highest pitch and the highest frequency. High frequency notes have a higher pitch than low frequency notes. You can see this if you look at the strings vibrating. The thin string vibrates faster than the thick bass string.

On an oscilloscope screen, the waves from a high pitch note will be closer together than the waves from a lower pitch note (Figure 11.12).

Quality

A tuning fork vibrating at a frequency of 256 Hz produces the note we call middle C. The same note can be played on a piano, a guitar, a violin or any other musical instrument. Someone listening would know that different instruments were being used because the note would sound

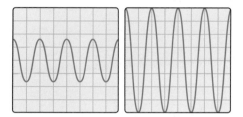

Figure 11.11 On an oscilloscope, louder sounds have taller wave traces.

> The **pitch** of a note depends on the frequency of the sound waves.

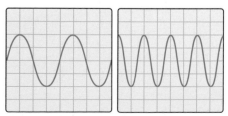

Figure 11.12 If the controls on an oscilloscope are not changed, higher frequency sounds produce more waves on the screen.

The **quality** of a note is determined by its waveform.

different. If you look at the wave traces produced by the different instruments on an oscilloscope, you can see why. Each wave trace shows a different shape or waveform. This is what gives each musical instrument its particular sound or **quality**.

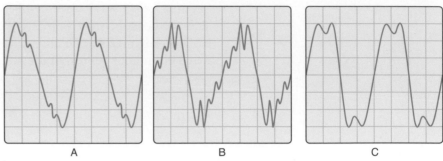

Figure 11.13 These notes from three different instruments will not sound the same. They have the same frequency and amplitude but a different waveform and therefore a different quality.

An electronic synthesiser can be programmed to produce any waveform. The synthesiser can be made to sound like any instrument you want.

❹ Figure 11.14 shows the oscilloscope traces produced by three different tuning forks.
   a) Which of the tuning forks is vibrating with the smallest amplitude?
   b) Which of the tuning forks is giving the loudest sound?
   c) Which of the tuning forks has the lowest frequency?

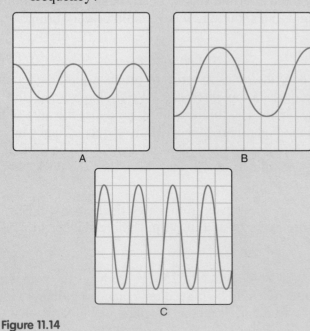

Figure 11.14

❺ Figure 11.15 shows the oscilloscope trace produced by a car siren.
   Describe how the sound is changing.

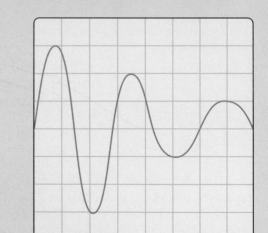

Figure 11.15

6 Explain why a note played on a violin sounds different to the same note played on a harp.

7 Figure 11.16 shows the waveform produced by an electronic synthesiser.
Copy Figure 11.16 and add to your diagram a second waveform for a louder note of lower pitch.

8 What are the three main characteristics that make one note sound different from another note?

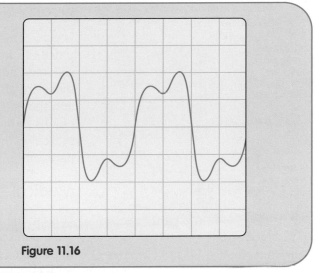

Figure 11.16

11.4 What is ultrasound and how is it used?

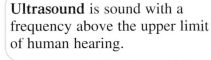

Ultrasound is sound with a frequency above the upper limit of human hearing.

Any sound with a frequency too high for humans to hear is called **ultrasound**. Although humans cannot hear ultrasound, many animals can.

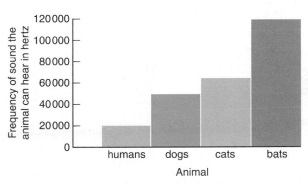

Figure 11.17 The range of sounds that some animals can hear

Although we cannot hear ultrasound, we can compare the amplitudes and frequencies of different ultrasounds by converting the waves into an electronic signal and displaying this on an oscilloscope. Ultrasound waves can be produced in the laboratory with a signal generator connected to a loudspeaker.

A narrow pulse of high-frequency ultrasound will pass through most substances without spreading out. If the ultrasound meets a boundary between two different materials, some will be reflected and some will be transmitted. A detector can pick up the pulse of partially reflected ultrasound and display it on an oscilloscope screen. The longer it takes the reflected pulse to reach the detector, the further the boundary is from the detector. This simple idea is the basis for many of the industrial and medical applications of ultrasound.

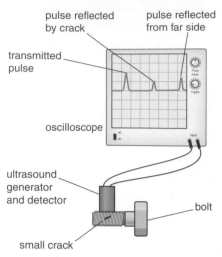

Figure 11.18 Looking for cracks in a metal bolt

Quality control in manufacturing

Hidden cracks in metal castings and concrete can be found by sending a pulse of ultrasound into the material. The transmitted pulse and any reflected pulse are displayed on an oscilloscope or computer screen. If there are no cracks, just two pulses will be seen, the transmitted pulse and the pulse reflected from the far side of the material. Any hidden cracks in the material will also reflect ultrasound, giving additional pulses on the screen. This technique is used to find cracks in aircraft parts and railway lines.

Medical scanning

Ultrasound is used to produce an image of an unborn baby. Pulses of ultrasound are transmitted directly through the abdomen of the mother to the fetus in the uterus. Some of the ultrasound is reflected every time it meets a boundary between different tissue types. A detector picks up the reflected pulses, which are then processed by a computer to give a visual display. This early image of the fetus lets the doctor check that the baby is developing normally. Pre-natal scanning also offers parents the chance to find out the sex of their unborn baby.

An advantage of using ultrasound rather than X-rays is that, unlike X-rays, ultrasound waves do not harm the fetus. Although ultrasound transmits energy into the body, there is not enough energy to ionise cells.

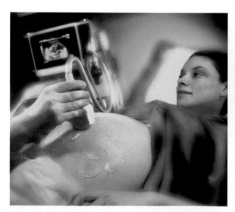

Figure 11.19 This pregnant woman is having a pre-natal scan. The combined ultrasound transmitter and detector is moved over the woman's abdomen on a layer of gel. Without the gel, most of the ultrasound would be reflected at the air/skin boundary.

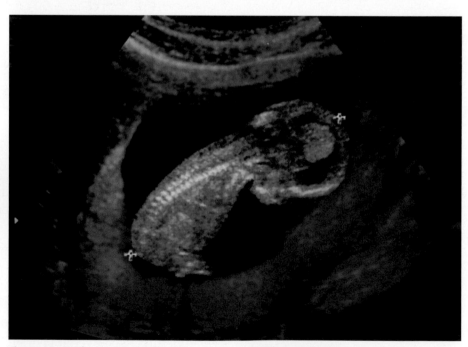

Figure 11.20 The image produced by a pre-natal ultrasound scan

Radiographers can also use the reflections shown in ultrasound scans to investigate damaged ligaments and organs such as the stomach and heart. Ultrasound scans can also examine tumours inside the body.

9 Name two animals that can hear sounds with a frequency above 60 000 Hz.

Cleaning and smashing

Ultrasound can be used to clean jewellery and delicate objects like watch or clock parts without the need to take them apart. The object is placed in a tank of liquid with an ultrasound generator. The high frequency sound waves through the liquid and through the object shake small specks of dirt and grease off the object.

Dentists sometimes use the vibrations from an ultrasound probe to remove tartar from teeth.

In hospitals, ultrasound vibrations can be used to smash kidney stones without the need for an operation. The small pieces pass out of the body in the urine.

Measuring distance using ultrasound

Figure 11.21 shows the oscilloscope trace produced when an ultrasound pulse is transmitted through a metal casting with a serious internal flaw. The settings on the oscilloscope can be adjusted to determine the distance of the flaw below the surface of the metal casting and to find the size of the flaw.

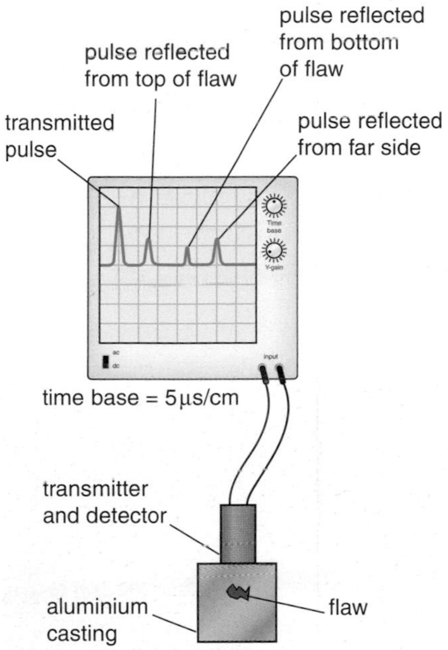

Remember from Section 7.4 that each horizontal division on the oscilloscope represents a certain length of time. This is called the time base setting.

Look at Figure 11.21. The time base setting = 5 μs/cm (5 μs = 0.000 005 s). This means that each centimetre on the oscilloscope screen represents a time of 0.000 005 s.

The distance between the two pulses reflected at each side of the flaw = 2 cm

∴ The time between the two pulses being detected
= 2 × 0.000 005 s = 0.000 010 s

This is the time taken by the pulse to travel through the flaw and back again.

Therefore the time taken to travel through the flaw
= 0.000 010 ÷ 2 = 0.000 005 s

Using the equation:

$$\text{distance} = \text{speed} \times \text{time}$$

and taking the speed of ultrasound through air as 340 m/s,

$$\text{distance} = 340 \times 0.000\,005 = 0.0017\,\text{m} = 1.7\,\text{mm}$$

So the distance across the flaw (its thickness) is 1.7 mm.

pulse reflected from top of flaw

pulse reflected from bottom of flaw

transmitted pulse

pulse reflected from far side

time base = 5μs/cm

transmitter and detector

aluminium casting

flaw

Figure 11.21 The size and position of a hidden flaw in an aluminium casting can be determined using ultrasound.

10 Use information in Figure 11.21 to calculate:
   a) the distance between the top of the casting and the first edge of the flaw. The speed of ultrasound in aluminium is 5100 m/s;
   b) the distance from the top to the bottom of the casting.

11 A trawler is using ultrasound pulses to locate a shoal of fish. There is a time difference of 0.3 s between the pulse being emitted and the reflected pulse from the shoal of fish arriving back at the trawler. Calculate how far the shoal of fish is from the trawler.
(Speed of ultrasound in water = 1500 m/s.)

Summary

✓ Sound waves are produced when objects vibrate.

✓ Sound waves are **longitudinal waves**.

✓ A longitudinal wave is one in which the energy transfer is in the same direction as the vibrations causing the wave.

✓ Sound waves cannot travel through a vacuum.

✓ When sound waves are reflected they obey the same rule of reflection as light rays.

✓ Sound is refracted when the material through which it is travelling changes density.

✓ The loudness of a sound increases as the amplitude of the sound increases.

✓ The **pitch** of a musical note gets higher as the frequency increases.

✓ The **quality** of a musical note depends on its waveform.

✓ The range of human hearing is usually taken as 20 Hz to 20 000 Hz.

✓ **Ultrasound** is any sound with a frequency above the upper limit of human hearing.

✓ Ultrasound is used for pre-natal scanning and for cleaning and quality control in manufacturing.

✓ Distance can be determined from the oscilloscope trace produced by transmitted and reflected ultrasound pulses.

❶ a) The amplitude, frequency and quality of a note can be changed. Which of these characteristics could be changed to make a note:
  i) louder; *(1 mark)*
  ii) sound completely different; *(1 mark)*
  iii) have a lower pitch? *(1 mark)*
 b) Most people hear sounds with frequencies between 20 Hz and 20 000 Hz.
  i) What are sounds above 20 000 Hz called? *(1 mark)*
  ii) State one way in which these sounds can be produced. *(1 mark)*

❷ A ship very close to a cliff sounds its fog horn. An echo of the sound is heard.
 a) What causes the echo? *(1 mark)*
   Sound travels at 330 m/s. The echo is heard after 4 seconds.
 b) How long does it takes for the sound from the fog horn to reach the cliff? *(1 mark)*
 c) Use the equation below to calculate the distance of the ship from the cliff.

   distance = speed × time *(2 marks)*

❸ Figure 11.22 shows a vet using an ultrasound scanner. The vet wants to see if the dog has damaged any of the ligaments in its shoulder.

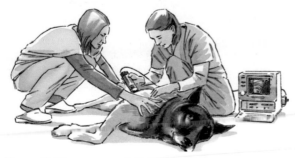

Figure 11.22

 a) Explain how ultrasound can produce an image of the ligament. *(3 marks)*
 b) Give two non-medical uses for ultrasound. *(2 marks)*

❹ Figure 11.23 shows pulses of ultrasound being used to locate a submarine. The transmitted and reflected pulses are shown on an oscilloscope.

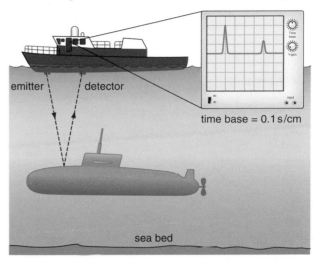

emitter   detector

time base = 0.1 s/cm

sea bed

Figure 11.23

 a) Use the information in the diagram and the equation below to calculate how far the submarine is underwater. (Speed of ultrasound in water = 1500 m/s.)

   distance = speed × time *(3 marks)*

 b) Describe how the oscilloscope pattern will change once the boat has gone past the submarine. *(2 marks)*

EXAMQUESTIONS

Chapter 12
How do motors, generators and transformers work?

At the end of this chapter you should:

✓ know that electric currents can produce magnetic fields;
✓ understand that a conductor carrying an electric current in a magnetic field may experience a force, and that the size of the force can be increased by increasing the current or increasing the strength of the magnetic field;
✓ know how forces produced in magnetic fields can be used to make things move in devices such as electric motors;
✓ understand that when a conductor 'cuts' through a magnetic field, a potential difference is induced and a current flows if the conductor is part of a complete circuit;
✓ know how the size of the induced potential difference can be increased;

✓ know that a transformer consists of two coils of wire wound on an iron core;
✓ understand that an alternating current in the primary coil produces a changing magnetic field around the secondary coil, which induces an alternating potential difference across the ends of the secondary coil;
✓ know that transformers are used to step-up (increase) or step-down (decrease) alternating potential differences;
✓ be able to decide the type of transformer needed for a particular application.

Figure 12.1 Electric motors drive many appliances. Washing machines, hair dryers, food processors, electric drills and vacuum cleaners all use electric motors. This cut-away view of an electric drill shows the motor inside.

12.1 Magnetic poles and magnetic fields

Magnets are manufactured and used in lots of different machines. These include motors, generators, TVs and computers.

When a magnet is dipped into a box of pins, the pins cling to it. A similar thing happens when iron filings or steel paper clips are used. But this does not happen with brass screws. The ends of the magnet where most of the pins cling are called the **poles**.

Magnets will only attract metals and alloys which contain iron, cobalt or nickel. Steel, which is an alloy of iron, is attracted by magnets. Brass, which is an alloy of copper and zinc, is not.

> The **poles** of a magnet are the parts of it where the magnetism is strongest.

North poles and south poles

If a bar magnet is hung from a thread, it always comes to rest in a north–south direction (Figure 12.2). The end (pole) of the magnet, which always points north, is called the north-seeking pole, or just north pole for short. The pole of the magnet which points south is called the south-seeking pole or south pole. Because of this, a small magnet can be used as a compass.

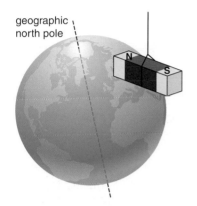

geographic north pole

Figure 12.2 A freely suspended magnet will always come to rest in a north–south line on the Earth.

Forces between poles

When the poles of two magnets are brought near each other, we find that:
- like poles (i.e. two north poles or two south poles) repel one another;
- unlike poles (i.e. a north pole and a south pole) attract one another.

Magnetic fields

Strong magnets can attract magnetic materials from some distance away or even through other materials like paper and wood. The space around a magnet, where its magnetic force acts, is called a **magnetic field**.

You can investigate the shape and direction of the magnetic field around a bar magnet using a small plotting compass, as shown in Figure 12.3.

> A **magnetic field** is the space around a magnet where its magnetic force acts. Lines of magnetic force show the shape of the field.

Put the bar magnet on a sheet of paper and place the plotting compass near one of its poles. Mark the ends of the compass needle with dots. Use the second dot as the starting point for the next position of the compass. Continue like this until the other pole of the bar magnet is reached or the field becomes too weak to detect. Then join up the dots as shown in Figure 12.3. These lines that you get are called lines of magnetic force.

Figure 12.4 shows the lines of magnetic force (magnetic field patterns):
a) around a single bar magnet;
b) between separate north and south poles;
c) between two separate north poles.

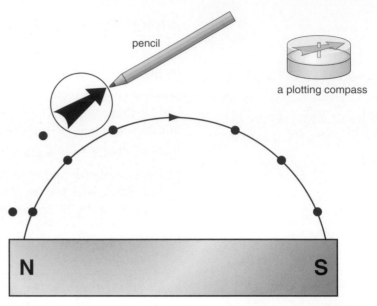

a plotting compass

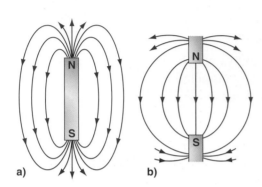

a)　　　　b)

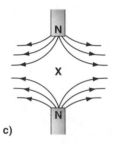

c)

Figure 12.4 The lines of magnetic force between magnets in different positions

Figure 12.3 Using a small plotting compass to investigate the magnetic field around a bar magnet

Notice the following points.
- The direction of a magnetic field, shown by arrows on the lines of magnetic force, is always away from a north pole and towards a south pole.
- Lines of magnetic force never cross. They show the direction of the magnetic field at a particular point and the magnetic field can have only one direction at one point.

Look at point X in Figure 12.4c. Here, the field from one north pole is equal but opposite to that from the other north pole. The fields cancel each other and X is called a neutral point.

❶ Explain the following terms.
a) magnetic field;
b) lines of magnetic force;
c) neutral point.

❷ Redraw parts a) and b) of Figure 12.5 showing the lines of magnetic force (magnetic field patterns) between the bar magnets. Show the

direction of the magnetic field with arrows on the lines of force and show the positions of any neutral points with the letter X.

❸ The north pole of a compass points towards the magnetic north of the Earth. Explain why this means that magnetic north really behaves like the south pole of a magnet.

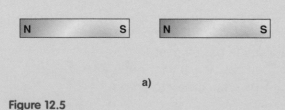

a)

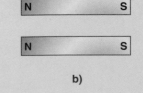

b)

Figure 12.5

12.2 Magnetism from electricity

Temporary magnets can be made by passing electric currents through wires. The magnetism that is produced by electric currents is called **electromagnetism**.

The magnetic field around a straight wire carrying a current

The magnetic field around a straight wire can be investigated using the apparatus in Figure 12.6. When the current is switched on, a magnetic field is produced around the wire. The magnetic field exerts a force on the compass needle causing it to point along the line of magnetic force. Notice that the lines of magnetic force are circles around the wire.

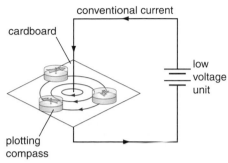

Figure 12.6 Investigating the field around a straight wire carrying an electric current

- When the current is reversed, the compass points in the opposite direction. This shows that the magnetic field and the magnetic force have reversed.
- When the current is switched off, the magnetism disappears. This shows that the magnetic field is only temporary.

The direction of the magnetic field around the wire can be predicted by the right hand grip rule. Pretend to grip the wire with your right hand so that your thumb points in the direction of the conventional current from the positive to the negative terminal (see Section 7.1). Your fingers will now curl round the wire in the direction of the magnetic field.

Check that you can follow this in Figure 12.6.

The magnetic field around a coil carrying a current

Figure 12.7 shows a coil of wire around a cardboard cylinder.
- When the switch is closed, a current flows through the coil and the magnetic field appears.
- If the current is switched off, the magnetic field disappears.

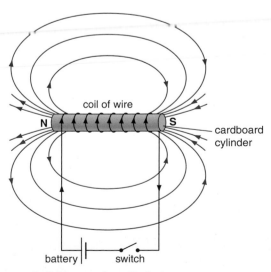

Figure 12.7 The magnetic field around a coil of wire.

By using the right hand grip rule at any point in the coil, you can predict the direction of the magnetic field.

Notice that the magnetic field around the coil is like that around a bar magnet.

You can do three things to make the magnetic field around the coil stronger:
- use a larger current;
- have more turns in the coil;
- put an iron bar (core) inside the coil.

The coil in Figure 12.7 can be used as an electromagnet. The magnetism will appear when the current is switched on and disappear when the current is switched off.

Large electromagnets are used in scrap-yards and factories to pick up steel and iron objects. Small electromagnets are used in buzzers, electric bells, circuit breakers and electric motors.

❹ Figure 12.8 shows two plotting compasses labelled A and B. A is above a wire and B is below the wire. Draw diagrams to show the positions of the needles in A and B when:
a) there is no current in the wire;
b) a small current passes from north to south along the wire;
c) a very large current passes from north to south along the wire.

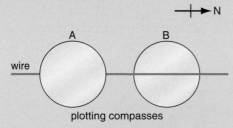

Figure 12.8

❺ Figure 12.9 shows a cardboard tube with a coil of wire around it carrying an electric current.
a) Copy the figure and draw in the direction of the needles in plotting compasses A, B, C and D.
b) Label the ends of the coil as N or S for north and south poles.

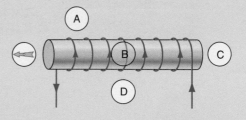

Figure 12.9

Activity – How does a circuit breaker work?

You should recall from Section 7.5 that circuit breakers prevent wires and cables from overheating and causing fires when faults occur in the electricity supply. They also prevent painful electric shocks and possible death to people using electric appliances in which a fault occurs. Small electromagnets are used in circuit breakers like the one in Figure 12.10.

When the current through the circuit is less than 15 amps, the force of attraction from the electromagnet is not sufficient to compress spring A further and attract the iron bolt. However, if a fault occurs in the rest of the circuit, a current greater than 15 amps will flow and this is sufficient for the circuit breaker to operate.

❶ Look carefully through the jumbled sentences below. Copy them out in the correct order to explain how the circuit breaker works. Start with the first statement in the list and finish with the last statement in the list.
   - A fault occurs in the circuit near the electric drill.
   - The iron bolt moves towards the electromagnet out of its slot in the plunger.
   - The force of the electromagnet attracts the iron bolt.
   - A current greater than 15 amps flows through the electromagnet.
   - Spring B can now move the plunger away from the contacts.
   - The metal ends of the plunger move away from the contacts.

   - The circuit is broken and the current ceases to flow.

❷ Suppose you wanted to make the circuit breaker more sensitive (so that it would operate at a lower current, for example when the current was only 5 amps).
   Suggest two modifications to the circuit breaker that would make it more sensitive.

❸ Describe briefly what you would do to check whether the circuit breaker in Figure 12.10 is operating accurately and breaking the circuit when the current reaches 15 amps.

❹ A circuit breaker which should operate at 15 amps was tested five times. The currents required to break the circuit in these five tests were 12.5, 13.5, 13.0, 12.7 and 13.3 amps.
   a) Calculate the average value of the current required to break the circuit.
   b) How large is the error in the current required to break the circuit?
   c) Is this error a random error, a systematic error or a zero error?

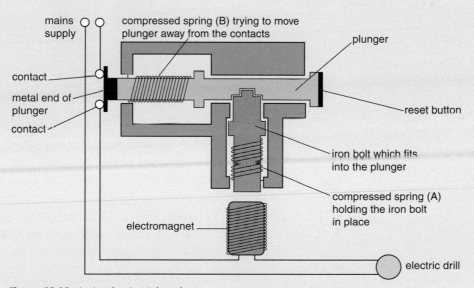

Figure 12.10 A simple circuit breaker

The motor effect

The **motor effect** occurs when a conductor carrying an electric current is placed in a magnetic field. The conductor experiences a force and, if this force is large enough, the conductor will move.

From the earlier sections of this chapter, we know that electric currents in wires and coils produce magnetic fields. If these wires and coils are near strong permanent magnets, the wires and coils may move. This movement is caused by interaction between the magnetic field produced when a current flows in the wires and coils and the magnetic field from the permanent magnet.

This combination of electricity and magnetism which causes movement is called the **motor effect**. This is how electric motors create movement. When a motor like that in Figure 12.1 operates, electrical energy is transformed into kinetic (movement) energy.

Studying the motor effect

We can study the motor effect using the apparatus in Figure 12.11. The thin strip of aluminium is held by supports between the poles of a strong magnet.

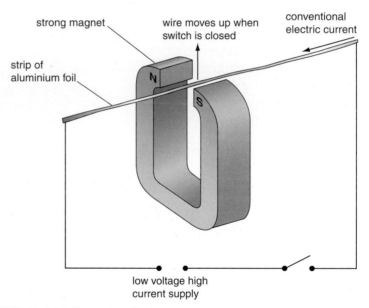

Figure 12.11 Studying the motor effect

- When the switch is closed, the thin aluminium strip moves upwards.
- If the current is reversed, the aluminium strip moves down.
- If the magnet is reversed, the aluminium moves down.
- If both the current and the magnet are reversed, the aluminium moves up again.

There must be a force on the aluminium strip making it move up or down. In order to understand this force we need to consider the magnetic field from the permanent magnet and the magnetic field produced when a current flows through a conductor.

What causes the motor effect?

Figure 12.12 shows the way in which the two fields combine. When there is no current in the conducting wire, the magnetic field will go straight across between the poles of the magnet. When a current flows through the conducting wire, it produces a circular magnetic field. Below the wire, the magnetic field due to the current in the wire is in the same direction as the field from the magnet, but above the wire the magnetic field due to the current is in the opposite direction to the field from the magnet. This means the field is stronger below the wire but weaker above it. The wire is pushed upwards by the stronger field below.

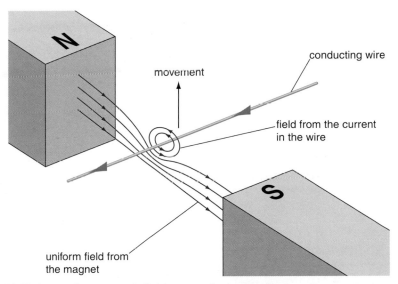

Figure 12.12 Interacting magnetic fields cause the motor effect.

The size of the force on the conductor can be increased by:
- increasing the strength of the magnetic field by using a stronger magnet;
- increasing the size of the current in the conductor.

If the direction of the field from the magnet or the direction of the current in the conductor is reversed in Figure 12.12, the field will be stronger above the conductor than below it. So, reversing the magnetic field or reversing the current will reverse the direction of the force and cause the conductor to move down.

Notice that the force on the conductor is greatest when the conductor and the permanent magnetic field are at right angles to each other. In this position the field produced by the current in the conductor is parallel with that from the magnet. This results in the biggest difference in the overall strength of the field above and below the conductor, so the force on the conductor is strongest.

However, if the conductor is parallel to the magnetic field from the magnet, the field produced by the current in the conductor will be at right angles to that from the magnet. In this case, the two fields cannot affect each other. There is no difference in the overall strength of the field above and below the conductor and therefore no force on the conductor.

12.4 Simple electric motors

An electric motor like the simple motor shown in Figure 12.13 uses the motor effect.

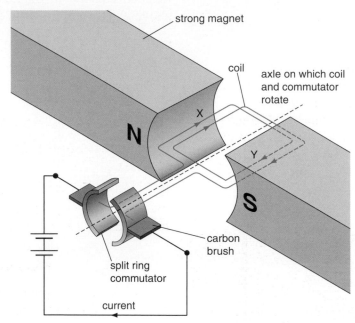

Figure 12.13 A simple electric motor. Only two coils are shown to make the figure as clear as possible.

6 Name three appliances (machines) that use electric motors.

7 The carbon brushes on a motor are made of graphite. Give two reasons why graphite is ideal for use as the brushes.

8 Look at Figure 12.13.

   a) Why is the motor more likely to stop turning when the coil is in the vertical position?
   b) Why do you think the pole pieces of the magnet are curved?
   c) What will happen if the terminals of the battery are reversed?
   d) What will happen if both the terminals of the battery and the poles of the magnet are reversed?

The rectangular coil of wire lies between the poles of a strong magnet. The coil is connected to an electrical supply by two carbon brushes and a split metal ring called a commutator. The carbon brushes (contacts) press lightly against the outside of the commutator, so that it can rotate with the coil. When a current flows through the coil, it rotates due to the motor effect.

When the coil is horizontal, side X of the coil moves down and side Y moves up. The forces on the coil rotate it anticlockwise until it becomes vertical. When the coil is vertical, the gaps in the commutator are next to the brushes, so there is no current through the coil.

As the coil passes the vertical position, the two halves of the commutator change contact from one brush to the other. Side Y now starts to move down and side X starts to move up. The coil continues to rotate anticlockwise as long as the current flows. Notice how the split-ring commutator cleverly allows the coil to continue rotating the same way.

Commercial motors are more complicated than the simple motor in Figure 12.13.
- They use electromagnets, not permanent magnets, because permanent magnets slowly lose their magnetism.
- They have coils with hundreds or even thousands of turns to increase the turning force.
- The coils are wound on an iron core to make the magnetic field stronger.

12.5 Generating electricity

The **generator effect** occurs when a conductor cuts through magnetic field lines. An electrical potential difference is induced across the ends of the conductor and a current flows if the conductor is part of a complete circuit.

Figure 12.14 The movement of the bicycle wheel causes this dynamo to generate electricity. The electric current will light a small lamp.

In Section 12.3 we found that a conductor carrying an electric current in a magnetic field can move. This is the motor effect. We can summarise the motor effect as:

$$\text{electricity} \xrightarrow{+\ \text{magnetism}} \text{movement}$$

The motor transforms electrical energy into kinetic (movement) energy.

This process can also be reversed. If a conductor moves through a magnetic field, an electrical potential difference is generated. A current flows if there is a complete circuit. So,

$$\text{movement} \xrightarrow{+\ \text{magnetism}} \text{electricity}$$

In this case, kinetic energy is transformed into electrical energy. Potential differences produced in this way are described as **induced** and the electric currents produced are called induced currents.

This effect is called the **generator effect**. The generator effect is used to generate electricity using dynamos for bicycle lights, alternators in cars and generators in power stations.

Figure 12.15 shows an experiment to study the generator effect. The coil is connected to a sensitive centre-zero ammeter.

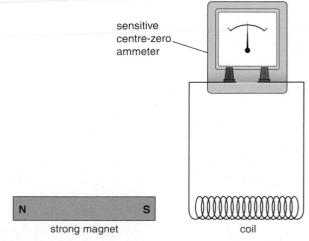

Figure 12.15 Moving a magnet near a coil shows the generator effect.

Figure 12.16 The generator effect is used in the security gates at airport terminals. As passengers walk through a security gate, metal objects (conductors) on their clothing or in their pockets cause changes in the magnetic field around the gate. This induces tiny electric currents which set off an alarm to warn the security staff.

The results of the experiment show that:
- an electrical potential difference is induced across the ends of the coil and a current flows if the magnet is moved into or out of the coil;
- if the magnet is stationary, no potential difference is induced and there is no current;
- the current flows one way when the magnet moves in and the other way when the magnet moves out;
- the induced current is also reversed if the polarity of the magnet is reversed;
- the generator effect also occurs and a current is induced if the magnet is stationary and the coil moves.

The induced potential difference and the induced current are greater if:
- the magnet or the coil moves faster;
- the magnet is stronger;
- the coil has more turns;
- the area of the coil is greater.

If you repeatedly move the magnet into and out of the coil, the current flows forwards then backwards, forwards then backwards, etc. This is an alternating current (see Section 7.4). We can use this idea to generate an alternating current in a simple alternating current (a.c.) generator.

---

9 a) Suppose you have a magnet, a coil of wire and a sensitive meter. Say how you would use them to generate an electric current.
   b) What changes would you make to your equipment to increase the size of the electric current?

10 Figure 12.17 shows a coil connected to a centre-reading ammeter and a magnet moving towards the coil. Notice that the pointer on the ammeter is pointing to the left of centre.

Draw the centre-reading ammeter when:
a) the magnet is stationary in the position shown in Figure 12.17;
b) the magnet is stationary and almost inside the coil;

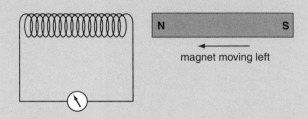

Figure 12.17

c) the magnet moves away from the coil to the right;
d) the south pole of the magnet is nearer the coil as it moves left towards the coil;
e) the coil is turned round and the magnet is moved as in Figure 12.17.

12.6 # The simple a.c. generator

Figure 12.18 shows a simple a.c. generator. The ends of the coil are connected to slip rings which rotate with the coil. Carbon brushes (contacts) connect the slip rings to the rest of the circuit.

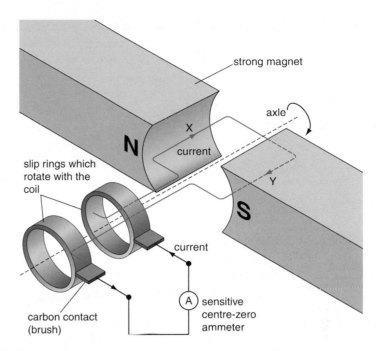

Figure 12.18 A simple a.c. generator

As the coil rotates in the magnetic field, it's like the coil moving towards and then away from the magnet repeatedly in Figure 12.15. This induces an alternating current in the coil.

Figure 12.19 shows how the potential difference induced in the coil changes as it rotates.

- In position (i), the coil is vertical. In this position, sides X and Y are moving parallel to the field and not cutting through the field. No potential difference is generated.
- When the coil has rotated through 90° to position (ii), side X is moving down and side Y is moving up. These sides are cutting through the magnetic field at the fastest rate, so the induced potential reaches its highest value.
- In position (iii), the coil is vertical again, so there is no induced potential difference.
- In position (iv), the coil is horizontal and the maximum potential is generated again. This time the potential is in the opposite direction to that in position (ii) because side X is now moving up and Y is moving down.
- In position (v), the coil is exactly as it was in position (i) and the cycle begins again.

Power stations use huge a.c. generators to produce electricity. Usually, they have a powerful rotating electromagnet rather than rotating coils. The advantage of this is that the coils are stationary so slip rings and brushes are not needed. This also avoids damage to the slip rings and brushes by friction and sparks. Generators like this in which the magnet moves rather than the coil are sometimes called dynamos.

Positions of the coil

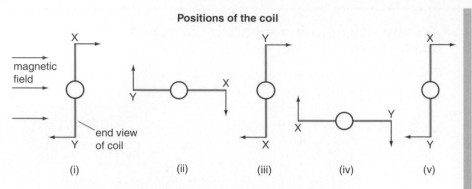

The potential difference generated in the coil

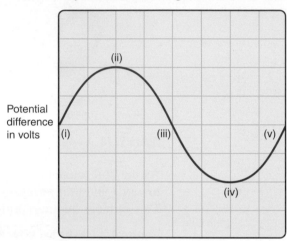

Figure 12.19 Relating the position of the coil to the induced potential difference in an a.c. generator

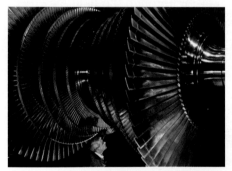

Figure 12.20 This huge steam turbine is being lowered into place as part of a power station generator.

The rotating electromagnet is usually driven by steam turbines. The steam is produced using coal, oil, natural gas or nuclear fuel as the energy source (see Section 2.4 and Figures 2.10 and 2.11). The current produced in the coils is an alternating current. Some power stations in Scotland and Wales use the energy from falling water to drive the turbines. Electricity generated in this way is called hydroelectricity (see Section 2.6).

⑪ Look closely at Figure 12.19.
   a) Why is there no current through the ammeter when the coil is stationary?
   b) i) What arrangements are necessary to get an induced electrical potential in the coil?
      ii) What additional arrangement is necessary to get a current through the ammeter?
   c) What is the purpose of the slip rings?
   d) What is the purpose of the carbon contacts (brushes)?
   e) Explain why the current generated is an alternating current.

Activity – Generating electricity to light a bicycle lamp

Figure 12.21 shows a simple device used on a bicycle to generate electricity and light a small lamp.

1 What is the name for this device?

2 Which part of the device moves?

3 Why does the device generate electricity?

4 a) Why does this device not require slip rings or brushes?

    b) What is the advantage of not having slip rings and brushes?

5 a) Will the current produced be an alternating current or a direct current?

    b) Explain your answer to part a).

6 a) How will the light from the lamp change as a cyclist increases speed from a standing start?

    b) What is the disadvantage of lighting a bicycle lamp with a device like this rather than with a battery?

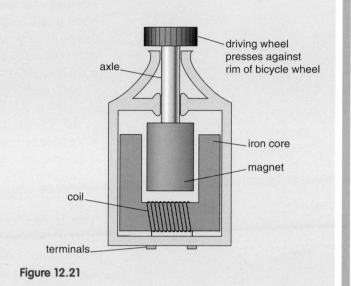

Figure 12.21

 ## How do transformers work?

> A **transformer** is used to change a potential difference. An a.c. current in the primary coil induces an a.c. potential difference in the secondary coil.

You may remember from Section 2.3 that transformers can change the potential difference across a circuit and so change the current flowing in the circuit. A transformer has two coils of wire wound on an iron core. Sometimes, the primary and secondary coils are wound side by side as in Figure 12.22. In other transformers, one coil may be wound on top of the other.

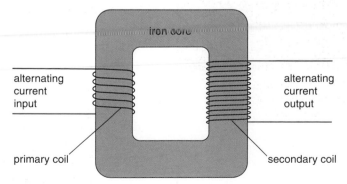

Figure 12.22 A transformer

In Section 12.5 we found that an induced current can be generated in a coil provided:
- it is part of a complete circuit; and
- the magnetic field around the coil is changing.

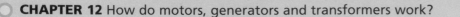

This means that an alternating current in the primary coil of a transformer will produce a magnetic field which is always changing in the iron core and around the secondary coil. This induces an alternating potential difference across the ends of the secondary coil. The greater the number of turns in the secondary coil, the greater is the induced potential difference.

- In a step-up transformer, the potential difference across the secondary coil is greater than the potential difference across the primary coil. Step-up transformers have more turns in the secondary coil than in the primary coil.
- In a step-down transformer, the potential difference across the secondary coil is less than that across the primary coil. Step-down transformers have fewer turns in the secondary coil than in the primary coil.

The induced potential difference (p.d.) across the secondary coil is directly proportional to the number of turns in the secondary coil. This means that if the number of turns in the secondary coil doubles, the induced potential also doubles, and if the number of turns is five times greater, then the induced potential is five times greater.

In general, we can say that the potential difference (p.d.) across a coil is proportional to its number of turns, N.

$$\text{p.d.} \propto N$$

So, the potential differences across the primary and secondary coils of a transformer are related by the equation:

$$\frac{\text{p.d. across the primary}}{\text{p.d. across secondary}} = \frac{\text{number of turns on primary}}{\text{number of turns on secondary}}$$

In symbols, we can write this as:

$$\frac{\text{p.d.}_p}{\text{p.d.}_s} = \frac{N_p}{N_s}$$

Example

Figure 12.23 shows an adaptor plug containing a small transformer. The transformer is used to operate a small 6 V radio from the 230 V mains supply. If there are 690 turns on the primary coil, how many turns are there on the secondary?

Using:

$$\frac{\text{p.d.}_p}{\text{p.d.}_s} = \frac{N_p}{N_s}$$

$$\Rightarrow \frac{230}{6} = \frac{690}{N_s}$$

$$\therefore N_s = \frac{690 \times 6}{230} = 18 \text{ turns}$$

Figure 12.23 An adaptor containing a small transformer to operate a 6 V radio from the 230 V mains supply

In this example, the transformer is a step-down transformer.

Transmitting electricity

Figure 12.24 A large transformer at a power station

After electricity has been generated at a power station, it is transmitted via the National Grid to our homes, schools and workplaces. This is where transformers play a crucial part.

Large power stations generate electricity at 25 000 volts. This is then stepped-up to 400 000 volts before electricity is transmitted through power lines to where it is needed as part of the National Grid (see Figure 2.7).

Transformers can change the voltage, but they cannot give out more energy than is put in. So, if the transformer raises the voltage, it must lower the current.

If the voltage is stepped up from 25 000 to 400 000 volts for the grid system, then the current will be reduced by the same proportion. This is a big advantage because a smaller current has a smaller heating effect in the cables. This means less energy is wasted in heating up the power lines. The smaller currents also allow the use of thinner cables and the pylons can be spaced further apart. However, transmission at such high voltages requires greater insulation.

The very high voltages in the National Grid must be reduced for use in our homes and workplaces. This is done by step-down transformers at substations, which reduce the voltage to 230 V.

---

12 a) Name the three main parts of a transformer.
b) Why are transformers useful?

13 a) What does a step-up transformer do to:
   i) the voltage;
   ii) the current;
   iii) the electrical energy being transmitted?
b) Why is electrical energy transmitted at high voltages in the National Grid?

14 A transformer does not work if the primary coil is connected to a battery. Why is this?

15 What type of transformer (step-up or step-down) should be used for the following applications?
a) Changing the mains voltage to 20 V for use with a set of Christmas tree lights.
b) Changing the grid voltage from 400 000 V to 11 000 V for a large industrial plant.

16 Copy Table 12.1 below and fill in the blank boxes.

Turns in primary coil	Turns in secondary coil	Primary p.d. in volts	Secondary p.d. in volts	Step-up or step-down
5000		25 000	275 000	
200	40	240		
	600	2	12	

Table 12.1

17 When the switch is closed in Figure 12.25, the ammeter attached to coil B kicks to the right. For a short time, a current flows through coil B. Say what happens to the ammeter during the following operations.
a) The switch is opened.
b) The switch is closed and it stays closed while a steady current flows through coil A.
c) With the switch closed, coil A is moved closer to coil B.
d) With the switch closed, coil A is moved away from coil B.
e) The battery is replaced by an alternating current supply which has a frequency of 1 Hz and the switch is closed.

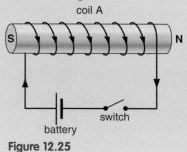
coil A

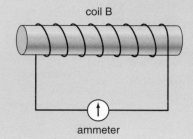
coil B

Figure 12.25

Summary

✓ A **magnetic field** is the space around a magnet where its magnetic force acts. The magnetism is strongest at the **poles** of a magnet.

✓ A magnetic field can be shown as a series of field lines. The direction of a magnetic field, shown by arrows on the lines of magnetic force, is always away from a north pole and towards a south pole.

✓ **Electromagnetism** is the magnetism produced by electric currents.

✓ The **motor effect** occurs when a conductor carrying an electric current is placed in a magnetic field. The conductor experiences a force and if this force is large enough, the conductor will move.

The force on the conductor is greater when:
– a stronger magnet is used;
– a larger current is used.

In the motor effect,

$$+ \text{ magnetism}$$
$$\text{electricity} \longrightarrow \text{movement}$$

✓ The **generator effect** occurs when a conductor 'cuts' through a magnetic field. An electrical potential difference is **induced** across the ends of the conductor and a current flows if the conductor is part of a complete circuit.

The induced current is greater if:
– the magnet or the coil moves faster;
– the magnet is stronger;
– the coil has more turns;
– the area of the coil is greater.

In the generator effect,

$$\text{movement} \xrightarrow{+ \text{ magnetism}} \text{electricity}$$

✓ A **transformer** consists of two coils of wire wound on an iron core. An induced current is obtained in the secondary coil if an alternating current passes through the nearby primary coil.

✓ Step-up transformers increase the potential difference across the secondary coil compared to that across the primary coil.

✓ Step-down transformers decrease the potential difference across the secondary coil compared to the primary coil.

✓ Step-up transformers are used to increase the voltage generated in power stations to 400 000 volts for transmission in the National Grid.

✓ Step-down transformers later reduce the voltage to 230 volts for use in our homes and workplaces.

✓ The potential differences across the primary and secondary coils of a transformer are related by the equation:

$$\frac{\text{p.d. across primary}}{\text{p.d. across secondary}} = \frac{\text{number of turns on primary}}{\text{number of turns on secondary}}$$

❶ Figure 12.26 represents a simple transformer used to light a 12 V lamp. When the a.c. input is supplied to the primary coil, the lamp is very dim.

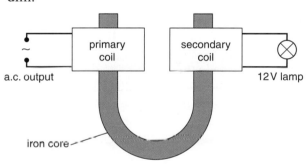

Figure 12.26

a) Copy and complete the sentences below using words in the box.

> Current   induces   magnetic field
> primary   secondary

The alternating current input in the _____ coil produces a continuously changing _____ in the iron core and therefore across the secondary coil. This _____ an alternating potential difference across the ends of the secondary coil. If the secondary coil is part of a complete circuit, an induced _____ will flow from the _____ coil.
(*5 marks*)

b) Suggest two ways to increase the voltage at the lamp without changing the power supply. (*2 marks*)

❷ Electrical energy is transmitted around the country in the National Grid through cables at very high voltages.
a) Why are the transmission cables suspended high above the ground? (*1 mark*)
b) Why are transformers an essential part of the transmission system? (*2 marks*)
c) Suggest one reason why the electricity is transmitted using alternating current.
(*1 mark*)
d) Why are such high voltages used? (*3 marks*)

❸ The shock waves from earthquakes can be detected by seismometers. Figure 12.27 shows a simple seismometer.

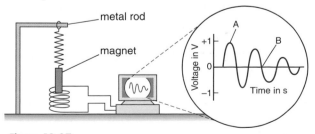

Figure 12.27

The seismometer has a bar magnet suspended vertically from a spring and just inside one end of a coil. The spring is hanging from a metal

EXAMQUESTIONS

support that transmits vibrations from the ground. The potential difference (voltage) induced in the coil is displayed on a computer.

a) What happens to the magnet when there is an earthquake? *(1 mark)*

b) Why is a potential difference induced in the coil? *(1 mark)*

c) Why is the induced p.d. an alternating p.d.? *(1 mark)*

d) How is the magnet moving when the induced p.d. has its highest value at A? *(1 mark)*

e) How is the magnet moving when the induced p.d. is zero at B? *(2 marks)*

f) State two ways in which the seismometer could be made more sensitive in order to detect smaller earthquakes. *(2 marks)*

4 a) Figure 12.28 shows a simple diagram of a motor. As the current flows from the battery, the coil and split-ring commutator rotate anticlockwise.

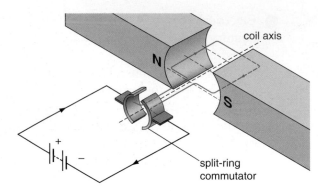

coil axis

split-ring commutator

Figure 12.28

i) Why does the side of the coil nearer the north pole of the magnet always move downwards? *(2 marks)*

ii) How does the split-ring commutator help to ensure that the coil continues to rotate in the same direction? *(3 marks)*

iii) Why is graphite an ideal material for the contact brushes? *(2 marks)*

b) Without changing the coil, suggest two ways in which you could make it rotate faster. *(2 marks)*

5 A power station generates 200 MW of power at a voltage of 25 000 V. A transformer with 64 000 turns in its secondary coil links the power station to the National Grid at a voltage of 400 000 V.

a) Write down the equation which relates the number of turns in each coil of the transformer to the potential difference across each coil. *(2 marks)*

b) Calculate the number of turns in the primary coil of the transformer. *(2 marks)*

c) The cost due to heat losses in the cables of the National Grid goes down as the cable is made thicker Why is this? *(1 mark)*

d) The cost of installing the cables of the National Grid goes up as the cable is made thicker. Why is this? *(2 marks)*

Chapter 13
What is the life history of stars?

At the end of this chapter you should:

✓ know that the Sun is just one star in the Milky Way galaxy;
✓ know that the Universe contains billions of galaxies;
✓ understand that stars change and go through a life cycle;
✓ appreciate the role of gravitational attraction in the life cycle of stars;

✓ understand what radiation pressure is and its role in the life cycle of stars;
✓ know what a supernova is;
✓ know that all naturally occurring elements are produced from fusion reactions within stars.

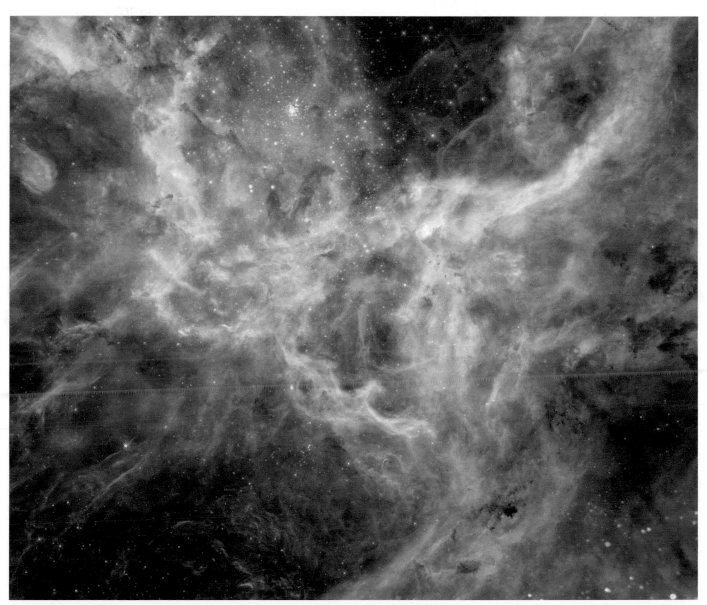

Figure 13.1 The Tarantula nebula in the southern constellation of Dorado is so big that light takes 1000 years to travel from one side to the other. This huge mass of gas and dust is the birthplace for a new generation of stars.

13.1 ## Stars, galaxies and the Universe

The Sun is a massive hot ball of brightly glowing gas. Deep within the Sun, nuclear fusion reactions take place. These reactions produce vast amounts of energy, causing the Sun to emit the whole range of electromagnetic waves. Compared to other stars, the Sun is quite small and not very bright. But it is our closest star, so other stars look tiny in comparison because they are so much further away.

The **Milky Way** is the galaxy that contains our own Solar System.

Each galaxy contains a vast number of stars all held together by gravitational forces. The Sun is just one of around 100 000 million stars in the **Milky Way** galaxy. Figure 4.5 shows what the Milky Way would look like if you could see it from the side and from above. Figure 13.2 shows what the Milky Way looks like from the Earth.

Figure 13.2 Seen from Earth, the Milky Way galaxy looks like a wide band of tiny bright stars.

The Milky Way is not the only galaxy in the Universe. Using large telescopes (see Section 4.2) millions of galaxies can be seen in all directions in space. The Universe is made up of billions (thousands of millions) of galaxies. Each galaxy has as many stars as the Milky Way. Galaxies are very far apart. One of the closest galaxies to the Milky Way is the Andromeda galaxy. It can be seen by the naked eye, but it still takes the light from Andromeda 2.2 million years to reach the Earth.

❶ Use the equation;

$$\text{distance} = \text{speed} \times \text{time}$$

to work out how far it is from the Andromeda galaxy to Earth. Remember that light travels at 300 000 kilometres per second.

Figure 13.3 The Andromeda galaxy is one of our nearest galaxies.

13.2 The life cycle of a star

Stars do not last forever. They go through a life cycle from birth to death.

The birth of a star

Like all stars, our Sun was formed from a **nebula**, a huge cloud of gas and dust. The gas was mainly hydrogen with about 20% helium.

Over millions of years the force of gravity pulls clumps of dust and gas particles together, squeezing them into a smaller and smaller volume. These gravitational forces also pull in more and more particles, so the mass of the clump increases. As the particles accelerate towards each other the gravitational potential energy they lose is transformed into kinetic energy. When the particles crash together, kinetic energy is transformed into thermal energy and the temperature increases. Eventually, the temperature at the centre reaches about 15 000 000 °C, which is high enough for **nuclear fusion** reactions to start. This process involves hydrogen nuclei fusing together to form helium nuclei, as we saw in Section 8.6. Hydrogen fusion produces a lot of energy, so the compressed gas ball starts to emit immense amounts of heat and light. Once the gas ball has started to produce its own radiation, it is called a star.

Scientists think that at the same time as the Sun was formed, smaller

> A **nebula** is a huge cloud of dust and gas from which stars are formed.
>
> **Nuclear fusion** is the joining of small nuclei to form larger nuclei.

Figure 13.4 In the constellation Orion (see Figure 4.2), one of the bright objects isn't a star at all. It's a nebula lit up by the light of hundreds of hot, young stars.

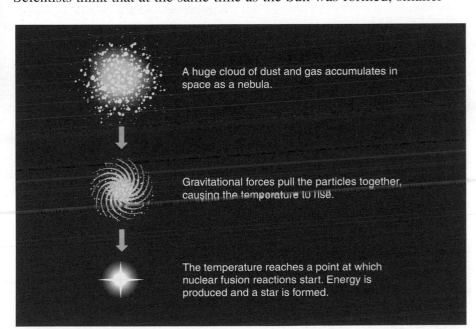

A huge cloud of dust and gas accumulates in space as a nebula.

Gravitational forces pull the particles together, causing the temperature to rise.

The temperature reaches a point at which nuclear fusion reactions start. Energy is produced and a star is formed.

Figure 13.5 The birth sequence of a star

bodies also formed from the same nebula. These bodies were too small for the temperature to rise enough for fusion reactions to start, so they did not produce their own heat and light. Instead of becoming stars, they became the planets and moons of the Solar System.

❷ Explain how a star is formed.

❸ What is a nebula?

❹ What process provides the energy needed for a star to produce its own heat and light?

Radiation pressure is the pressure exerted on a surface exposed to electromagnetic radiation.

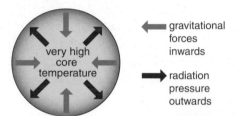

gravitational forces inwards

radiation pressure outwards

very high core temperature

Figure 13.6 The gravitational forces acting towards the star's centre are opposed by the radiation pressure, which pushes outwards.

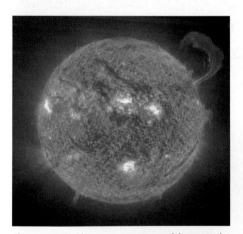

Figure 13.7 The Sun is in its stable period with enough hydrogen left to shine for about 5000 million years.

The stable period of a star

The energy produced by nuclear reactions in the core of a star travels outwards as radiation – mainly light. Radiation exerts a force on any surface it hits. This is called the **radiation pressure**. The higher the core temperature of a star, the greater the radiation pressure.

During the main period of its life, a star remains in a stable state. The gravitational forces pulling the star's matter inwards are balanced by the enormous outward radiation pressure. The star doesn't shrink or expand. This period of stability may last for billions of years. Our Sun is in its stable period, and is about halfway through its life. It will continue radiating energy from nuclear fusion reactions in its core until it runs out of hydrogen in about 5000 million years.

Nearing the end of life

As the star's supply of hydrogen runs out, the high radiation pressure produced by the fusion reactions decreases. Without this outwards pressure, gravitational forces cause the star's core to contract. This increases the temperature of the core, making it hotter than it was during the stable period. The core is now mainly helium. Eventually, the core temperature becomes high enough for further, more complex nuclear fusion reactions to occur.

The new fusion reactions produce a higher outward radiation pressure than before. At this point the inward gravitational forces are unable to balance the radiation pressure and the star expands. It expands so much that the outer layers cool to about 3000 °C. Because the surface is cooler it looks red (only red-hot, not white-hot), so this type of star is called a red giant. When our Sun reaches this stage it will be so large that the Earth will get burned to cinders inside it!

The death of a star

What happens next depends on the size of the star. Small stars like our Sun will contract and the surface will become very hot. This will cause the star to glow white-hot, becoming a type of star called a white dwarf. Eventually, the light from the white dwarf fades and the star ends its life as a black dwarf.

Stars many times the size of our Sun first expand to form red supergiants (very large red giants). These collapse and die in a different way from smaller stars. As gravitational forces cause a red supergiant to collapse huge amounts of energy are released, causing the outer layers to blow up in a spectacular explosion called a **supernova**. Afterwards the remnants at the centre of the original star contract even further to form an incredibly dense body called a neutron star. If the neutron star shrinks any further, the gravitational forces will become so strong that nothing, not even light, can escape from its surface. It is then a black hole.

A **supernova** is the explosive death of a star.

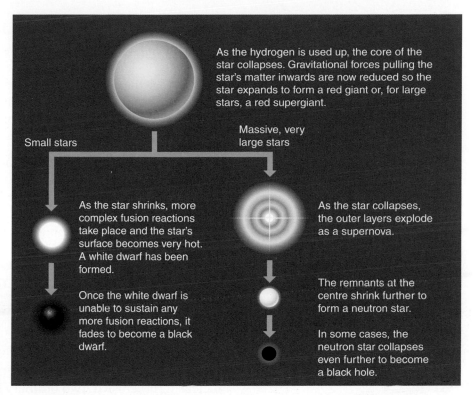

As the hydrogen is used up, the core of the star collapses. Gravitational forces pulling the star's matter inwards are now reduced so the star expands to form a red giant or, for large stars, a red supergiant.

Small stars

Massive, very large stars

As the star shrinks, more complex fusion reactions take place and the star's surface becomes very hot. A white dwarf has been formed.

As the star collapses, the outer layers explode as a supernova.

Once the white dwarf is unable to sustain any more fusion reactions, it fades to become a black dwarf.

The remnants at the centre shrink further to form a neutron star.

In some cases, the neutron star collapses even further to become a black hole.

Figure 13.8 Stars die in different ways, depending on their size.

Figure 13.9 The Crab nebula is the result of a supernova. The supernova was recorded by Chinese astronomers in 1054 AD. It was so bright that it was visible in daylight for over 3 weeks.

At the end of their stable period, some large stars expand to form very bright stars called blue supergiants. During its short life, a blue supergiant can change to a red supergiant and back again several times. Eventually its fate is the same as that of a red supergiant: it will explode as a supernova.

⑤ For the time between its birth and its death, a star is stable. Explain why the star is stable.

⑥ Describe the stages that a large star passes through, from its stable period until it becomes a black hole.

⑦ Describe what will happen to our Sun from the time it starts to run out of hydrogen until it becomes a black dwarf.

13.3

The role of nuclear fusion in the evolution of the elements

The Universe has not always been as it is now. Early on, the Universe consisted mainly of hydrogen, but it now contains a variety of elements. Where did these elements come from? The answer is from nuclear reactions within the stars.

Nuclear fusion reactions do not happen easily. Nuclei are positively charged and positive charges repel. The closer the nuclei get to each other, the stronger are the repulsive forces pushing them apart. If two nuclei are to fuse (in a fusion reaction) they must overcome the forces of electrostatic repulsion keeping them apart. At the very high temperatures deep inside a star, nuclei have enough energy to do this.

The formation of helium from hydrogen

The fusion reactions in a star start with hydrogen, the most abundant gas, to create helium.

Remember that during nuclear fusion, two nuclei are joined together to form just one larger nucleus and energy is released. For each helium nucleus (^4_2He) created, two ordinary hydrogen nuclei (^1_1H) and two neutrons (^1_0n) must fuse. This does not happen all at once.

From Figure 8.12 you can see that the fusion of hydrogen nuclei (^1_1H) and neutrons (^1_0n) to form helium nuclei (^4_2He) involves two stages. In the first stage, a hydrogen nucleus (^1_1H) fuses with a neutron to form a heavy hydrogen (deuterium) nucleus (^2_1H).

$$^1_1\text{H} + {}^1_0\text{n} \rightarrow {}^2_1\text{H}$$

In the second stage, two heavy hydrogen nuclei (^2_1H) fuse to form a helium nucleus (^4_2He).

$$^2_1\text{H} + {}^2_1\text{H} \rightarrow {}^4_2\text{He}$$

The formation of carbon and other light elements

When the star runs out of hydrogen it collapses. This causes the core temperature to rise rapidly up to $100\,000\,000\,°\text{C}$, while the outer layers expand into a red giant. In the hot core of a red giant, more complex fusion reactions start to happen. First, helium nuclei are converted to carbon. The carbon nuclei then fuse with other nuclei to form new elements of even higher mass, up to and including iron. The following equation shows one example, carbon fusing with helium to form oxygen.

$$^{12}_6\text{C} + {}^4_2\text{He} \rightarrow {}^{16}_8\text{O}$$

Other small nuclei fuse to form nuclei of heavier elements, such as silicon and iron.

8 Explain why the heaviest elements are only formed in a supernova.

9 Under what conditions will carbon nuclei fuse with the nuclei of other elements?

10 What evidence do scientists have for thinking that the Solar System was formed from 'recycled' materials?

The formation of heavy elements

Once we get to iron, the process changes. For iron to fuse with other elements, large amounts of energy must be absorbed, not emitted. This energy can only come from the huge amounts of energy released when a massive star collapses and then explodes in a supernova. So, the fusion of iron and the creation of the heaviest elements occurs only in a supernova.

The explosion of stars as supernovae causes new, heavier elements to be formed by fusion and also scatters them throughout the Universe. When gravity starts to pull the remnants of the explosion together into a nebula, the whole life cycle of a star starts again. However, the future star starts life with a richer supply of heavier elements than earlier generations of stars.

Nuclei of the heaviest elements are present in the Sun's outer layers, and atoms of these elements are present in the inner planets of the Solar System. This is the evidence that scientists have for thinking that our Sun and the rest of the Solar System were formed from the remains of a supernova – a case of recycling on an astronomical scale!

Summary

✓ A galaxy is a vast number of stars held together by gravitational attraction.

✓ The **Milky Way** is the galaxy that contains our Solar System.

✓ The Universe is made up of billions (thousands of millions) of galaxies.

✓ A **nebula** is a huge cloud of dust and gas from which stars are formed.

✓ **Nuclear fusion** is the joining of small nuclei to form larger nuclei.

✓ When hydrogen nuclei fuse to form a helium nucleus, energy is produced.

✓ **Radiation pressure** is the pressure exerted on a surface exposed to electromagnetic radiation.

✓ A star is stable when the inward gravitational forces are balanced by the outward radiation pressure.

✓ A **supernova** is the explosive death of a giant star.

✓ Fusion processes in stars produce all the naturally occurring elements.

✓ The heaviest elements are created only in a supernova.

✓ Supernova explosions scatter the elements throughout space.

❶ Copy out the statements A, B, C and D.
   A It is made up of billions of galaxies.
   B One of the many stars in the Milky Way galaxy.
   C The process of changing hydrogen to helium.
   D The name given to an exploding star.

Match each of the statements A, B, C and D to a word from the box below.

> Earth   fusion   fission   neutron
> Sun   supernova   Universe

(4 marks)

❷ Stars go through a life cycle of change.
   a) Explain how a star is formed.   *(3 marks)*
   b) Why does the amount of hydrogen in a star decrease?   *(1 mark)*
   c) Describe what happens to a very large star from the time it runs out of hydrogen.   *(4 marks)*

❸ a) What name is given to the process by which stars produce energy?   *(1 mark)*
   b) Explain the link between a supernova and a neutron star.   *(2 marks)*
   c) What is a black hole?   *(2 marks)*

❹ For most of its lifespan a star is stable.
   a) Explain, in terms of the forces acting, why a star is stable.   *(3 marks)*
   b) What happens to end the stable period of a star's lifespan?   *(1 mark)*
   c) Why, at the end of its stable period, will our Sun not produce a supernova?   *(1 mark)*

❺ The Solar System contains atoms of the heaviest elements.
   a) Where were these elements formed?   *(1 mark)*
   b) Explain how these elements are formed.   *(2 marks)*
   c) What does this tell you about the age of the Solar System compared to the age of most of the stars in the Universe?   *(1 mark)*

Index